An Introduction to
Childhood Studies

An Introduction to Childhood Studies

Edited by Mary Jane Kehily

Open University Press
Maidenhead · New York

Open University Press
McGraw-Hill Education
McGraw-Hill House
Shoppenhangers Road
Maidenhead
Berkshire
England
SL6 2QL

email: enquiries@openup.co.uk
world wide web: www.openup.co.uk

and Two Penn Plaza, New York, NY 10121-2289, USA

First published 2004

A catalogue record of this book is available from the British Library

ISBN 0 335 21267 0 (pb)   0 335 21268 9 (hb)

Library of Congress Cataloging-in-Publication Data
CIP data applied for

Typeset by RefineCatch Limited, Bungay, Suffolk
Printed in Great Britain by MPG Books Ltd, Bodmin, Cornwall

Contents

The editor and contributors

David Buckingham is Professor of Education at the Institute of Education, University of London, where he directs the Centre for the Study of Children, Youth and Media. He has directed several major research projects on young people's relationships with the media and on media education, and has lectured on these topics in more than 20 countries worldwide. He is the author of numerous books, including *Children Talking Television* (Routledge 1993), *Moving Images* (Manchester University Press 1996), *The Making of Citizens* (Routledge 2000), *After the Death of Childhood* (Polity Press 2000) and *Media Education: Literacy, Learning and Popular Culture* (Polity Press 2003).

Rachel Burr has a background in social work and research interests in child-focused human rights, international aid agencies and children of the streets and orphanages of Vietnam. Recent publications include 'Global and local approaches to children's rights in Vietnam', *Childhood*, 9(1) and 'Ethics of doing anthropological fieldwork', *Anthropology Matters*, 3. She is currently visiting fellow at the University of Wisconsin, Madison, USA.

Diana Gittins works as a freelance writer and consultant. She has taught in higher education for many years and also runs creative writing workshops. She is the author of four works of non-fiction: *Fair Sex*, *The Family in Question*, *The Child in Question* and *Madness in its Place*. She was a Hawthornden Fellow in 1993 and has published a collection of poetry, *Dance of the Sheet*. Her first novel is currently with her agent.

Peter Hunt is the first specialist in children's literature to be appointed Professor of English at a UK university (Cardiff). He has written or edited 16 books on the subject, and over 250 articles. He has lectured at over 100 universities in 19 countries, and has published six children's books.

Chris Jenks is Professor of Sociology at Goldsmiths College, University of London. His previous books include *Rationality, Education and the Social Organization of Knowledge* (Routledge 1976), *Worlds Apart – Readings for a Sociology of Education* (with J. Beck, N. Keddie & M. Young) (Collier-Macmillan 1977), *Toward a Sociology of Education* (with J. Beck, N. Keddie and M. Young) (Transaction 1977), *The Sociology of Childhood* (Batsford 1982), *Culture* (Routledge 1993), *Cultural Reproduction* (Routledge 1993), *Visual Culture*

(Routledge 1995), *Childhood* (Routledge 1996), *Theorizing Childhood* (with A. James and A. Prout) (Polity 1998), *Core Sociological Dichotomies* (Sage 1998), *Images of Community: Durkheim, Social Systems and the Sociology of Art* (with J.A. Smith) (Ashgate 2000), *Aspects of Urban Culture* (Sinica 2001), *Culture: Critical Concepts* (four volumes) (Routledge 2002), *Transgression* (Routledge 2003), *Subculture: The Fragmentation of the Social* (Sage 2004), and *Urban Culture* (four volumes) (Routledge 2004) . He is interested in sociological theory, post-structuralism and heterology, childhood, cultural theory, visual and urban culture, and extremes of behaviour.

Mary Jane Kehily is a lecturer in the Faculty of Education and Language Studies at The Open University, UK. She has a background in cultural studies and education, and research interests in gender and sexuality, narrative and identity and popular culture. She has published widely on these themes. Recent publications include *Sexuality, Gender and Schooling* (Routledge 2002) and (with Joan Swann) *Children's Cultural Worlds* (Wiley/Open University 2003).

Daniel Monk is a lecturer in law at Birkbeck College, University of London. Previously based at Keele University, where he taught child law to professionals working with children, he has written extensively about sex education, school exclusions, children's rights and constructions of childhood in education law generally. He is currently researching home education. He co-edited *Legal Queeries* (Cassell 1998) and *Feminist Perspectives on Child Law* (Cavendish 2000) and is assistant editor of *Child and Family Law Quarterly*.

Heather Montgomery is a social anthropologist who works for The Open University, contributing to the course 'Childhood 0–18'. She has worked in Thailand conducting research among young prostitutes there, published by Berghahn in 2001 as *Modern Babylon? Prostituting Children in Thailand*. She writes on children's rights, sexual abuse and the anthropology of children and childhood.

Wendy Stainton Rogers is a senior lecturer at The Open University and also head of its Research School. A psychologist by training, she has carried out extensive research within the area of childhood, particularly into the social policy, law and practice issues connected with child protection. She has also carried out research on children's sexuality and the application of postmodern theory to child care practice. She has published widely on these themes.

Valerie Walkerdine is Professor of Psychology at the University of

Wales, Cardiff. Her recent publications include *Challenging Subjects: Critical Psychology for a New Millennium* (Palgrave 2002), *Growing up Girl: Gender & Class in the 21st Century* (with H. Lucey and J. Melody (Macmillan 2000), *Mass Hysteria: Critical Psychology and Media Studies* (with L. Blackman) (Macmillan in press), *Feminism and Psychology Reader* (Sage 1996) and *Daddy's Girl: Young Girls and Popular Culture* (Macmillan 1997).

Foreword
Martin Woodhead

One afternoon recently I carried out a small-scale ethnography at a major academic bookstore in central London. I observed the book-browsing habits of students and scholars interested in children and childhood. I already had extensive personal experience of searching for books on this subject and wasn't surprised by what I found. Several people navigated quickly to specific sections of the store, approaching the book displays with purposeful gaze, seeking out specific categories of interest, such as 'Cognitive Development', or 'Child Protection' or 'Primary Education'. Typically they scanned shelves for specific topics or authors, or pounced on the latest additions before leaving, apparently well satisfied, often with purchase in hand. But another eager book-buyer very quickly appeared disoriented, despite the helpful guide to sections of the store. This customer was altogether less focussed – even disorganized – in their book browsing, initially moving from area to area, shelf to shelf in an apparently random fashion. Then after a while they appeared to develop a browsing strategy, first scanning shelves headed Anthropology and Sociology, then alighting eagerly on a small section marked Sociology of Childhood before moving on quickly through Social Policy, Social Welfare and Social Work, stopping off briefly in Women's Studies, Cultural and Media Studies, Development Studies, with a final glance at Social History. Their journey through the store was slow. They left looking frustrated, and empty-handed. I recognized this customer as a kindred spirit, perhaps with academic roots in a particular discipline, but with interests that don't fit traditional areas of childhood study. Perhaps they were one of a growing number who identify their work as 'Childhood Studies'.

Interest in 'Childhood Studies' is for many born out of frustration with the narrow versions of 'the child' offered by traditional academic discourses and methods of inquiry, especially a rejection of the ways psychology, sociology and anthropology traditionally partition and objectify 'the child' as subject to processes of development, socialization or acculturation. The appeal of an interdisciplinary Childhood Studies is about a more integrated approach to research and teaching around children's lives and well-being, a more 'joined-up' view of 'the child in context', which has also become a priority for policy and for professional training. For others, Childhood Studies is built around a rejection of the essentialism endemic in traditional theorizing, in favour of recognizing the multiple ways childhood is socially constructed and reconstructed in relation to time and place, age, gender, ethnicity etc. Childhood Studies also represents a critique of the ways children's lives are regulated in modern societies, an emphasis on recognizing children as social actors, and empowering their participatory rights in all areas of social life, including child research.

This book explores many of these debates around the study of children and childhood – a welcome addition to the resources available in the growing field of Childhood Studies. Mary Jane Kehily's plan to edit this 'Introduction to Childhood Studies' grew out of her teaching within the newly established Open University degree programme in Childhood and Youth Studies, especially as a member of the team writing four introductory textbooks for course *U212 Childhood*. Those books were published by Wiley in association with The Open University in 2003 under the titles 'Understanding Childhood', 'Childhoods in Context', 'Children's Cultural Worlds' and 'Changing Childhoods'. Many of the themes from that series are included in the present volume, with chapters contributed by a distinguished group of scholars representing a wide range of perspectives.

The definition of Childhood Studies is still open to debate, not least because visions for inter-disciplinarity vary. This is hardly surprising for a relatively new area of scholarship. In some ways it may even be desirable if the field is to be flexible and responsive to the challenges facing modern childhoods within a global context. But the momentum towards establishing Childhood Studies is clear enough, signalled through this and many other books published in recent years, along with the success of dedicated journals and new undergraduate and postgraduate programmes being established across several continents.

Before too long, I look forward to re-visiting that London bookshop to carry-out a follow-up ethnography of book-browsing, when I hope Childhood Studies will have been recognized, with a shelf – or better still a section – of its own!

Martin Woodhead
Professor of Childhood Studies
The Open University, UK
May 2004

1 Understanding childhood: an introduction to some key themes and issues

Mary Jane Kehily

Recent developments in education and the social sciences have seen the growth of childhood studies as an academic field of enquiry. Over the last decade or so childhood studies has become a recognized area of research and analysis, reflected in the success of publications such as James and Prout (1997) *Constructing and Reconstructing Childhood* and Stainton Rogers and Stainton Rogers (1992) *Stories of Childhood: Shifting Agendas of Child Concern*. A growing body of literature points to the importance of childhood as a conceptual category and as a social position for the study of a previously overlooked or marginalized group – children. Childhood studies as a field of academic endeavour offers the potential for interdisciplinary research that can contribute to an emergent paradigm wherein new ways of looking at children can be researched and theorized. This book aims to bring together key themes and issues in the area of childhood studies in ways that will provide an introduction to students and practitioners working in this field.

In this chapter I aim to introduce and comment upon some of the key themes and issues that will be revisited throughout the book. I want to begin by asking the question, 'What is childhood studies anyway?' Is it a collation of already existing knowledges about children and childhood or does the term constitute a new academic field? An obvious point to acknowledge is that the study of children and childhood has been part of a diverse range of academic disciplines for a very long time. Different disciplines have developed different ways of approaching the study of children, using different research methods driven by a far from coherent set of research questions. For some disciplines (such as sociology and cultural studies) childhood as a concept is specifically addressed, while for other disciplines (such as psychology and education) the focus has been upon the child or children. In order to develop an insight into the diversity of childhood studies as a field of inquiry, the book is divided into three parts: historical approaches to childhood, sociocultural approaches and policy perspectives. These offer a different and sometimes distinct way of looking at children and childhood, providing the reader with a conceptual framework for understanding the field. Each part is considered in more detail below.

Historical approaches to childhood

Historical studies provide a rich source of knowledge about children and childhood in the past and the present. Many of the issues that concern contemporary studies of childhood have a historical trajectory that eluci- dates and informs the present in powerful ways. Issues of concern for con- temporary scholars of childhood such as child labour, the gulf between the experience of childhood in the West and the non-western world, and west- ern anxieties about children in the new media age can be usefully explored by recourse to history. Historical approaches suggest that childhood was reconceptualized in the UK between the late nineteenth century and the beginning of World War I (Steedman 1990; Gittins 1998). These studies demonstrate that concerns with child poverty and ill health produced a significant shift in the economic and sentimental value of children. Over a fairly short historical period the position of working-class children changed from one of supplementing the family income to that of a relatively inactive member of the household in economic terms, to be protected from the adult world of work and hardship (Cunningham 1991). A contemporary US-based study elaborates upon this theme by indicating that children's contribution to the family in western contexts is economically worthless but emotionally 'priceless' (Zelitzer 1985). Zelitzer's study suggests that child- ren's 'value' lies in their ability to give meaning and fulfilment to their parents lives. Further historical research suggests that childhood provides a site for thinking about the self and locating selfhood; a way of mapping and developing human interiority (Steedman 1995). Seen from this perspective, the child represents an extension of the adult self, a symbolic link with one's own childhood invoking a psychic dynamic between the past and the present.

   Some of these themes can be seen in the work of Henry Mayhew, a nine- teenth-century social commentator who observed and documented the lives of working-class people in London. His detailed descriptions in *London Labour and the London Poor* (first published 1861), provide us with a rich social history of life and conditions in nineteenth-century England. Mayhew's encounter with an 8-year-old street vendor, the Watercress Girl, documents his feelings of surprise at meeting a child who, to his mind, is not a child. Mayhew's sense of surprise rests upon his observation that a child of 8 has 'lost all childish ways'. Mayhew begins by positioning her as a child and speaking to her about 'child- ish subjects' such as playing with toys, playing with friends and going to the park. The Watercress Girl, however, is not familiar with this aspect of childhood and has no experience of playing for pleasure. Her experiences are centred round a few streets in London where she lives and works. Mayhew draws our attention to the material circumstances of the girl's existence: she is pale, thin and unused to eating regular hot meals; she is unkempt and inadequately clothed; she no longer attends school; and she has become accustomed to a life of hardship that includes occasional bouts of physical abuse. Mayhew is moved by the child's description of her life to the point where he finds her account 'cruelly pathetic'. From his description we can deduce something of what Mayhew's expectations of childhood may be. It would be reasonable to suggest that Mayhew views childhood as a period of life where play and carefree pleasure should be indulged, where the child is protected from the adult world of work and is cared for, kept warm and well fed. The encounter between Henry Mayhew and the Watercress Girl can be seen in a couple of interrelated ways. First, it is possible to understand Mayhew's surprise as a moment where the imagination is held in check by the reality of experience. The Watercress Girl challenges Mayhew's concept of childhood and disturbs his notion of what a child is and how a child behaves. Hence his difficulty seeing someone so young, talking to her as a child, while simultaneously recognizing that she is not childlike and in fact is 'in thoughts and manner, a woman'. Second, the account can be seen and understood in terms of social class. As a middle-class man, Mayhew is confronted with a working-class childhood which he does not recognize and has not experienced. Mayhew's description of the Watercress Girl may indicate that, from his perspective, the girl has been deprived of her childhood. The theme of lost or stolen childhood is one that remains part of popular contemporary discourses of childhood.

Contemporary images of children in advertisements, television and film also comment on the concept of childhood in ways that bespeak a particular relationship with the past. Barnardo's is a leading children's charity based in the UK. About 20 years after Henry Mayhew's encounter with the Watercress Girl, Dr Thomas John Barnardo became so concerned about the plight of street children in the East End of London that he opened an orphanage. This children's home became a model for the setting up of others throughout the UK and Barnardo's name has since been associated with the institutional care of children and young people. Barnardo's no longer run children's homes but they continue to be involved in many charitable projects to support children and young people. Barnardo's describe their approach to caring for children in the twenty-first century in the following way:

> Children have only one chance of a childhood. They deserve to be protected from harm, to enjoy good emotional, mental and physical health, and to feel that they belong in their home, at school and in their local community.

> Barnardo's believes that it is never too early or too late to offer a helping hand – and to give the most disadvantaged youngsters the chance of a better childhood and a brighter future.
>
> (Barnardo's 1999)

Like other charities Barnardo's rely upon donations from the public and are constantly engaged in fundraising ventures to support their work and promote the public profile of the organization. In October 1999, Barnardo's launched an advertising campaign in newspapers and magazines to raise awareness of their work with children. The series of advertisements portrayed children in a variety of 'adult' situations: homelessness, drug and alcohol abuse, prostitution, suicide and prison. The image of a baby injecting drugs, aroused a great deal of controversy. The Advertising Standards Authority received 28 complaints from individuals and organizations that considered the advertisement to be shocking and offensive. In the face of public protest, Barnardo's replaced the image with one of a happier baby without the syringe and tourniquet. But why is the image such a shocking one? It could be argued that the power of the image lies in the fact that it deliberately and self-consciously transgresses boundaries. While it is generally accepted that adults have knowledge of the world of drug use, it is usually assumed that children should be protected from such knowledge. To see a baby who is not only exposed to the reality of drug use but actually participating in it can be seen as a violation of generally held sensibilities about appropriate knowledge and behaviour. Yet all drug users were, of course, once babies. And this is the point that the Barnardo's advertisement makes very forcefully. Childhood leads inevitably to adulthood and furthermore the child's environment and experiences can have a bearing on adult life. In the advertisement the image and the text work together to create this message. The text reads:

> John Donaldson. Age 23. Battered as a child, it was always possible that John would turn to drugs. With Barnardo's help, child abuse need not lead to an empty future. Although we no longer run orphanages, we continue to help thousands of children and their families, at home, school and in the local community.
>
> (Barnardo's 1999)

The visual and textual juxtaposition of John Donaldson, baby, and John Donaldson age 23 makes a direct link between a battered childhood and drug abuse in adulthood. In this sense the image is stark and uncompromising. From the perspective of the charity, the link between abused childhood and troubled adulthood calls for intervention and change encapsulated in the Barnardo's logo, 'Giving children back their future'. Henry Mayhew and Dr Barnardo both view working-class children as poor and impoverished in many ways; their sense of lack is material, emotional and experiential. The Barnardo's advertisements suggest that children deserve to have a future and that they represent the future. As such, Mayhew and Barnardo both contribute to a view of childhood defined by its social status as a subordinate group in need of protection in order to be prepared for adulthood. Of course, it is adults who are claiming a future for children rather than children themselves, and this brings us to another point. Mayhew and Barnardo both position children as essentially passive – things happen to them that they do not choose and cannot control. Issues of agency and powerlessness remain central to contemporary discussions of childhood, emerging across several chapters in this volume.

The idea that childhood innocence should be preserved is a pervasive one and can be seen to operate on many different levels. Henry Mayhew's account implies that children should be protected from the harsh realities of life. The advertisements featured in the Barnardo's campaign may be aligned with this sentiment but go further to indicate that the child is an adult-in-the-making and therefore requires quality care and attention. The *idea* of childhood that can be discerned in Mayhew's account and Barnardo's advertising reflect two discourses that underpin contemporary understandings of childhood – the Romantic discourse and the discourse of *tabula rasa* (blank slate). Drawing upon the work of French philosopher Jean-Jacques Rousseau (1712–78), the Romantic discourse claimed that children embody a state of innocence, purity and natural goodness that is only contaminated on contact with the corrupt outside world. The Romantic vision of the child ascribed children a spirituality that placed them close to God, nature and all things good. Children's purity should be respected and protected in order for them to express themselves freely and creatively. These ideas about children were taken up in England by William Wordsworth who famously claimed that 'The Child is father of the Man' ('My Heart Leaps Up', 1802). The *tabula rasa* discourse draws upon the philosophy of John Locke who developed the idea that children come into the world as blank slates who could, with guidance and training, develop into rational human beings. Within this discourse the child is always in the process of becoming, an adult-in-the-making with specific educational needs that adults should take seriously. It is the responsibility of adults to provide the appropriate education and control to enable children to develop into mature and responsible citizens (for a further discussion of discourse informing childhood see Montgomery 2003). The Romantic and *tabula rasa* discourses along with a third discourse – the Puritan – postulating that children are potentially wicked or evil, underpin many contemporary discussions of childhood and are elaborated upon further in many chapters of this book.

The theme of representations is taken up in Chapter 2 to illustrate the ways in which the concept of childhood has been constructed over time. Using a range of historical examples, Diana Gittins points out that childhood is an adult construction that changes over time and place. Moreover, she suggests that the concept of childhood serves to disguise differences between children, especially in relation to social categories such as gender, ethnicity and social class. The chapter provides a clear and insightful discussion of the Ariès thesis, an influential historical study that analysed paintings to argue that childhood is a modern invention that emerged from the beginning of the sixteenth century. Gittins points out that the development of childhood as a concept was class-specific, reflecting the values and practices of a rising European middle class that increasingly differentiated adults and children, girls and boys.

Creating children as a special category of people also creates the need for cultural products and practices that set children apart from adults. Toys, books and artefacts made specifically for use by children are often referred to as the *material culture* of childhood. In Chapter 3, Peter Hunt explores this aspect of children's culture and discusses the historical relationship between children's books and the concept of childhood. He points out that children's literature is an unreliable resource for understanding childhood. Children's literature creates or constructs a version of childhood that is then addressed in children's books. Important power struggles can be played out within children's literature as it is of course adults who write and children who read the books. Viewed across time, the literature can be seen as a site where competing versions of childhood can be defined and struggled over. The earliest books for children were produced for the middle classes and had a strong didactic purpose, providing children with moral and religious education. In recent times, children's writers appear to be on the child's side, creating an alliance with other children against adults. The potency of children's literature lies in the residual image of childhood it leaves behind – the safe, decent world of the Famous Five or the wonderful fantasy world of action heroes. Hunt suggests that a significant change in children's literature occurred during the 1970s. This period was marked by the introduction of neo-realist themes – dark tales portraying a nightmarish world, usually outside the bounds of children's fiction. In contemporary children's literature, children are positioned as perceptive and reflexive subjects, more knowing than the adults around them. Finally, Hunt suggests that children's books reflect the aspirations of adults for children – aspirations that can be variously identified as: the child as last refuge of a collapsing society; child as consumer; and child as rebellious individual.

In Chapter 3 of the section on historical approaches to childhood, Mary Jane Kehily and Heather Montgomery consider childhood in relation to issues of sexuality. Contemporary discourses, drawing heavily on Romantic themes, position children as sexually innocent. Exploring ideas of innocence and sexual knowledge historically through anthropology, it is apparent that childhood sexuality is a highly contested domain contingent upon time and place. Through discussion of a range of examples from different times and geographical locations, the chapter points out that the meanings ascribed to sexuality and sexual practice are a matter of interpretation for both adults and children. The chapter suggests that the idea of childhood innocence in the West retains its strength as an adult *ideal*, something which adults would *like children to be*. In many western contexts adults appear keen to maintain symbolic boundaries that play out the powerful social taboo commented upon by Stevi Jackson (1982), that children and sex should be kept apart. However, a Foucaultian perspective indicates that the presence of boundaries also creates the conditions for multiple acts of trangression. The eroticization of children in the West, particularly girls, can be seen in this light. The chapter points to the potential of literature and popular culture to illustrate and illuminate these themes in films such as *The Wizard of Oz* and novels such as *Lolita*. The chapter concludes with the thought that the construction of childhood innocence reveals much more about adults than children.

Sociocultural approaches to childhood

Part 2 considers the ways in which the study of childhood has been approached within the social sciences and cultural studies. Here the focus is largely upon the contemporary period of the late twentieth century to the present day. The late twentieth century was marked by an interest in forms of reflexivity. Academics working within the confines of disciplinary boundaries posed questions concerning the nature and status of academic inquiry such as 'How do we know what we know?' and 'How far does research bring into being the subject it purports to study?' The argument could be made that, in conducting research on children, researchers also produce a version of 'the child' and indeed a version of childhood. The recognition that there may be different ways of being a child and different kinds of childhood is important to the development of contemporary approaches to childhood. Central to contemporary approaches is the understanding that childhood is not universal; rather, it is a product of culture and as such will vary across time and place.

The disciplines of psychology and sociology have made a significant contribution to contemporary understandings of childhood. In general, psychological research has focused upon the individual child, while sociological research has been interested in children as a social group. In the early twentieth century, developmental psychology became established as the dominant paradigm for studying children (Woodhead 2003). Developmental psychology documented the stages and transitions of western childhood. Within this framework, childhood is seen as an apprenticeship for adulthood that can be charted though stages relating to age, physical development and cognitive ability. The progression from child to adult involves children in a developmental process wherein they embark upon a path to rational subjectivity.

Sociological approaches by contrast have been concerned with issues of socialization; ways of exploring how children learn to become members of the society in which they live. The differences between the two approaches are outlined and discussed in an academic intervention that sets out the parameters for a 'new sociology of childhood' (James and Prout 1997). James and Prout propose that 'the immaturity of children is a biological fact of life but the ways in which it is understood and made meaningful is a fact of culture' (p. 7). They suggest that there is a growing body of research that identifies an emergent paradigm for the study of childhood. Key features of the paradigm, as outlined by James and Prout, are:

- childhood is understood as a social construction;
- childhood is a variable of social analysis;
- children's relationships and cultures are worthy of study in their own right;
- children should be seen as active social agents;
- ethnography is a useful method for the study of childhood;
- studying childhood involves an engagement with the process of reconstructing childhood in society.

The differences between psychological and sociological approaches to childhood are frequently emphasized and mobilized as part of a move to critique the universalism of child development (James and Prout 1997; Jenks, this volume). In Chapter 5, Chris Jenks discusses the different ways in which developmental psychologists and sociologists have approached childhood. His chapter points to the influence of Piaget and, by contrast, the conceptual grounds of sociological thought. Finally, Jenks' chapter offers a series of models of the child that provide an overview of sociological approaches to childhood. While it is instructive to think about the differences between developmental psychology and sociology, it is also helpful to hold onto the commonalities and points of continuity between the two approaches. Socialization also calls into being an adult-in-the-making, a child that is in the process of becoming a responsible citizen, albeit a more socially orientated one. The histories of developmental psychology and sociology can be seen as engagements with the project of liberalism – the production and regulation of rational and civilized adult citizens (see Walkerdine, this volume). There is a further methodological point to be made in support of developmentalism. As Martin Woodhead (2003) notes, many of the critiques of Piagetian approaches overlook the research goals and practices that informed the investigation of children's thinking and learning. Woodhead points out that Piaget's approach was child-centred: to encourage greater respect for children's thinking and behaviour; to attempt to understand children's perspectives on their own terms.

Valerie Walkerdine's chapter aims to think about the place of psychology in the understanding of childhood. She notes that developmental psychology has played a central role in the scientific study of children since the end of the nineteenth century. The sociological critique of this body of literature has had the effect of purging psychology from childhood studies only to replace it with forms of neuroscience. Walkerdine suggests that psychology can contribute to our understanding of childhood and can be understood within the context of a historically specific political moment of western democratic societies. Walkerdine explores the experience of schooling in nineteenth-century England as a process designed to address national problems of crime and pauperism. Education would teach moral values and good habits. This investment in pedagogy produced a new way to understand the *nature* of children. From this perspective, developmental psychology provides valuable insights into childhood as a process of adaptation marked by the staged progression towards adulthood. Walkerdine points out that childhood is always produced as an object in relation to power. Moreover, the modern western conceptualization of the child exists in circuits of exchange between the western and the non-western world. Walkerdine suggests that it is important to move beyond dualisms to understand how people become subjects within specific local practices and, further, to understand how subject positions and practices operate within complex circuits of exchange. In conclusion, Walkerdine outlines three approaches to rethinking the place of psychology in childhood: situated learning and apprenticeship; Actor Network theory; and Deleuze and Guattari's notion of assemblages.

The final chapter of Part 2 shifts the focus to a consideration of children's culture. Approaching childhood from a cultural perspective draws upon the work of Raymond Williams (1961, 1989) who famously claimed that 'culture is ordinary'. Williams referred to culture as a 'way of life' that makes sense to individuals in a particular community. This perspective also sees culture as a form of action – it is not just something that people have, it is also what they *do* (Kehily and Swann 2003). David Buckingham's chapter considers the relationship between new media technologies and childhood, and particularly the ways in which children's lives have been shaped and changed in the new media age. Buckingham observes that technology, like the idea of childhood itself, is often invested with our most intense fears and fantasies. These fears and fantasies usually fall into two camps: technology as dangerous and threatening or technology as a form of liberation and empowerment. In the age of the internet, the computer becomes a convenient place to dump worries and frustrations. Countering this view is the Romantic-inspired idea that children are naturally creative and can use new technologies in positive and empowering ways. Buckingham suggests that both these perspectives are symptomatic of the sentimental ways in which children are viewed in western societies. He points to the technological determinism that underpins much discussion of new media, a way of looking that assumes technology will bring change in and of itself. New media technologies, however, rely upon many of the forms and conventions of old technologies. While much research refutes the idea that computer games, for example, are antisocial, very little is known about how children perceive, interpret and use new media. Finally, Buckingham calls for the need to connect macro and micro perspectives, to situate children's relationships with media within the texture of their daily lives while also taking account of the economic and political forces at stake.

In thinking about children's cultural worlds it is important to acknowledge the rich vein of school-based studies that have contributed to an understanding of childhood from the perspective of children themselves. This body of literature explores the many ways in which children make sense of the world around them and take their place in that world through everyday cultural practices. Many of the studies adopting this approach capture something of the *experience* of being a child. In an influential early study based in the UK, Charlotte Hardman (1973) sought to discover whether there is in childhood a self-regulating autonomous world that does not necessarily reflect early development of adult culture. Inspired by the Opie's (Opie and Opie 1969) *Children's Games in Street and Playground*, Hardman suggested that children should be studied in their own right and should be treated as agentic social actors. She developed an analysis of children's culture based upon participant observation of children in a primary school. She suggested that culture could be represented diagrammatically as interlocking circles in which children constituted one segment of a society's set of beliefs, values and social interactions. Hardman's generative approach called for the 'muted voices' of children to be heard. This call was taken up by Bill Corsaro (1985) in his study of children at a nursery school in the USA. Like Hardman, Corsaro's ethnographic observations of children at play offer a compelling and richly detailed analysis of children as active meaning-makers.

Berry Mayall (1994, 2002) has further explored childhood from the perspective of children themselves. Mayall's study argues that children constitute a part of the social order that can be seen in terms of generation. Mayall suggests that children's contribution to the social order should be recognized. Specifically, she points to the significant role that children play in relationship work: providing support, making and maintaining relationships in families and taking on care activities.

Other studies of children's cultural worlds have drawn attention to childhood as a gendered experience. Barrie Thorne's (1993) US-based study of children, gender and play uses ethnographic methods to study the social worlds of boys and girls (aged 9–10) in a public elementary school. Her study captures the energetic and highly-charged nature of children's cultural worlds where friendship involves engagement in imaginative forms of physicality, talk and action. To the adult researcher the rapid movements of children at play appeared haphazard and chaotic. However, after several months of observation Thorne began to make sense of children's play from the perspective of children themselves. Thorne's analysis suggests that children's friendships have a structure and an internal logic that makes sense to the children involved. Through patterns of friendship and rituals of play, children create meanings for themselves and others. An example of this cited by Thorne is the way in which children use everyday objects such as pencils, crayons, erasers, toy cars, magnets and lip gloss. Thorne suggests that these objects acquire symbolic significance among friends. In the school context, where children have little power, these objects become significant as tokens of friendship that can be bartered and exchanged. Thorne observed that the objects constituted a flourishing 'underground economy' and indicated that among the children she studied, they acquired use-value in contexts where patterns of trade marked circles of friendship in the following ways: 'as a focus of provocation and dispute, as a medium through which alliances could be launched and disrupted, as sacraments of social inclusion and painful symbols of exclusion, and as markers of hierarchy' (Thorne 1993: 21).

Thorne identified a further example of children creating meanings through friendship in playground chasing games. Here Thorne describes and comments upon the widespread invocation of 'cooties' or rituals of pollution in which individuals or groups are treated as carriers of contagious 'germs'. Thorne documented the experiences of some unfortunate children whose undesirability was captured and pronounced by the tag 'cootie queen' or 'cootie king'. Thorne suggests that, in general, girls are seen as a source of contamination, referred to by boys in one school as 'girl stain'. This involved boys treating girls and objects associated with girls as polluting while the reverse did not readily occur. Thorne's analysis of these games points to the relationship between children's cultural worlds and the broader context of power relations in which they exist:

> When pollution rituals appear, even in play, they enact larger patterns of inequality, by gender, by social class and race, and by bodily characteristics like weight and motor coordination . . . In contemporary US culture even young girls are treated as symbolically contaminating in a way that boys are not. This may be because in our culture even at a young age girls are sexualized more than boys, and female sexuality, especially when 'out of place' or actively associated with children, connotes danger and endangerment.
>
> (Thorne 1993: 75–6)

Thorne points to the further significance of gender in children's cultural worlds through her conceptualization of 'borderwork', a term used to characterize the ways in which children tend to form single-sex friendship groups that serve to create and strengthen gender boundaries. Thorne suggests that children's friendship patterns create a spatial separation between boys and girls that they work to maintain through play and social interactions more generally. Drawing up boundaries, however, also creates opportunities for transgression, crossing the line to disrupt gender-appropriate behaviour or 'border crossing' as Thorne terms it. While most children adhered to gender-defined boundaries, Thorne did notice that border crossing appeared to be acceptable among girls or boys who had achieved a position of high status within their peer group.

Valerie Hey's (1997) study of girls' friendships in the UK points to some under-acknowledged features of same-sex friendship groups. Hey's ethno-graphic study of girls (aged 11–18) in two secondary schools challenges many assumptions relating to girls' friendship with each other. Hey suggests that feminist researchers have a tendency to romanticize girls' friendships, to view them through the celebratory lens of girls' capacity for sharing, caring and mutual support. By way of contrast, Hey documents and discusses the frequent interactions between girls that centre upon the less than supportive practices of bitching, falling-out and rituals of exclusion. In Hey's account girls can be seen to be engaged in patterns and practices of friendship that are fuelled by tensions and conflict as much as support and care.

Frosh *et al.*'s (2002) study of boys and masculinity illustrates some striking features of boys' friendships. Their interview-based study of boys (aged 11–14) in the UK suggests that boys' relationships with each other are structured around the contradictions of masculine identities. Many of the boys they spoke with saw masculinity and toughness as inextricably linked, thus making it difficult for them to discuss feelings of emotional closeness and intimacy within male friendship groups. In individual interviews with Rob Pattman, however, many boys did discuss feelings of intimacy and vulnerability at school and within the family. Frosh *et al.* particularly comment upon the ways in which conforming to masculine norms may constrain boys and leave them with few opportunities for expressing their feelings. The studies of Thorne, Hey and Frosh *et al.* contribute to an understanding of childhood by problematizing the notion of gender as a 'natural' self-evident feature of children's lives in western societies.

Policy perspectives on childhood

Part 3 is concerned with issues of policy and the ways in which policies relating to children may produce moments of conflict and contradiction when they collide with the realities of children's lives. In Chapter 8, Wendy Stainton Rogers points out that social policy is motivated by a concern for children. Issues of deprivation and disadvantage, and ways to alleviate them, become central to social policy perspectives on children. Earlier in this chapter, we discussed the work of Barnardo, whose concern for children in poverty provided the impetus for the institutional care of children in the UK. This identification of a 'need' followed by social action has been a feature of policy-based approaches. Generally speaking, social policies attempt to make positive interventions in people's lives. In the context of contemporary western child-hoods, Kellmer Pringle (1974) outlined the four basic needs of children as:

- the need for love and security;
- new experiences;
- praise and recognition;
- responsibility.

The discussion of children's needs, however, is commonly based upon assumptions and value-laden judgements about children. Martin Woodhead (1997) notes that the focus on children's needs remains a powerful rhetorical device for constructing versions of childhood – prescribing care and education and evaluating the quality of adult-child relations. In a move to deconstruct western notions of childhood, the universalism of the 'needs' discourse has been critiqued and replaced by a discourse of children's 'rights'. The shift in orientation from needs to rights reflects an endeavour to understand and take into account the child's point of view. Chapter 8 discusses these themes in more detail.

In the UK, social policy is premised upon taking decisions and courses of action that are in 'the best interests of the child'. This aim resonates with global legislation on children, particularly the United Nations Convention on the Rights of the Child (UNCRC) (1989). The UNCRC suggests that adult intervention on behalf of children should be guided by actions that promote the 'best interests' of the child or group of children. The UNCRC places children's rights in the context of human rights and stresses the importance of rights for *all* children. The rights of children are outlined as a set of legally binding principles designed to protect and promote children's welfare in areas such as health, education and the family. The UNCRC acknowledges the vulnerability of children and discusses their rights in relation to the 'four Ps': protection, provision, prevention and participation (for a further discussion of children's rights and the UNCRC see Lansdown 2001; Burr and Montgomery 2003; Burr, this volume).

Issues of policy and legislation commonly rely upon top-down initiatives whereby adults attempt to 'do the right thing' by children. Some studies, how-ever, have developed a child-centred approach to issues of rights. Priscilla Alderson (1993, 2000) takes an innovative approach to children's rights in research that explores children's abilty to understand and make decisions on their own behalf. In studies of, for example, children's ability to consent to surgery and share in the organization and management of schools, Alderson tackles the issue of children's rights from the perspective of children themselves. Her studies document and portray a richly-textured world in which children are indeed capable of exercising rights and making decisions concerning their welfare by themselves and for themselves.

Wendy Stainton Rogers' chapter focuses on practical ways in which childhood can be promoted or made better by adults working within the state policy of England and Wales. Stainton Rogers offers a critical commentary on the notion of the child's 'best interests' by providing us with illustrative examples that unsettle established notions of childhood and welfare – for example, 14-year-old Zadie raises issues that address the tension between children's autonomy and their need for protection. Stainton Rogers points to the limitations of the needs discourse and the rights discourse when it comes to acting in Zadie's best interests. She suggests that a quality of life discourse offers more scope for developing sensitive approaches to children and families. Moreover, a consideration of quality of life has the potential to recognize the strengths of individuals and families in ways that move beyond forms of individualizing and pathology.

Chapter 9 further explores the theme of children's rights by looking at the UNCRC in relation to the experiences of street children in Vietnam. Rachel Burr introduces the reader to the UNCRC and provides useful background information regarding its almost worldwide ratification. Here the impact of the UNCRC is examined in the light of sociocultural influences upon childhood experiences in South-East Asia. Burr argues that the UNCRC represents a particular model of childhood informed by western thinking that has implications for children in non-western contexts. Burr's empirical evidence from Vietnam suggests that, as presently constituted, this child-focused international human rights law is fundamentally grounded in individual rights and therefore remains unable to accommodate societies in which communal rights are the norm. In a critique of the UNCRC Burr draws upon her ethnographic study to show that because the self as 'I' is not universally recognized the UNCRC itself holds little meaning for many societies where communal values take precedence over individual rights. Burr points to the clear tensions between the aims of the UNCRC and local practices in Vietnam. She points out that despite the almost universal ratification of the UNCRC, children's rights are not universal; they are played out differently in different cultural contexts with inevitable points of dissonance and conflict. Seen from the perspective of children themselves in Vietnam, Burr's study illustrates that top-down attempts to give children autonomy are not necessarily having their intended impact.

In Chapter 10, Daniel Monk explores the ways in which childhood is shaped by the law. Perceptions of law and the legal profession frequently paint a picture of law as complex, rather dry and, depending on the circumstances, a burden or a source of protection. The aim of this chapter is to dispel these commonplace assumptions. Monk demonstrates that the law relating to children is not simply a code of behaviour or a rule-book that tells us what children can do or how adults (parents and authorities) should behave towards them. Rather, it can be seen as an increasingly significant site for the construction and legitimization of contemporary knowledge about childhood. In other words, law is not simply functional but productive. This approach requires that we think of law and read law as a contingent cultural and social text. This chapter introduces the reader to some of the key works and underlying principles of critical, feminist and socio-legal perspectives on childhood. It does not deal with these approaches in an abstract or purely theoretical fashion but applies them through an examination of three distinct and currently controversial areas of law:

- Child sexuality;
- Domestic violence and contact disputes in family law proceedings;
- Juvenile justice and the criminal child.

A common question and theme underlying all three areas is the extent to which the law listens to the voice of the children concerned and acknowledges their individual subjectivities. Monk highlights this point and explores the extent to which children can be understood to be 'rights holders' and the degree to which the increased focus and acceptance of a 'children's rights' discourse has and is able to challenge the objectification of children by law. The three areas have been selected to reflect a wide range of legal categories (public, private family, criminal, education and health law) and a variety of legal sources (statute, case law and codes of practice). Monk does not attempt to provide a comprehensive coverage of child law; rather, he demonstrates that there is not one uniform coherent image of the child in law but, rather, that law engages in dialogue with a range of other discourses and tells many different stories of childhood.

The struggle for childhood

Chapter 10 is underpinned by the twin images of children as either innocent angels or evil devils. The Romantic-inspired child of innocence also calls into being its opposite – the demonic child. This duality is often used in the media and can be seen in contemporary views and images of childhood generally. Childhood figures in the contemporary British and North American imagination exist in an idealized state, but children who break out of this state, especially through crime, are increasingly penalized and demonized. Childhood innocence is celebrated and protected, while individual children who transgress are vilified. Their behaviour places them beyond the realm of 'proper' children and normal childhood. As Scraton (1997: 167) observes: 'The conceptualisation of "evil" within the aberrant child has long traditions with religious, academic and child-care institutions. It resides permanently beneath the surface which presents a veneer of tolerance and understanding in direct contrast to the forces released once children and young people step out of line'.

The cases below detail two murders committed by children in Britain and Norway. A comparison of these two cases illustrates the point that childhood innocence is an adult construct rather than an intrinsic and natural part of childhood. The cases also illustrate that there is no appropriate age or developmental stage where children can be said to understand moral reasoning. Children's capacity to understand the consequences of their actions is dependent upon sociocultural context. Chapter 10 suggests that the ways in which children's capacities are enshrined in law and social policy are far from coherent.

Liverpool, UK: the Bulger case

The murder of James Bulger was a key event in Britain in the 1990s and the repercussions continue in contemporary Britain. This event acts as a symbol for much of what is deemed to be wrong with British children and led to many newspaper editorials and commentaries on the nature of childhood, even though the case itself was remarkable for its very rarity. The number of children killed by other children over the last 150 years has remained extremely low and totally constant (Smith 1994). In 1993, James Bulger, a 2-year-old boy, was shopping with his mother in Liverpool and wandered off. He was found and led away by two 10-year-old boys, Jon Venables and Robert Thompson, who subsequently assaulted and killed him and left his body on a railway line. The case appalled people in Britain for many reasons: the age of the murderers; the fact that they were caught on a closed-circuit television camera and images of them abducting James were broadcast on national television; and the indifference of passers-by, who seeing James in distress being led away by his killers did nothing to help. The case opened up an enormous public debate over the nature of children and childhood and the contrasting representations of children, with children such as James representing pure innocence and his killers pure evil.

Sections of the British public and media reacted to the two killers in an emotive way. As the boys were taken to court a mob gathered outside the courtroom screaming for them to be given the death penalty. The courts decided that although they were below the usual age of criminal responsibility they should be tried as adults, in an adult court with none of the privileges usually accorded to children in such circumstances. They were found guilty and sentenced by the judge, Mr Justice Morland, to be detained 'for very, very many years, until the Home Secretary is satisfied that you have matured' (quoted in Morrison 1998). Mr Morland suggested that their minimum sentence should be eight years for 'retribution and deterrence', which two days later was increased by the Lord Chief Justice to ten years. After those ten years were up, the decision about their detention would be reviewed although they were given no maximum sentence. The reaction to the boys by sections of the press was dramatic and often they were portrayed as monsters. In the words of the judge, 'The killing of James Bulger was an act of unparalleled evil and barbarity', while one police officer was quoted as saying, 'I truly believe they are just evil'. A colleague of his reinforced this with the words, 'You should not compare these boys with other boys. They were evil' (Morrison 1998). The newspapers weighed in. The *Sun's* headline read, 'The Devil Himself Couldn't Have Made a Better Job of Two Fiends'; The *Mirror* called the boys 'Freaks of Nature', noting that although they had 'the faces of normal boys . . . they had hearts of unparalleled evil' and the *Daily Star* said simply, 'How Do You Feel Now You Little Bastards?' (Davis and Bourhill 1997: 47).

Eighteen months later, the issue was still bitterly contested with certain tabloid papers backing James Bulger's parents' campaign to have the murderers locked up indefinitely with no hope of release. Partly as a result of this public pressure, the then British Home Secretary, Michael Howard, increased the tariff to 15 years. The lawyers for Venables and Thompson appealed against this at the Commission on Human Rights in Strasbourg. They took the case to the European Court of Human Rights which ruled in 1999 that, although Venables and Thompson had not been subject to cruel, degrading or inhuman treatment, their trial had been unfair and violated their human rights because they had not been able to understand the proceedings. The laws of criminal responsibility in England and Wales and the role of the law in demonizing Venables and Thompson are considered in more detail in Chapter 10.

Blake Morrison attended the trial of Venables and Thompson as a reporter. He went on to write a best-selling book about the experience, *As If*, in which he argues that Venables and Thompson remain innocent despite their crime:

> I have a four-year-old who believes the man in the moon is real – who believes that the moon *is* a man. Other four-year-olds have similar beliefs. They think the mannequins in shop windows are dead people. They think the sea's there because someone left the tap running. They wonder who the sun belongs to, and whether heaven has a floor, and why people aren't in two all the way up. I know seven-year-olds who believe in the Easter Bunny and the tooth fairy. I know nine-year-olds who believe in Father Christmas. (I know forty-year-olds who think

God lives in the sky and wears a white gown.) Long may it last, this belief in magic ... But don't tell me four-year-olds know the difference between right and wrong.

And eight-year-olds, ten-year-olds? They understand the difference better, but can they act on that understanding? Did I? At ten I stole a Ferrari – a Dinky toy belonging to my cousin Richard ... I knew what I was doing was wrong but desire – such a good feeling, which as a child I hadn't learnt to distrust – made it feel right ... I had a moral sense but not moral conviction. How could I have had conviction? I was a child.

Rousseau writes of a boy killing a bird *without knowing what he does*. The phrase is reminiscent of Christ's: 'Forgive them father, for they know not what they do.' Special pleading from the cross; that people sometimes kill in ignorance, even innocence, and should not be eternally punished for their sin.

The basis of *doli incapax* is similar: that before the age of reason, children can't be held responsible. When does the age of reason begin? Every country has its own answer, its own baseline; it's eight in Scotland, ten in England, Wales and Northern Ireland, twelve in Canada, thirteen in Israel, fifteen in Norway, sixteen in Cuba – and in Romania eighteen. The mad arbitrariness. And see how low the British come. Low is the word. Maybe Rousseau was right, or no less wrong than we are, to measure reason in inches rather than years: 'Childhood has its ways of seeing, thinking and feeling which are proper to it'. Nothing is less sensible than to want to substitute our for theirs, and I would like as little to insist that a ten-year-old be five feet tall as that he possess judgement. Robert [Venables] is four foot six, Jon [Thompson] is four foot eight ... If children of four know the difference between right and wrong, let them be jurors. Let ten-year-olds for sure. Wouldn't it be more appropriate for T[hompson] & V[enables] to be tried by ten-year-olds, rather than adults, since this would mean, as juries are supposed to mean, judgement by one's peers? I try this question out, saying it out aloud ... but the answer comes back: of course not. Ten-year-olds as jurors? I wouldn't trust their maturity, their judgement, intelligence, the qualities said to be present in T & V when they killed James ...

God knows, adults find it hard enough to act on their knowledge of right or wrong. Can children, whose sense of right and wrong is newer but dimmer, fresher but fuzzier, act with the same clear moral sense? Do they grasp that hurting someone is much more wrong than stealing and truanting (which T & V had got away with for months)? Do they have a sense of the awful irreversibility of battering a child to death with bricks? Can death have the same meaning for them as it has for an adult? I submit your Honour, that the answer to these questions is no, no, no and no.

(Morrison 1998: 99)

Morrison argues that, as children of 10, James Bulger's killers could have had no real sense of the consequences of their actions and that therefore they cannot be seen as truly guilty or held responsible. He is arguing from a belief that all children are innocent because they do not know. Others, in the media and the justice system, saw the learning of knowledge, especially about right and wrong, as a continuum and that by 10, children should know not to kill and what the consequence of beating and abusing a smaller child will be. The nature of the debate crystallizes round the notion of innocence. Morrison raises the question of innocence and guilt while others, such as the newspaper editors quoted above, suggest James' killers were innately evil and that normal children, the innocents, had to be protected from these aberrations.

Trondheim, Norway: the Raedergrd case

A year after James' death, the small Norwegian town of Trondheim was hit by a similar tragedy. In 1993, 5-year-old Silje Marie Raedergrd was playing with two 6-year-old male friends when the game turned violent. They stripped her, beat her unconscious and then ran away, leaving her to freeze to death in the snow. The similarities with the Bulger case were striking; what is stunning is the differences in perception of children and the way the authorities and Silje's mother reacted. Trondheim is a close-knit community and although many people in the town knew who the killers were, their names were never published and they were protected from the media. The boys lived on the same housing estate as Silje and her family and as soon as news of her murder was made public, the police and the local schoolmaster opened up the school that both the boys and Silje attended and talked to both children and parents, stressing how safe the children were and appealing for calm and no vengeance. Meanwhile the mother of one of the boys who had killed Silje said, 'Please remember that we are dealing with small children here. I cannot continue living here if my son is to be called a killer for the rest of his life' (Franklin and Petley 1996: 150). Two days later, the killers went back to this school, accompanied by psychologists. There were no protests and no parents withdrew their own children. The *Guardian* reported the local paper's attitude: 'the culprits were just six years old; how did they know what they were doing? In Norway, where the age of criminality is 15 – as opposed to 10 in Britain – they were treated as victims not killers' (Hattenstone 2000).

Silje's mother's reaction also contrasts starkly with the UK case. The day after the murder she appealed that the boys should be left alone and not subject to a witch-hunt. She said: 'I forgive those who killed my daughter. It is not possible to hate small children. They do not understand the consequences of what they have done . . . I can sympathise with the boys' parents. They must be going through a lot now. I do not know all of them yet, but they are welcome to contact me if they so wish' (Franklin and Petley 1996: 150). Despite the fact that she still suffers from post-traumatic stress as a result of her daughter's murder and rarely goes out, Silje's mother maintains that the boys should not be imprisoned: 'No they were punished enough by what they did. They have to live with that. I think everybody has got to be treated like a human being. The children have to be educated, have to learn how to treat other people so they could get back into society' (Hattenstone 2000).

A comparison of these two cases reveals that once again, ideas about children's innocence are tied to ideas about age, what children can be expected to know and how far and at what age they have developed a moral consciousness and ability to reason. If Thompson and Venables had been Norwegian, there would have been no question about whether or not they should stand trial – they simply could not, because the Norwegian legal system does not recognize that children under the age of 15 can know what they are doing. The biggest difference in the cases, however, was the discussion they provoked about the very nature of childhood. The children in Trondheim were seen as much as victims as Silje herself and were counselled and reintegrated into society as soon as possible. The crime, while shocking, occasioned no great debate about childhood. In Britain however, the murderers have become symbolic of evil children out of control. The killers of James Bulger are now 20. They are out of prison, have been given new names and identities and have moved away from Liverpool. Their case also prompted questions about the very nature of modern children. Were these killers straightforwardly evil as the police had believed? Were they an aberration or was there something pathological in the nature of childhood itself? *The Sunday Times* claimed that the case was symptomatic of the inherent evil in children: 'We will never be able to look at our children in the same way again . . . parents everywhere are asking themselves and their friends if the Mark of the Beast might not also be imprinted on their offspring' (28 November 1993).

Childhood was in itself a dangerous place that had to be controlled and regulated by parents and adults. In the concern (some would say moral panic) surrounding children at the time, children were no longer seen as inherently innocent until corrupted but possessing 'the Mark of the Beast' which could emerge at any time. Others have taken this further, arguing that:

> Children everywhere were described in terms reserved for hated enemies, they were subject to a 'relentless outpouring of rage and hatred' (Davis and Bourhill 1997: 56); the air was saturated with what Scraton (1999 unpublished paper) has recently termed the 'ideological whiff of child-hate'. The cumulative impact of child

contempt has reached its crescendo. The demonization of children was symbolically established.

(Goldson 2001: 39)

These two different cases show the two extreme views of childhood apparent in much of western thinking. In Trondheim, the children were seen as entirely innocent because they were children. In Liverpool, they were evil, their innocence corrupted, and were afforded none of the privileges and tolerance that their age would have usually brought. In the former case the children were innocent because they did not know; in the latter, they were evil precisely because they did. In so many western images and understandings of children, as this chapter has explored, this dualism is inherent in studies of children. Their childhood is based around their innocence, whether that is defined as sexual, emotional or physical. Once their innocence has gone, so has their childhood, and once that has disappeared they are subject to the same pressures and difficulties as adults, whatever their age and whatever their understanding. They are entitled to no protection, no sympathy and no special pleading. They are no longer children. As Marina Warner (1994: 43) observes:

> We call children 'little devil', 'little monsters', 'little beasts' – with the full ambiguous force of their terms, all the complications of love, longing, repulsion and fear . . . But the child has never been seen as such a menacing enemy as today. Never before have children been so saturated with all the power of projected monstrousness to excite repulsion and even terror.

PART 1
Historical Approaches to Childhood

2 The historical construction of childhood

Diana Gittins

Introduction

Over the past decades more and more books have been published that seek to analyse, describe, reconstruct and represent childhood in the past. Some say childhood used to be more painful and cruel, others claim the reverse. Some argue that all children are essentially the same in the way they develop and that therefore childhoods do not differ in basic ways, while others contend that childhood is always socially and historically constructed. The very notion of a history of childhood, as with the concept of childhood itself, can be, and often is, contested.

Approaches to studying the history of childhood vary quite considerably, but generally fall into three broad categories: first, the study of the changing material conditions of families and households through time, focusing primarily on their socioeconomic situations; second, attempts by 'psycho-historians', drawing on Freudian theory, to reconstruct and try to understand the emotional and psychological changes in childrearing and the experience of childhood in the past; third, the study and description of legal and political changes in governmental attitudes to childhood, childrearing and children by those interested in the history of social policy.

Increasingly, however, and particularly with the development and influence of postmodernist theory, some historians have become interested in what children and childhood have meant to adults, how those attitudes changed and developed, and ways in which they can be analysed, particularly drawing on representations of childhood over time. It is this aspect I want to focus on primarily here, while at the same time acknowledging that all of the categories outlined above are to a great extent interrelated in any discussion. First, however, it is necessary to consider what exactly is meant by childhood.

What is childhood?

Because each and every one of us has been a child, we all believe we know what childhood is – or was. Yet as adults, it is always something past and lost, invariably filtered through memory. Memories of our own childhoods inform our ideas about who we think we are, who we think we were, and what we believe childhood should be for others. Yet memory is a slippery fish and operates often simultaneously at different levels, arguably being reconstructed over time. Early memories can be affected by later images, narratives and experiences. Some seem clear, rational and conscious, while others lurk largely unacknowledged at an unconscious level. The trickeries of memory, of course, can be manipulated by those who do not want children to remember abusive acts. How can the truth and rationality of a memory ever be decided, and by whom?

Arguably we use *images* to a great extent to express real feelings and experiences which the images/memories represent. Furthermore, there are discourses within our culture that define what childhood should be, and these may be as influential in forming our ideas of an image as our own memories. While we like to think of ourselves as logical and rational beings who behave consistently and coherently, more and more it is accepted that we are fragmented, contradictory and complex beings. As a result, what we would like to think of as clear and rational ideas of what childhood is, and was, is arguably a tangled web of ideas, often illusory, which disguise much more complex meanings. It could be said that childhood, rather than a real and material state of being, is more an adult construction that, while apparently simple, in fact disguises a multitude of contradictory memories, desires and myths: 'Childhood, the invention of adults, reflects adult needs and adult fears quite as much as it signifies the absence of adulthood. In the course of history children have been glorified, patronised, ignored, or held in contempt, depending upon the cultural assumptions of adults' (Walther 1979: 64).

How can childhood be invented by adults? Surely, it is a fact that a baby is a biological reality, an embodied being that is entirely physiological? Indeed, a baby *is* a material and biological reality. Yet at the same time, every baby born is born into a social world, a linguistic world, a gendered world, an adult world full of discourse, with complex and contradictory meanings. The helpless and totally dependent human infant, without control or language, is given meaning by adults from the first minute its parent(s) start to interact with it in the context of a wider culture.

The concept of 'child' concerns an embodied individual defined as non-adult, while the notion of 'childhood' is a more general and abstract term used to refer to the status ascribed by adults to those who are defined as not adult.

How that status is conceived – by adults – varies and changes: sometimes it has been defined by physical and/or sexual maturity, sometimes by legal status, sometimes by chronological age alone. The state of being a child is transitory and how long it lasts is culturally and historically variable; in western countries a child may become economically active now at the age of 15 or 16, while in the past, and in some Third World countries still today, children as young as 5 or 6 go out to work. In Britain a child may drink alcohol at home from the age of 5, but not in a public house until the age of 18. The age of criminal responsibility was 7 in Britain before 1933; now it stands at only 10, while in Spain it is 16. This means that in Britain a child of 10 can be treated as an adult in the legal system, while still treated as a child in almost every other aspect of its life. 'Child' has also served to define social groups perceived as inferior: colonized people, slaves, women:

> Even as late as the eighteenth century, the French and German words *garçon* and *Knabe* referred to boys as young as six and as old as thirty or forty. In part, such confusions stemmed from the fact that such terms also denoted status or function . . . among Irish peasants it is still common to call unmarried, propertyless men 'boys', regardless of their age, because this denotes their low status in a community where marriage and inheritance mark one of the most important social boundaries.
>
> (Gillis 1981: 1)

'Child' therefore defines not just physiological immaturity but also connotes dependency, powerlessness and inferiority. Child*hood*, however, focuses more on the general state of being a child, does not refer to an individual child and suggests the existence of a distinct, separate and fundamentally different social group or category. It only has meaning in the context of a binary relationship with adulthood and implicit in it is the idea that it is universal.

Yet the very idea of childhood has *not* always been there, and has changed over time, just as definitions of it, and when it ends, vary between different cultures. For boys in most western countries, for instance, beginning work full-time was usually a mark of transition into adulthood, while for girls it has usually been marriage (or childbirth) that marked the transition, regardless of the age at which they married. Only in recent years has this begun to change. Childhood, therefore, is arguably a construction, a fiction interwoven with personal memories: cultural representations that serve to disguise difference between children – whether in terms of gender, ethnicity, class or physical ability. It hides power relationships and inequality. In short, childhood has been historically constructed and needs to be understood in relation to ideas about what children should be and have meant to adults over time, and why such ideas and beliefs have changed.

All history is arguably a reconstruction from what little remains of fragmentary sources over the ragged course of time: records are burned, lost, shredded (if written); forgotten and distorted if passed on orally; gravestones offer only names and dates. Whole cultures are wiped out by invaders and colonizers who for political reasons will often choose to destroy and ignore their predecessors, to deliberately help them become lost to time. There may be detailed and rich records for royalty and the aristocracy at certain times, but little or nothing to give accounts of those who worked for them or lived nearby, toiling hard to survive. A good historian looks for silences and gaps as much as for that which is stated and recorded. Records exist in places for school attendance and have often been used to make sweeping generalizations about childhood, but at a time when only boys went to school, what do they tell us of girls? Some sermons from centuries past survive in which preachers pontificate about how children should be brought up – but do parents in real life follow the words of preachers verbatim? Have they ever? How can we possibly know?

Ariès and representation

Philippe Ariès, a social historian, first drew attention to the idea that childhood is socially and historically constructed, not biologically given or fundamentally 'natural'. He argued that attitudes to children have changed over time, and with these changing attitudes a new concept developed: childhood. He claimed that in the Middle Ages children mixed freely with adults, and although adults were not indifferent to children, they were less concerned with their development and well-being than has been, arguably, the case in modern European society. Children were seen more as little adults, as adults-in-the-making, than as separate individuals forming part of a distinct social/age group:

> In mediaeval society the idea of childhood did not exist; this is not to suggest that children were neglected, forsaken or despised. The idea of childhood is not to be confused with affection for children: it corresponds to an awareness of the particular nature of childhood, that particular nature which distinguishes the child from the adult . . . In mediaeval society, this awareness was lacking . . . as soon as the child could live without the constant solicitude of his mother, his nanny or his cradle-rocker, he belonged to adult society.
> (Ariès [1960] 1986: 125)

Ariès' work has had enormous impact on how historians and social scientists think of childhood, even though there has been much debate as to the reliability of his methods and sources.

Ariès based much of his theory on the lack of representations of children in medieval art, thereby drawing attention to the central importance of representation and how it is integral to the construction of meaning. 'Representation' refers to both texts and images, but for the purposes of this discussion I will only refer to visual representation. The idea of representation is basically that images cannot be accepted as true reflections of their sources, but are always reconstructed in such a way that they are separate from, distinct from, and other than, those sources. A painting of the Christ child, for example, does not convey a 'true' picture of Christ as a child: the artist would have used an ordinary baby as a model; the background and details would have been specific to his culture at that time or come from his imagination; details such as a halo and a lamb were part of a range of symbols used to connote meanings and messages seen as central to Christ – innocence, holiness, and so forth. Most importantly, as Chaplin (1994: 1) argues, representation can be understood as articulating and contributing to social processes. Paintings of Jesus were part and parcel of western values and beliefs and this in turn informed and affected patterns of interaction and behaviour in the wider social and political world.

Images are immensely powerful and more easily recalled than words, but it is important to remember that they are material products which have been constructed by (invisible) others for a specific purpose. Representations 'are not just a matter of mirrors, reflections, key-holes. Somebody is making them, and somebody is looking at them. They have a continued existence in reality as objects of exchange; they have a genesis in material production. They are more "real" than the reality they are said to represent or reflect' (Kappeler 1986: 3).

We in the twenty-first century are so inundated with and totally used to images wherever we go and wherever we turn that it is hard to remember that the proliferation of imagery is a historical development, and a very recent one at that: photography, cinema, videos, television, advertising are all historically very recent and as a result the impact of one single image is arguably much less than it would have been in the past. Images – representation – are a very powerful means of communication, and a particular kind of communication.

Images do not convey empirical information in the way that words in a text can, and often do. Images often convey emotion, trigger associations and memories, and can evoke multiple meanings, some of which may not even be recognized by the viewer. Seeing a picture of a small child, for example, may evoke feelings of empathy or vulnerability, stir unconscious memories of fear or anxiety, or suggest ideals of innocence and a wish to protect. If that child is also designated as representing Jesus, a whole extra body of messages and assumptions imbues it. None of these, however, is necessarily explicit to the viewer. Charles Peirce put forward a theory that outlined the importance of visual art as a form of communication, and in this he proposed a typology of signs: *iconic*, *indexical* and *symbolic*:

The *iconic* sign proposes a 'fitness' of resemblance to the object it signifies, as a portrait represents the sitter. The *indexical* sign has a concrete, actual relationship to the signifier – usually of a sequential, causal kind – in the sense that smoke is an index of fire. The *symbolic* sign signifies by virtue of a contract or rule . . . It therefore requires the active presence of the interpretant to make the signifying connection. In this triad, the iconic, indexical and the symbolic signs are not mutually exclusive. Rather, they are three modes of a relationship between signifier and object . . . which co-exist in the form of a hierarchy in which one of them will inevitably have dominance over the other two . . . While an image of a table may propose a 'fitness' of resemblance to the table it signifies (iconic signal), this is not the only message that the image gives off. It may symbolise upper-class affluence and dinner parties (a large, well-polished, ornately carved table) or it may symbolise poverty and toil in the kitchen (a small, plain, rickety, scratched table). Colour often signifies symbolically.

(Chaplin 1994: 88–9)

What interested Ariès in medieval art was that painters at that time did not portray childhood as in any way distinct from adulthood. Children, he maintained, when and if they were represented in art, were painted as little adults. They were not represented as if they were perceived as 'other' or forming part of a distinct social group set apart from adults. Yet from the late Middle Ages children *did* begin to be differentiated from adults in paintings. In western art they became an important subject for representation alone as well as in family portraiture.

Paintings are usually commissioned by a particular person for a particular purpose. If the painter wants to be paid (usually indisputable), he or she needs to produce work that pleases the patron. To do so may often mean creating a representation which flatters, disguises or in some way enhances the impression/memory/appearance of what and who is being represented. During the Middle Ages, paintings were overwhelmingly created for churches and religious purposes; they illustrated religious themes and drew heavily on symbolism. At a time when the majority of the population was illiterate, they told visual and symbolic stories to congregations to bring home the message of Catholic ideology. They were not concerned with representing a reality of the material world and certainly had no interest in portraying everyday life and ordinary concerns. Any children who were represented in medieval iconography were almost invariably in the context of religious teaching and beliefs; they did not purport to stand for any embodied child, but were used as a symbol of the soul, or to represent the idea of a holy childhood:

The touching idea of childhood remained limited to the Infant Jesus until the fourteenth century, when ... Italian art was to help to spread and develop it ... At this time the theme of a Holy childhood developed and spread. It became more profane. Other childhoods were portrayed. From this religious iconography of Childhood, a lay iconography eventually detached itself in the fifteenth and sixteenth centuries.

(Ariès [1960] 1986: 33, 35)

From the fifteenth century onwards, however, there was an increasing division in the way children were represented, arguably as a result of the influence of the humanism of Renaissance art, but also undoubtedly part of wider and far-reaching changes in the socioeconomic world: the growth of capitalism, the rise of the bourgeoisie and new ideas and ideals about families and family life.

Historians agree that profound changes occurred around the sixteenth century that affected ideals of, and most probably behaviour concerning, families, family life and childhood. It was a time when capitalism was developing and the feudal order, especially in England, was crumbling; it was a time when new religious beliefs affected how people thought of their world, a time when discoveries, technological and scientific changes were all contributing to profound changes in western culture. Exactly *how* such changes affected families, households, childrearing and childhood, however, is very much open to debate. Families, households and childhoods already varied and differed widely according to class and region, and speaking of them as if they were universal is highly misleading; data and resources are scarce and what theories and generalizations are, and have been, made are by definition provisional, uncertain and liable to contradiction.

Historians of the modernization school have argued that there was a revolution in child care and attitudes to children in Early Modern Europe, notably during the sixteenth century with the rise of Puritanism. Their theories have been based largely on the recorded sermons of preachers at that time which, they argue, show how parents were exhorted by religious leaders to be severe with even the youngest of children in order to eradicate the sin that they believed was innate in everyone from birth.

Protestantism, but especially Puritanism, stressed the importance of individual responsibility to God in the sense that individuals could not obtain forgiveness from sin just through confession or, as was common in medieval Catholic Europe, through the purchase of indulgences. Instead, women and men were instructed to strive to live out the precepts of a Christian life on a daily basis in the everyday world. To put such emphasis on correct behaviour in daily life as well as maintaining a lifelong commitment meant that a rigorous training and socialization in Christian values and behaviour was essential. Such behaviour had to be taught. Not surprisingly, these new religious beliefs brought about a shift in attitudes to childrearing and, by implication, to the importance of childhood generally. Arguably, childhood during this period became a battleground where parents fought to inculcate morality and good behaviour in a committed struggle to save the souls of their children (Demos 1970; Greven 1970).

These fundamental changes in religious belief and their impact on behaviour and childrearing undoubtedly had a considerable effect on the nascent bourgeoisie from the time of the Reformation onwards. Puritan preachers exhorted parents to supervise their children rigorously from the earliest age; play was seen as dangerous and disobedience in any form was taken as a religious affront. The Calvinists, who believed in predestination and actively sought signs of salvation, stressed early conversion and a rejection of all frivolity as the sole way of escape from what was seen as a child's – and also humanity's – essentially depraved nature. Yet there is little way of knowing if these precepts and exhortations were in fact followed by all to the extreme degree demanded by religious zealots.

A group of historians known as 'psychohistorians', for instance, have interpreted these broad historical changes as ones which had a very negative effect on children, childrearing and childhood. Lloyd de Mause put forth what he called a 'psychogenic theory of history' in which he maintained that, first, the evolution of parent-child relations constitutes an independent source of historical change; second, that the history of childhood is a series of closer approaches between adult and child; and third, that childrearing practices are the very condition for the transmission and development of all other cultural elements (de Mause 1976: 4). Like modernization theorists, psychohistorians see parent-child relations as gradually improving in a linear and progressive way from a time when children were valued hardly at all and even sacrificed (literally), to modern cooperative and loving relationships. Influenced by Freudian theory, psychohistorians tend to focus on key stages of childhood, such as weaning and toilet training, and give pre-eminence to the idea of the unconscious. The overriding goal of Puritan preachers to ensure parents eradicated sin from their children has been seen by psychohistorians as having very destructive and negative effects on children and childhood at that time, with a great deal of suffering and cruelty assumed to have been experienced.

Pollock (1983, 1987), however, argues that there is good evidence to support the thesis that Puritan parents were gentle, loving and caring with their children and sees this as almost a universal trait: 'parents have always valued their children: we should not seize too eagerly upon theories of fundamental change in parental attitudes over time . . . There are some basic features of human experience which are not subject to change' (1983: 17). Emotional relations between adults and children, Pollock maintains, are biologically given rather than socially or historically constructed; her theory is, in fact, a socio-biological one. While it is undoubtedly a reasonable claim to make that parents have always valued and loved their children, what her theory lacks is any scrutiny and analysis of the *meaning* of words such as 'love' and 'value' in past times. What we in the twenty-first century may define as loving behaviour towards our children most probably has little in common with what 'love' meant to fifteenth-century parents living in an icy hovel with barely enough to feed seven hungry pest-infested children.

The meaning of words does not remain static, but change over time and according to the context in which they are used. The meaning of words is constantly subject to subtle shifts and changes in the course of social interaction as well as over time. Zelitzer (1985), for example, argued that the 'value' parents put on children up until the nineteenth century was largely an economic one; as children ceased to be economically valuable, they became 'emotionally priceless'. The meaning of children to parents, and thus the meaning ascribed to childhood, changes and varies. While it cannot be denied that children have always tended to have emotional importance to parents, the exact nature and content of that emotional importance cannot be seen as universal. In this way, childhood also must be seen to have and convey different meanings at different times and in different social situations.

One way in which we can get some idea of changing meanings ascribed to childhood over time is, as Ariès made clear, through representation. From the sixteenth century onward, child portraits became increasingly popular among the wealthy; these represented, for the first time, and in a stylized form, historically specific children. At the same time, religious images of children, especially naked boys (*putti*) proliferated. *Putti*, small naked Eros figures, became prevalent in paintings in the sixteenth century, and were originally popularized by Titian:

> Like the medieval child – a holy child, or a symbol of the soul, or an angelic being – the *putto* was never a real, historic child . . . This is all the more remarkable in that the theme of the *putto* originated and developed at the same time as the child portrait. But the children in fifteenth and sixteenth century portraits are never . . . naked children. Nobody could visualise the historical child, even when he was very small, in the nudity of the mythological and ornamental child, and this distinction remained in force for a long time.
>
> (Ariès [1960] 1986: 42)

Arguably, such a division between a 'real' iconic child and a symbolic child made sense at the time because people would never have expected religious representations of children to be realistic; the purpose of religious representations differed from representations of real children, and that was very clear at the time. This shift in how children were represented, their increasing differentiation from adults and thus the development of a new concept – childhood – was paralleled with other changes. It coincided, for instance, with the development of specialized clothing for children, the growth of education and an increasing amount of literature aimed exclusively at children.

To say 'children', however, is deceptive and misleading, because it was in fact *boys* who were first singled out as a distinct and different social category: 'Boys were the first specialised children. They began going to school in large numbers as far back as the sixteenth century' (Ariès [1960] 1986: 56). Both girls and boys were dressed similarly in petticoats until they were 6 or 7 as a sign of subordination and submission (as well as convenience – they wore no underclothes and simply urinated on the ground). At the age of 7, however, boys were 'breeched' and from then on their dress became totally different from that of girls. Girls were dressed from early on as miniature women, while the clothes boys wore from the age of 7, although similar in certain ways to those of grown men, were nevertheless distinct in certain key areas. In the eighteenth century, for instance, boys began to wear special suits called 'skeleton suits', which were different both from their father's clothing and from that of girls:

> Trousers were the common uniform of some subordinate classes of men, including laborers, sailors, and European peasants. A young boy's trousers therefore symbolized his subordination to the men of the family, but the vocabulary of submission was now borrowed from the dress of lower-class males rather than that of upper-class women. Boys as young as three or four were dressed in skeleton suits, recognizing their masculinity long before they reached maturity . . . [it] separated young boys from the mass of women, girls and very small children in petticoats, and placed them in a special category. The skeleton suit drew equal attention to the wearer's age and sex, for it was worn neither by miniature men nor by asexual children but by boys. It also divided the development of a boy into three clear stages: three or four years of infancy in frocks, about six years of boyhood in the skeleton suit, and another four or five years of youth in a modified adult costume.
>
> (Calvert 1982)

They were not just *boys*, however, but also *middle-class* boys. The construction of childhood historically was therefore not just about increased differentiation between age groups, but was also clearly articulated by gender and by class. The historical development of childhood in western Europe was articulated through boyhood. The context of this in the material world was the increasing power of the middle classes who, to a great extent, differentiated themselves from both the aristocracy and the working classes in terms of family and a developing domestic ideology which was premised on new and clearer differentiation between women and men, boys and girls, adults and children, family and the outside world. Home was becoming defined as distinct from work and new ideas of dependency were developing in which women and children were increasingly seen as dependent on their fathers/ husbands. Yet the way in which these changes were constructed through discourse suggested that they were effectively universal: they were presented and represented not as 'the middle-class family', but as '*the* family', not as 'middle-class boyhood' but as '*childhood*'.

The concept of childhood as it developed was historically and class specific, while at the same time disguising both gender and class differences. The term suggests all childhoods are equal, universal and in some way fundamentally identical: it disguises more than it reveals and denies the fact that the meanings and assumptions inherent in it (innocence, dependency) were constructed by a certain social group at a certain point in time, but later used to define what all families and all childhoods should be. The wide range of legislation on child labour, child prostitution and compulsory education can be viewed in the context of these new definitions, forged by the rising bourgeoisie to define and describe their own way of life and then translated into a universal discourse of how everyone else should be. As a result, childhood has become, in a real sense, a myth. Roland Barthes ([1972] 1987: 143) argues that myth 'is depoliticised speech . . . myth does not deny things, on the contrary, its function is to talk about them; simply, it purifies them, it makes them innocent, it gives them a natural and eternal justification'. Myth denies the complexities and contradictions of history and historical construction, giving them 'the simplicity of essences . . . it organises a world which is without contradictions because it is without depth' (Barthes [1972] 1987: 143).

Nature and childhood

One of the ways in which myths can develop is through representation, which was, of course, central to Ariès' theory. Indeed, the development of individual portraits of children and the growth of family portraiture testify to the efflorescence of new bourgeois domestic ideology from the eighteenth century onwards. Moreover, representations of children (and by implication, childhood) increasingly equated them with nature. But what exactly is nature? It is often used to describe groups or phenomena seen as other than, separate from or in opposition to, 'culture'. Gardens, parks, fields of corn we so readily proclaim as 'natural' are in fact constructed by humans, both physically and semantically. The very concept of nature has changed and varied over time, and has for several centuries also been equated with childhood:

This relationship between children, childhood and nature has existed at a number of different levels. It is as complex as our ideas about nature itself: the state of childhood may be seen as pure, innocent, or original in the sense of primary; children may be analogised with animals or plants, thereby indicating that they are natural objects available for scientific and medical investigation; children could be valued as aesthetic objects ... but they could equally well be feared for their instinctual, animal-like natures. Two fundamental points ... arise out of the association between children and nature: First, the polyvalency of nature led to a variety of concepts of childhood, and second, these diverse meanings of childhood were deeply imbued with moral values.

(Jordanova 1989: 6)

In the seventeenth century, the dominant idea of nature was that of a dichotomization between body and mind, which came to a peak with Descartes and the rise of scientific rationalism. Animals at this time were downgraded, while children were increasingly compared to angels and seen as needing more careful protection and nurturing. There was much concern with demarcating more carefully the boundaries between humans and animals, and farmers at the time began to move animals out of their homes and into separate accommodation. Any sign of 'animal-like' behaviour from small children was dealt with most severely.

Yet by the eighteenth century, as the new middle classes became increasingly powerful and urbanization and industrialization gathered pace, ideas about nature had changed dramatically. In particular, there was a shift from mechanical ideas of nature that made a sharp differentiation between body and mind, and in which the body was seen as akin to a machine, to 'organicist' views:

In the late eighteenth century, life was commonly associated with activity and plasticity, with the adaptive powers of organisms to respond to the environment, and with organisation, that is, the structural complexity of a living being, a concept used to explain the special properties of animals and plants. Life as a notion of synthesis, system and fusion ... A rigid demarcation between mind and body thus made no sense ... the moral and the social emerged out of the natural organisation of living matter.

(Jordanova 1986: 106–7)

Ideas about childhood were also changing markedly at this time, with women and children being seen more and more as closer to nature, in a scheme in which 'nature' was increasingly seen as a positive and somewhat mysterious force. Paintings at this time increasingly represented children with pets. Girls were often portrayed in less constrained clothes than in the past, often painted with gardens or similar natural setting as backgrounds; indeed, by the nineteenth century the garden itself had become a metaphor for childhood. As childhood – and especially girlhood – became more and more associated with nature, so childhood became increasingly sentimentalized, culminating in such classic sentimental representations as the 'Bubbles' advertisements in the early twentieth century, where nature, purity, inno-cence and transience are portrayed in a sentimental way and used to sell a wide and increasingly diverse variety of products. From then on the myth of a universal childhood, with all its denial of historicity and difference, becomes entrenched in western culture.

Critiques of Ariès

Yet what is the relationship between reality and representation? To answer that would require a protracted investigation of philosophical debates on the nature of reality; but it is a key area in which Ariès' work has been criticized, and it continues in contemporary culture with controversies over, for example, the relationship between children watching violent videos and tele-vision and their violent behaviour in the material world. What can be said is that representation of children is something done by adults – in other words, it offers potential insight into what children and childhood *mean* to adults, what they have meant to them over time, and how (and perhaps why) those meanings have changed and varied.

Critics of Ariès point out that in focusing so closely on (religious) art, he ignored other sources that could contradict his theory:

> He mistook the absence of handbooks on child-rearing for lack of concern with children, instead of looking in medical treatises for relevant material: focusing on artistic representations of children as miniature adults, he ignored a mass of textual evidence ... for the recognition of childhood as a human stage with specific charac-teristics and needs.
>
> (Nelson 1994: 82)

Nelson was also critical of Ariès for neglecting the variety that existed in the Middle Ages in terms of class and place, as well as ignoring fundamental and important shifts that occurred during the different centuries that have come to be labelled as 'the Middle Ages'. As a result, she argues, Ariès underestimated the love medieval parents held for their children.

Ariès was also criticized by Martindale (1994) for ignoring 'immutable and universal elements' in the care and socialization of children by adults which 'were indeed present in the Middle Ages if one bothers to read the evidence'. He maintains, for instance, that there was in fact an intellectual schema in medieval Europe that dealt with the processes of infancy, childhood and adolescence. Furthermore, he criticized Ariès for suggesting that the high rate of infant and child mortality in the Middle Ages resulted in parents feeling emotionally indifferent to their children because they had to defend themselves against the almost inevitable probability of losing some of them. This, however, was not a central tenet of Ariès' thesis, but one put forward by modernization theorists such as Shorter (1975), Stone (1977) and Stearns (1975).

Conclusion

In spite of criticisms levelled at Ariès, many with some justification, there is no doubt that his work has had enormous influence on the study of childhood. By drawing attention to childhood as something that has been historically constructed, he gave an impetus to historical research on childhood which has indeed burgeoned since the 1960s, continues to the present day and has arguably been crucial in a general problematizing of ideas about, and meanings of, childhood itself. In this chapter I have attempted to trace some key developments in the concept of childhood through a focus upon historical approaches to the study of childhood, particularly in the domain of representations. Looking first at the concept of childhood itself, the chapter points out the differences between the child as an embodied individual and childhood as a historical and social construction that changes over time and place. Second, the chapter points to some of the ways in which images work to create meanings through the ways they are composed and the feelings they invoke in the viewer. Finally, the main body of the chapter has considered some key changes in western societies that have had a profound effect upon families, family life and childhood. Here the rise of the middle class and the meanings ascribed to social categories such as women and children, boys and girls have played a crucial part in the development of childhood as a specifically modern construct. The concept of childhood remains imbued with significance that encodes what children *mean* to adults.

3 Children's literature and childhood

Peter Hunt

Terry Pratchett is a writer much concerned with the complicated relationship between childhood and children's literature. In *Hogfather*, one of his 'Discworld' novels (written for 'anyone old enough to understand'), Susan, the new governess, is taking her charges for a walk, and that walk suggests just how complex their relationship is:

> It was a quiet day for Susan, although on the way to the park Gawain trod on a crack in the pavement. On purpose.
>
> One of the many terrors conjured up by the previous governess's happy way with children had been the bears that waited around in the street to eat you if you stood on the cracks . . .
>
> 'Gawain?' she said, eyeing a nervous bear who had suddenly spotted her and was now trying to edge away nonchalantly.
>
> 'Yes?'
>
> 'You meant to tread on that crack so I'd have to thump some poor creature whose only fault is wanting to tear you limb from limb.'
>
> 'I was just skipping—'
>
> 'Quite. Real children don't go hoppity-skip unless they are on drugs.'
>
> He grinned at her.
>
> 'If I catch you being twee again I will knot your arms behind your head,' said Susan levelly . . .
>
> The previous governess had used various monsters and bogeymen as a form of discipline. There was always something waiting to eat or carry off bad boys and girls for crimes like stuttering or defiantly and aggravatingly persisting in writing with their left hand. There was always a Scissor Man waiting for a little girl who sucked her thumb, always a bogeyman in the cellar. Of such bricks is the innocence of childhood constructed.
>
> (Pratchett: 36–7)

Children's books have a very curious relationship with childhood, and are highly unreliable guides to what childhood was or is. This is not simply because childhood is such a diverse thing: it is because each writer (or syndicate, or publisher) creates or constructs the childhood that they then address. Children's books, therefore, are more likely to portray *attitudes* to childhood than any individual or culturally agreed childhood. Childhood shown in children's books is likely to be a model of how adults think it should be, or wish it was; or a demonstration of what it should *not* be (with more or less direct instructions to the parents as well as the child); or a picture of how adults *wish it had been* or *remember it to have been*. This is complicated partly because children's books are the site of a power struggle; given the fact that adults write and prescribe, and children read, it can be argued that it is impossible – even undesirable – to have a children's book that does not try in some way to manipulate its audience. As Joseph L. Zordano (2001: xv) observed: 'The vast majority of children's stories invite the child to identify with the adult's idea of what the child should be, leaving unquestioned the authority structure of adult and child always implied in the text . . .'.

If we add to this the fact that adults – and, it might seem, especially adults who write children's books – often have a curiously ambivalent relationship to both their own and other people's childhoods, then any image of childhood must be treated with great caution. It may be idealized and sentimentalized (as in A.A. Milne); or it may contain a subtext of a sublimation of an unhappy or traumatic childhood (as in Enid Blyton); or it may contain socially motivated, awful warnings (from Heinrich Hoffmann's satirical but frightening *Struwwelpeter* of 1845 to Robert Swindell's *Stone Cold* of 1993).

Francis Spufford, in his account of his childhood reading, *The Child That Books Built*, thought that in the 1960s and 1970s, the 'second golden age' of children's books, there was a coherent view of childhood in children's literature:

> Unifying this concurrence of good books, and making them seem for a while like contributions to a single intelligible project, was a kind of temporary cultural consensus: a consensus about what children were, and about where we all were in history . . . The new orthodoxy took it for granted that a child was a resourceful individual, neither ickily good nor reeking of original sin.
>
> (Spufford 2002: 18)

It's a nice thought, but even if such conformity and uniformity could be true, it takes no account of the gap between kinds of fiction and kinds of real life. Because writers wish to entertain by empowering children, or feel the need to protect an assumed innocence, books distort: endings resolve matters, extremes are moderated, people behave well, attitudes are balanced. Most of all, genre characteristics – the necessities of plotting – lead to things such as oppositional childhood: how many stories hinge on adults not believing what children tell them? Thus the most powerful children's writers – Carroll, Blyton, Dahl – appear to be 'on the child's side', creating an alliance against the *other* adults. The childhood that appears in books can therefore also often be what the adult thinks that the child *wants* to see.

And all *that* is further complicated by the individuality of readers: each child's reading of each book will be different in significant ways. The images of distressed and damaged childhood in Anne Fine's very dark 'comedy' *Madame Doubtfire* (1987) for example, will be read very differently by a child from a secure home or a child from a broken home (and even then it is impossible to guarantee any simple differences in the meanings that they make).

But despite all of that, we can assume that individual childhoods are strongly affected by the cultural influences around them, and that one of the stronger cultural influences is childhood as imagined by writers of children's books. The result is that children's literature has, in general terms, a symbiotic relationship with childhood: books give an image of childhood different from actuality, but the book is then imitated in real life.

There are some notorious examples of this. Imitation can operate at the simple level of fashion; when A.A. Milne and his brothers had their photographs taken in 1886, as Ann Thwaite points out in her biography of Milne:

> It is the year of *Little Lord Fauntleroy* and all three boys are wearing black velvet suits, with buttoned knickerbockers and large lace collars. Their flaxen hair curls picturesquely on their shoulders . . . It was certainly their mother's idea . . . sensible woman that she was in other ways. Not that there was anything eccentric about it. Many of the nice little boys in the neighbourhood were wearing similar suits . . . It was the hair that was the real problem. It was not cut until they were ten. It gave the wrong impression.
>
> (Thwaite 1990: 23)

(Other notable victims of this fashion were Ernest Shepard and Compton MacKenzie.)

On a larger scale, the survival and development of the British public schools owes something to the codes of behaviour given by Harriet Martineau's *The Crofton Boys* (1841), Thomas Hughes' *Tom Brown's Schooldays* (1857) and thousands of other books. In their fascinating study of girls' stories, *You're a Brick, Angela!* Mary Cadogan and Patricia Craig note the influence on the behaviour of girls of the school stories of Angela Brazil:

> whose energetic form captains and prefects are silly, exuberant and intense in a way which is highly caricaturable . . . [though] *they were*

> *taken seriously by several generations of pubescent readers* ... Silliness
> in young girls had been ignored altogether by the turgid Victorian
> writers ... or it was used as an occasion for moralizing ... Angela
> Brazil broke deliberately with tradition, by expressing the girls'
> attitudes from the inside ... Her girls can be ruthless, stupid, vain or
> pig-headed ...
>
> (Cadogan and Craig 1986: 179–80, emphasis added)

The influence of 'juvenile fiction' extended out to the British Empire.
Writers like G.A. Henty did not merely reflect male childhoods, they perpetu-
ated the attitudes of the manly, empire-building English schoolboy who
thought, in the words of van Eeghen in 1908, that 'he, personally, is equal
to two or more Frenchmen, about four Germans, an indefinite number of
Russians, and any quantity you care to mention of the remaining scum of the
earth' (quoted in Hunt 2001: 71).

The influence of fiction on real life seems to be strong, regardless of
whether the subject-matter is 'realism' or 'fantasy', and regardless of the
improbability of the *actions* of the children in the books. Take, for example, the
writer who has undoubtedly been read by more British children over a longer
time period than any other – Enid Blyton. What image of childhood did
she portray in her books, and what influence did it have? As most of her
books were fantasies, it might seem that the childhoods of Dick and Julian and
George and Anne (for example) are not relevant to our debate. But on the most
obvious level, she celebrates a stable, middle-class, middle England, with
certain standards of decency and certain gender placings. As David Rudd, who
has done a good deal to rehabilitate Blyton's reputation, has pointed out, the
absence of parents in her books 'is in line with Blyton's Froebel philosophy
that children should be left to their own devices as much as possible, and
should be given a rich, natural environment; then they will grow "straight"'
(Rudd 2000: 98).

For all their outlandish adventures, in what seems increasingly to be an
impossibly idyllic suburban and rural landscape, the 'Famous Five' and the
others provide a pattern for supportive, hierarchical behaviour which is part of
a tradition of family solidarity in children's books which stretches back, as
we shall see, for over 150 years. Blyton is a classic example of the potency of
popular literature, absorbed, as it were, through the reading pores of a nation;
what is absorbed is not, I think, the wish-fulfilment and the empowerment
within fantasy – we grow out of these. But residually we are left with a childhood that is ultimately safe, sunny, decent and co-dependent. Childhood
is circumscribed subconsciously, simultaneously idyllic and solipsistic;
childhoods like that (without the adventures) must either have existed, or (as
Jerome K. Jerome put it) were coloured at no extra charge. Either way, their
influence on adults, or on children growing into adults, is incalculable.

To trace the history of the relationship between childhood and children's books is thus infinitely complicated, but I have selected some influential 'landmark' texts. We must, however, bear in mind that with children's books, perhaps more than with any other form, it is the books overlooked by history, the books that were read and loved to pieces that have been just as influential. (This can be tested by asking anyone what the best-loved book in their childhood was; very often they can remember the feel, or the shape, or the colour, or the story, but not the title!)

The very earliest books directed at children were for the privileged few, primarily concerned with education, and specifically religious and moral education. The book generally accepted as the first illustrated book for children, *Orbis Sensualium Pictus* by Johan Amos Comenius (1592–1670) is a Latin primer (translated into English in 1659) and includes a page on 'Societas Parentalis: The Society betwixt Parents, and Children'. Childhood is seen in the context of a family structure:

> *Married Persons* (by the blessing of God) have issue, and become *Parents*.
> The *father* begetteth and the *Mother* beareth *sons* and *daughters* (sometimes *Twins*).
> The *Infant*, is wrapped in *Swadling-cloathes*, is laid in a *Cradle*, is suckled by the Mother with her *Breasts*, and fed with *Pap*.
> Afterwards it learneth to go by a *Standing-Stool*, playeth with *Rattles*, and beginneth to speak.
> As it beginneth to grow older, it is accustomed to *Piety*, and *Labour*, and is chastised, if it be not dutiful.
> *Children* owe to Parents Reverence and Service.
> The Father maintaineth his Children *by taking pains*.

That straightforward portrait of childhood could have been applied for the next 200 years, for Comenius also shows children at play, for example in the page 'Ludi Puerules: Boyes-Sport': '*Boys* used to play either with *Bowling-stones* or throwing a *Bowl* at Nine-pins, or striking a *Ball* through a *Ring* with a *Bandy* [bat], or scourging a *Top*, with a *Whip*, or shooting with a *Trunk* [blow-gun or pea-shooter] and a *Bow*, or going upon *stilts*, or tossing and swinging themselves upon a *Merry-totter* [swing].

Through the seventeenth and eighteenth centuries, books for children contain this contrasting view of childhood. On the one hand there is the insistence that the child be pious and respectful, and yet, in the background, are the *real* children romping and being disobedient.

Probably the most lasting of all the 'early' writers was Isaac Watts, whose *Divine Songs Attempted in Easy Language for the Use of Children* included such memorable verses as 'Against Quarrelling and Fighting' ('Let dogs delight to bark and bite,|For God hath made them so') and 'Against Idleness and Mischief' ('How doth the little busy bee|Improve each shining hour') which was so much a part of British culture that it was parodied by Lewis Carroll over 150 years later in *Alice's Adventures in Wonderland* (1865) as 'How doth the little crocodile/improve his shining tail . . .'.

The eighteenth century saw a battle between the Watts tradition and the more pragmatic popular booksellers; a compromise was often reached. John Newbery, one of the earliest pioneers of children's book publishing included in his *A Little Pretty Pocket-Book* (1744) an alphabet of games (Chuck-Farthing, Dancing Round the May Pole, Fishing, Hop-Scotch, and so on) each accompanied by a moral or Rule of Life. Newbery also stressed the gender difference in childhood: *A Little Pretty Pocket-Book* was sold with 'a Ball and Pincushion, the use of which will infallibly make Tommy a good Boy, and Polly a good Girl'.

To some twenty-first-century eyes, the dominant children's books of the period, whether by educational theorists such as Maria Edgeworth, following Locke and Rousseau, or the Evangelicals such as Sarah Trimmer, may seem to be dangerously repressive. Mary Martha Sherwood's huge best-seller, *The History of the Fairchild Family* (1818 and sequels) is constructed of episodes with a story showing children behaving well or badly (in the latter case they are punished), and ending with a moral and a prayer. In the significantly titled 'Story on the Absence of God', Henry defies his father, and will *not* learn his Latin grammar; Mr Fairchild flogs him with 'a small horse whip', sentences him to isolation and bread and water, and lectures him: 'I stand in the place of God to you, whilst you are a child; and as long as I do not ask you to do any thing wrong, you must obey me: therefore, if you cast aside my authority, and will not obey my commands, I shall not treat you as I do my other children'. Henry eventually sees the error of his ways, and he and his siblings come to respect the stance of their parents. As M. Nancy Cutt points out, however, this family is, in its own way, very caring indeed:

> The little Fairchilds were neither left to the care of servants nor handed over to the outside agencies of school, camp, or cinema. They had at all times their parents' undivided attention. Mr. and Mrs. Fairchild, though strict, are not unpredictable; they explain the reasons for prohibitions and punishments; they invite questions; they are loving and demonstrative . . . Most episodes end [with the children] kissed and reassured . . . tucked into bed by a mother who always had time for them, the little Fairchilds felt thoroughly secure.
>
> (Cutt 1974: 67–8)

Throughout the first half of the nineteenth century, the idea of the child as being inherently evil and needing to be firmly controlled was in tension with the 'romantic' idea of the child pure, free and close to God. Consequently, as the reference point of religion was gradually eroded, to be replaced (especially in the USA) by a concept of individual responsibility, the idea of what constituted acceptable behaviour in childhood changed. As early as 1839, in Catherine Sinclair's *Holiday House*, there is a distinct loosening of the constraints on childhood, and a toleration of playfulness and innocence. In this book, Harry and Laura are naughty children: among other exploits, Laura cuts her hair off, and Harry sets fire to the nursery. Rather than the kind of punishment that might have been meeted out by Mr Fairchild, they elicit this reaction from their uncle: ' "Did any mortal ever hear of two such little torments!" exclaimed Major Graham, hardly able to help laughing. "I wonder if anybody else in the world has such mischievous children?" ' And as for punishment: ' "Perhaps, Mrs Crabtree, we might as well not be severe with the poor boy on this occasion. As the old proverb says, 'There is no use in pouring water on a drowned mouse.' Harry has had a sad fright for his pains . . ." ' (Hunt 2001: 52–3).

The way in which attitudes changed can be illustrated by comparing Isaac Watts' verses with those of Robert Louis Stevenson in *A Child's Garden of Verses* (1885):

> A child should always say what's true,
> And speak when he is spoken to,
> And behave mannerly at table:
> At least as far as he is able.

> (Hunt 2001: 348)

The image of a loving and generally secure family or family unit forms the backbone of the image of childhood in children's books up to the present day, through Charlotte Yonge, Edith Nesbit, Arthur Ransome, Enid Blyton and on into the picture books of Shirley Hughes and contemporary popular reading such as Lucy Daniels' 'Animal Ark' series. We will return to these 'mainstream' books, but we need to recognize that many other significant images of childhood existed around them.

If the Victorian middle-class family provided the norm and the focus for childhood, it also recognized that there were other contrasting childhoods, both in terms of class and gender. In books aimed at girls, especially, the idea of middle-class benevolence was strong – and benevolence required an object: the deserving poor. Hence there arose a powerful genre, the 'waif' novel which, a sceptic might say, combined sentimentalism and self-righteousness with the maintenance of a comfortable status quo. A best-seller like Hesba Stretton's *Jessica's First Prayer* (1867) has as its eponymous character a ragged beggar girl whose mother is a drunken actress. She follows her casual benefactor to church:

> Jessica took a great interest in the minister's children. The younger one was fair, and the elder was about as tall as herself, and had eyes and hair as dark; but oh, how cared for, how plainly waited on by tender hands! Sometimes, when they were gone by, she would close her eyes, and wonder what they would do in one of the high black pews inside, where there was no place for a ragged, barefooted girl like her; and now and then her wonderings almost ended in a sob, which she was compelled to stifle.
>
> (Hunt 2001: 188)

Jessica learns to pray, and takes on the role of the innocent instructor of the adults; on the other hand, while she becomes respectable, she does *not* move out of her station in life.

The curious blending of this kind of tale with both evangelist thinking and a romantic empowerment of the child produced the fashionable idea of the 'ministering child' led by Mary Louisa Charlesworth's *Ministering Children* (1854). Poverty is not only material; it can also be spiritual, and Charlesworth wrote 'to show what ministering children are. There is no child upon earth who may not be a ministering child' (Hunt 2001: 115). Thus, in the first story, Ruth, a little girl who is very poor, comforts an even poorer child with a little food and a lot of the Bible, until she dies:

> But now the child's poor mother said she wanted Ruth to comfort her up, as she had done her dying child; and she begged Ruth to read to her, and tell her those beautiful stories out of the Bible, for she could not read herself. And so Ruth became a ministering child to the poor childless widow.
>
> When we see a child dressed neat and warm in her school-dress, we think she is well taken care of; but it is not always so; and sometimes the little school-girl or boy is much more hungry and faint than the child who begs his food in the streets. We cannot tell how it really is with poor children, or poor men and women, unless we visit them in their homes.
>
> (Hunt 2001: 115)

That 'we' is significant, in placing the child reader apart from the 'others', the children read *about*, and it thereby defines the idea of the *reading* child. The 'others' are often the underclass, those who Dickens portrayed in the death of Jo, the crossing-sweeper in *Bleak House*, in 1853: 'Dead, your Majesty. Dead, my lords and gentlemen. Dead, Right Reverends and Wrong Reverends of every order. Dead, men and women born with Heavenly compassion in your hearts. And dying thus around us every day.'

If girls were portrayed, or defined as demure, studious and benevolent, boys were *different*; this difference was both deep and long-lasting, and, once again, both reflects and perpetuates gender differences and sexism. Here is an example from 1906, setting out the past century's gendering of childhood:

> 'Well,' said the Doctor, 'you know men have to do the work of the world and not be afraid of anything – so they have to be hardy and brave. But women have to take care of their babies and cuddle them and nurse them and be very patient and gentle . . . Boys and girls are only little men and women. And *we* are much hardier than they are . . . and much stronger, and things that hurt *them* don't hurt *us* . . . And their hearts are soft, too . . . and things that we shouldn't think anything of hurt them dreadfully.'

It is perhaps surprising to find that division of roles being explicitly stated in a book by the proto-feminist Edith Nesbit (*The Railway Children*), but much the same happens in a radical (but realist) writer, Arthur Ransome. Here is the fate of Dorothea in *The Big Six* (1940):

> The Admiral had put her foot down. Dorothea was not to be allowed out after dark.
> 'She said ambushes were all right for boys and if there was a row I'd only be in the way. I told her it was my idea in the beginning, but she said I'd have to be content with that.'
> 'She's right, really,' said Dick.

And so on, through Blyton and her successors; critics have even found much the same attitude occurring, if residually, in J.K. Rowling's books.

Victorian boys, then, were stiff upper-lipped, clear-eyed and clean-limbed, the boys of *The Coral Island* manfully conquering the world for Britain. Henty's boys – who became models for their generation, were, as Guy Arnold put it, 'manly, straightforward, could give and take punishment . . . fearless, never lying, resourceful . . . [they] develop strong physiques . . . normally they are from sound middle-class families' (Arnold 1980: 31).

This was a position supported by females as well; Charlotte Yonge said in 1887 that 'Boys especially should not have childish tales with weak morality or "washy" piety, but should have heroism and nobleness kept before their eyes' (Jones and Watkins 2000: 5). Henty's heroes also, like generations of boys (that is, generations of boy readers), avoid women. As Henty said: 'I never touch on love interest. Once I ventured to make a boy of twelve kiss a little girl of eleven, and I received a very indignant letter from a dissenting minister' (Manville-Fenn 1976: 429).

Childhood became a matter of codes, ways of behaving that make you one of the insiders. In Martineau's early school story, *The Crofton Boys*, new boy Hugh is given some advice:

> 'You will find it in every school in England . . . that it is not the way of boys to talk about feelings – about anybody's feelings. That is the reason why they do not mention their sisters or their mothers – except when two confidential friends are together, in a tree, or by themselves in the meadows. But, as sure as ever a boy is full of action – if he tops the rest at play – holds his tongue, or helps others generously – or shows a manly spirit without being proud of it, the whole school is his friend.'

Hugh is later pulled off a wall and has to have his foot amputated, but never reveals the name of the bully involved. Such codes survived beneath the rather savage realism of Kipling's *Stalky and Co.*, and the low comedy of Frank Richards, to re-emerge in the codes of Rowling's Hogwarts School (popular literature is, after all, the most conservative of forms).

The same stereotyping of codes is found in girls' stories, with similar effects. As Cadogan and Craig point out, until the 1920s, girls' stories generally stressed 'feminine duty and domesticity'. The new storypapers for girls, led by *The School Friend* (from 1919, and largely written by men):

> projected a new image of responsible but lively girlhood . . . the hero-ine of every story should be active in her own interests . . . Girl readers began to consider not only fictional heroines but themselves as initiators rather than shuttlecocks of fate, or backers-up of men . . . Hundreds of thousands of girls in the 1920s and '30s lived out the Northcliffe code, and the example of . . . honest and robust pupils was often more effective than advice from schools and churches.
>
> (Cadogan and Craig 1986: 230–1)

The nineteenth-century image of childhood differed in the USA. In the family story, there was more emphasis on independence. In the pivotal *Little Women*, there is a picture of adolescent behaviour that must have appeared to British readers to be enviably unrestrained. As Mr Brooke says: 'Young ladies in America love independence as much as their ancestors did, and are admired and respected for supporting themselves'. In boys' stories there was a strong genre of 'self-help' stories of poor boys making their own way in the world, epitomized by Horatio Alger Jr's *Ragged Dick* (1868). This brought together the 'street urchin' books and the idea of boundless American opportunity, and the books were aimed at the working classes as well as the middle classes. In *Ragged Dick*, Dick the boot-black begins his upward move by depositing money in the bank:

Our hero took his bank-book, and gazed on the entry 'Five Dollars' with a new sense of importance . . . for the first time, he felt himself a capitalist; on a small scale, to be sure, but still it was no small thing for Dick to have five dollars which he could call his own. He firmly determined that he would lay by every cent he could spare from his earnings towards the fund he hoped to accumulate.

But Dick was too sensible not to know that there was something more than money needed to win a respectable position in the world . . . He . . . knew he must study hard, and he dreaded it . . . But Dick had good pluck. He meant to learn nevertheless and resolved to buy a book with his first spare earnings.

(Hunt 2001: 220)

This attitude is epitomized by William Makepeace Thayer's biography of President James Garfield, *From Log Cabin to White House* (1880) with Garfield's 'I can' attitude as a child continually emphasized.

Parallel to this was the 'bad boy' story, which began with Thomas Bailey Aldrich's *The Story of a Bad Boy* (1870), is most widely known in Mark Twain's *Tom Sawyer* (1876), and which culminated in the broad humour of *Peck's Bad Boy and His Pa* (1883). Here is a model for boyhood in which indiscipline is valued – 'Of course all boys are not full of tricks, but the best of them are. That is, those who are the readiest to play innocent jokes, and who are continually looking for chances to make Rome howl, are the most apt to turn out to be first-class business men' (Hunt 2001: 339).

Of course the 'bad boy' stories are overlaid by a certain nostalgia on the part of their (adult) authors, and if they offer children a subversive role it is a 'licensed' subversion. As always, the relationship of fiction to childhood is a complex one, and this complexity can be illustrated by two British texts, Lewis Carroll's *Alice's Adventures in Wonderland* (1865) and Richard Jefferies' *Bevis* (1882).

Alice's Adventures was originally written for a specific child – almost, it might be said, in collusion with a specific child for whom Carroll had a deep concern. Now, that in itself does not guarantee that the childhood portrayed is in any way authentic, but the book and its sequel, *Through the Looking Glass* do seem to constitute a critical portrayal of the 'luxurious captivity' of the Victorian female child. Alice is confined within the walls of the Victorian nursery; the characters she meets in her fantasy Wonderland – the Red Queen, the Duchess, the Mad Hatter and the rest – are caricatures of the insane adult world that she knows. She can only gain any power – knocking over the jury box full of eccentrics and reducing many of them to a pack of cards – in fantasy, and even that is betrayed at the end of the book, as Alice's sister mundanely explains away the dream: 'the rattling teacups would change to tinkling sheep-bells, and the Queen's shrill cries to the voice of the shepherd boy'. But for much of the book, the authorial voice does seem to be on Alice's side, and the result, disguised perhaps from adults by nonsense and political satire and parody, is a book that does *not* recommend a particular childhood.

At the opposite extreme in terms of what childhood can be is the amoral freedom portrayed in Richard Jefferies' *Bevis*, a book *about* childhood which was rapidly adopted by children. Bevis and his friend Mark have the freedom of a farm; they spend nearly six weeks – unmissed by parents (it is harvest time) – living on an island by themselves. They learn to swim and sail; they participate in an epic mock-battle with gangs of local boys; they build a hut, and make a gun, and kill virtually anything that moves with it. Here is Bevis at the end of the summer:

> There was a gleam in his eye, the clear red of his lips – lips speak the state of the blood – the easy motion of the limbs, the ringing sound of the voice, the upright back, all showed primeval health. Both of them were often surprised by their own strength. In those days of running, racing, leaping, exploring, swimming, the skin nude to the sun, and wind and water, they built themselves up of steel, steel that would bear the hardest wear of the world. Had they been put in an open boat and thrust forth to sea like the Viking of old, it would not have hurt them.

Many readers have, however, seen something curious, if not sinister, in the approach of Carroll, and to a lesser extent Jefferies, to the children they create. There is a manipulation, a sensuality, possibly even a prurience, that suggests that imaging childhood has become at best a therapy for the authors, rather than anything that can speak constructively to children. Disablement, illness and death are used to punish or control or 'suspend' children in a state of innocence – even when the child in question is the hero, as in Susan Coolidge's *What Katy Did* (1872) or Ethel Turner's *Seven Little Australians* (1894) and many other titles. This suggests a deep unease in society, a profound ambivalence towards freedom, especially of the female. As Reynolds and Yates (1998: 168) observe, 'It seems likely that at least some of the representations of dead or dying children from these periods . . . like their womanly counterparts, contain disguised erotic discourses and opportunities for sensual arousal'. This topic has been explored extensively by, for example, Nelson (1991), Kincaid (1992) and Carpenter (1985).

Childhood, then, was (and is) frequently *used* in texts, and perhaps one of the more innocent uses was in the popular romance, epitomized by the work of Frances Hodgson Burnett. Once you have taken the adult step of seeing childhood as a place of lost innocence, then it is a short step to giving fictional children the power that adults lack. Thus Burnett produced in Cedric Errol in *Little Lord Fauntleroy* (1886) perhaps the quintessential adult's-child, a mixture of ingenuousness and innocent toughness that charms his irascible, proud, aristocratic grandfather, the Earl of Dorincourt, and everyone else that he meets. This is what children *should* be like – although how far it represents a childhood to be emulated or envied is far from clear: 'What the Earl saw was a graceful childish figure in a black velvet suit, with a lace collar, and with lovelocks waving about the handsome, manly little face, whose eyes met his with a look of innocent good-fellowship'.

This popular image of the child developed in two quite contrasting ways, and it is tempting to see 'real' children as suffering or tolerating the images forced upon them by adults (or is that only a twenty-first-century view?). One development has survived rather better than the other. The heirs of Alice, in the 'real' world, were also the heirs of Jo March, individualists making their own way in the world, blended with the romantic fantasy of Burnett. Katy Carr, Rebecca Rowena Randall (of Sunnybrook Farm), Anne Shirley (of Green Gables) and Pollyanna Whittier are, in the modern idiom, feisty girls (in their different ways). They overcome their own problems and solve those of others, generally by open-heartedness and force of character: in their own worlds they are powerful. The difficulty is that their 'real' worlds are still fantasies; these optimistic childhoods are only adults' dreams.

The other development away from Cedric Errol was perhaps even more dubious in relation to reality. Cedric was seen to be, whether he was or not, a 'beautiful child' and whether it was the influence of pre-Raphaelite artists, the change in the size of families or a neo-romantic atmosphere, a fashion for the idea of the 'beautiful child' grew up. This was characterized by an intense sentimentalizing of childhood which, fuelled by a reaction to World War I which led writers to create an idyllic, protected childhood, kept the fashion going into the 1920s. Its most famous embodiment is A.A. Milne's Christopher Robin (although it should be remembered that the little boy in tunic and shorts was far from being a unique figure). But, for all his fame, Christopher Robin is not really a figure *for* children. Consider 'Buttercup Days' from *Now We Are Six* (1927): whose view of childhood is this?

> Where is Anne?
> Close to her man.
> Brown head, gold head,
> In and out the buttercups.

The antidote to this colonization of childhood was provided by a very different picture of childhood, this time initially written for adults – Richmal Crompton's William, who first appeared in 1919 and whose anarchic career ended, around 350 stories later, in 1970. William is as far from the perfect child as it is possible to get (and Crompton lampooned Christopher Robin in *William the Pirate* in 1932); Mary Cadogan sums up his appearance:

> Generally . . . his clothes are dishevelled and dirty, his carroty hair is
> spiky and upstanding, and his socks are crumpled around his ankles
> because he has used his garters as catapults. His liberally freckled
> face is often screwed into a scowl or allowed to sag into a vacuous
> look which William thinks conveys innocence, though it is more
> suggestive of imbecility.
>
> (Cadogan and Schutte 1990: 56)

The question must be, does William more than merely demolish? Does he
assert the strength of the subversive and if so, does he do it for *children*?

These and many other variations on the idea of childhood, influential
as they were, are satellites around the mainstream, family-oriented childhood that asserts 'norms' of behaviour. Couched in the Victorian ideal of the
unified family, notably in books such as Charlotte Yonge's *The Daisy Chain*
(1856), childhood was increasingly portrayed as being semi-independent of
parents; siblings acted as a group, as a unit, in circumstances very frequently
engineered by the absence of parent or parents.

Instrumental in this were Kenneth Grahame's two books *about* childhood, *The Golden Age* (1895) and *Dream Days* (1898) – sophisticated, ironic
books that did not speak to children but which posited children as intelligent
and knowing. The most influential exponent of this kind of childhood,
for children, was Edith Nesbit, whose books about the Bastable children are
widely regarded as setting a pattern for the twentieth century. In *The Treasure
Seekers* (1899), for example, the children are trying to restore their family
fortunes (their mother is dead, their father fallen upon relatively hard
times). A book-inspired scheme to make money by setting their dog on a
passing old man and then rescuing him misfires, but it brings out the best
in them:

> An then Oswald saw it was all up, and he said, 'Good morning,' and
> tried to get away. But Lord Tottenham said –
>
> 'Not so fast!' And he caught Noël by the collar. Noël gave a howl,
> and Alice ran out from the bushes. Noël is her favourite. I'm sure I
> don't know why. Lord Tottenham looked at her and said –
>
> 'So there are more of you!' And then H.O. came out.
>
> 'Do you complete the party?' Lord Tottenham asked him, and
> H.O. said there were only five of us this time.
>
> Lord Tottenham turned sharp off and began to walk away, hold-
> ing Noël by the collar. We caught up with him, and asked him where
> he was going, and he said, 'To the Police Station.' So then I said quite
> politely, 'Well, don't take Noël; he's not strong, and he easily gets
> upset. Besides, it wasn't his doing. If you want to take any one take
> me – it was my very own idea.'

> Dicky behaved very well. He said, 'If you take Oswald I'll go too, but don't take Noël; he's such a delicate little chap.'
>
> (Hunt 2001: 463)

With Arthur Ransome's *Swallows and Amazons* (1930) and its 11 sequels, childhood was portrayed as a time of freedom: the literary summer holiday had arrived. Ransome's children play (very seriously) away from the nursery and the town, in the Lake District, the Norfolk Broads and elsewhere, with parents discretely monitoring their activities. Despite the change of scene, Ransome is portraying a childhood in the Victorian ideal. The children know their places in the family, and look after each other, behaving in accordance with well-understood codes. Skills, dedication, respectability, loyalty, responsibility and 'mutual aid' imbue all that they do. In *Swallows and Amazons* John Walker's greatest trauma is when he is accused of lying; in *We Didn't Mean to Go To Sea* (1937) the children literally live or die by their own choices.

Ransome's legacy was 50 years of stories that portrayed childhood as a good place to be, but one that was inevitably a place to move on from. One day the children will grow up is the message, and now is the time to acquire the skills and dream the dreams. Thus that unsettling oddity, J.M. Barrie's *Peter Pan*, with its hero who did not wish to grow up but who remained ego-centrically and sadly excluded from real emotions, was not the model that writers adopted: increasingly, it came to be seen as the negative dream of regressive adults.

A major exception to this was Enid Blyton who, as we have seen, celebrated a traditional middle-class childhood. However, her unpopularity with adults, as David Rudd has pointed out, is not a matter of manners or ideology but 'because the adults feel shut out of [the books]'. The world Blyton creates does not look forward to children becoming adults: 'Forever saying the same, Blyton's works . . . celebrate *being* rather than *becoming*' (Rudd 2000: 204). The erosion, the destruction perhaps, of some protected, separate state of being called 'childhood' can almost be measured by attitudes to Blyton.

But for all Blyton's post-war Arcadias, the world was changing, and the writers of the 'second golden age' of children's books in the UK, from about 1945 until about 1970, display serious tensions in their construction of childhood. If we look at some of the most famous books of the 1950s and 1960s – *The Borrowers, Tom's Midnight Garden, The Wolves of Willoughby Chase* – it seems at first that the children portrayed, the childhoods offered to the readers, are very conventional: the values and the roles are much the same as before. But in all the books, it is the adults who are looking backwards (that is, both the adults in the books and the adult authors), and the children who are looking forward. Arietty, in *The Borrowers*, sees the displacement of the family as an adventure and a challenge, not a loss of better days; Tom Long finds himself breaking away from the sureties of thought of his uncle, and being damaged by the conventional comforts of his aunt. Dido Twite confronts the barriers of class and accepts the challenges of modern science. Most of all, adults are not reliable; they are no longer competent; the world that they have made for children is no longer admirable.

These changes crystallized around 1970, although you might not notice this in 'popular' literature for children. The heirs of Enid Blyton, the pony books, 'Animal Ark', the increasingly carefully-calculated series books and, indeed, a large majority of picture-books, all continued to portray balanced families, with children in subservient, generally gender-based roles. Even Roald Dahl, that deeply ambivalent master of displacement has, as the underlying drive of many of his books, the need for the child to move into or back to family. The *Harry Potter* books display very conventional roles for children.

It was in the work of the neo-realists that childhood changed and became a place of postmodern nightmares. The most obvious examples are in the 'teenage' market: Robert Cormier's *The Chocolate War* (1975), a school story in which our clean-cut new boy ends in a bleeding, defeated heap, and Judy Blume's *Forever* (1975), in which our clean-cut heroine has sex and doesn't get married or suffer any dire consequences, epitomize a new, pragmatic view of childhood. The responses to these books (Blume remains the most censored of American children's writers) demonstrates very clearly how strongly the idea of an innocent, pure, protected childhood persists, perhaps against all the evidence to the contrary.

In the UK, we can consider the case of Anne Fine, whose children's books are frequently centred upon disturbed children (*The Tulip Touch*, 1996), or dysfunctional families (*Madame Doubtfire*, 1988), or the problems of step-parenting (*Goggle-Eyes*, 1989; *Step by Wicked Step*, 1995), or problems of growing up in a skewed society (*Bill's New Frock*, 1989; *Flour Babies*, 1992). These are the childhoods that in the nineteenth century were the childhoods of the 'others'. And Fine's attitude is one that Arthur Ransome might not have recognized:

> Children are powerless. The people in their lives make tremendous changes for children and then deny both to themselves and the children the importance of the change and the anguish of the change . . . And so I think that the one thing I try and do in the children's books . . . is to give children a sense that, even though these cataclysmic things happen, it's not that things will change but that their feelings about it will change. It's not as bad as they think or even if it is as bad as they think they will come to terms with it . . . If the children's writer has a job, it is to interpret the world to the child. *You may bring some comfort.*
>
> (Podmore 1996: vi, emphasis added)

Which returns us to the central problem of how far childhood as portrayed in fiction can, or should, relate to reality. Can you show unremitting bleakness and hopelessness? As Ursula K. Le Guin said:

> what . . . is a naturalistic writer for children to do? Can he present the child with evil as an *insoluble* problem . . . To give the child a picture of . . . gas chambers . . . or famines or the cruelty of a psychotic patient, and say 'Well, baby, this is how it is, what are you going to make of it' – that is surely unethical. If you suggest there is a 'solution' to these monstrous facts, you are lying to the child. If you insist that there isn't, you are overwhelming him with a load he's not strong enough yet to carry.
>
> (Haviland 1980: 112–13)

Anne Fine takes a compromise position – 'I write as a citizen as well as a novelist. Children need some protection from the harshest adult realities' (Tucker 1998:7) – but others have not. The novels of Melvin Burgess about drug addiction (*Junk*, 1996), or Peter Dickinson's *AK* (1997) about a child soldier, or Robert Swindell's chilling *Stone Cold* (1993) about a serial killer of homeless teenagers, do not fudge their picture of the state of society. In Gillian Cross' *Wolf* (1990), Cassie lives in a world of council flats and squats and junk food, where parents and grandparents have become so corrupted that her father, a terrorist, is trying to kill her. We are a long way from the loving, pious family of Mr Fairchild, with its violent but loving certainties.

And so we have arrived at a world where children are portrayed as more knowing than the adults around them. In Terry Pratchett's 'Johnny Maxwell' books, the young are streetwise and media-savvy – to the extent that they understand the fictions they are in. In *Only You can Save Mankind* (1993: 27–8) Johnny becomes enmeshed in a fantasy based on a computer game. His friends are unimpressed:

> 'Well . . . your mum and dad are splitting up, right? . . . So you project your . . . um . . . suppressed emotions onto a computer game. Happens all the time . . . You can't solve *real* problems, so you turn them into problems you *can* solve. Like . . . if this was thirty years ago, you'd probably dream about fighting dragons or something. It's projected fantasy.'

Children's books have always been about the aspirations of adults for children – about offering models and images; and, as ever, the images offered now pull in different ways. One acknowledges the postmodern world, and shows childhood, paradoxically, as the last refuge of a collapsing society; but the child as constructed here has nowhere to go: adulthood is not a state to aspire to. And yet that childhood is being devoured by commercial media; 'commercial' writing, with its cross-media marketing, sees the child as consumer, and is obviously deeply involved in moulding a childhood which it then exploits. It also positions itself 'against' prescribed, educational reading matter, producing the illusion that the mass-consumers are somehow rebellious individuals.

Children's literature, in its portrayal of childhood, is a barometer of the pressures on childhood, a state that seems to many to be on the point of being pressurized out of existence. But perhaps there is still hope; as Anne Fine says, the ultimately optimistic pictures of childhood that she gives in her fictions are based, ultimately, on her own children: 'I try to show children as I think they are. Why should I think mine are the only keen-eyed, critical, sensitive, compassionate young people on the planet?' (Fine 2000: 162).

4 Innocence and experience: a historical approach to childhood and sexuality

Mary Jane Kehily and
Heather Montgomery

Introduction

The concept of childhood is frequently premised upon an idea of innocence in which ideas about childhood are constructed in opposition to a dangerous and potentially corrupting adult world. In this chapter we aim to explore the theme of innocence and lost innocence, particularly in relation to childhood sexuality. We are concerned to explore two key questions:

- Are children naturally sexual or asexual?
- Is sexuality something that children need protecting from?

Our starting point for exploring these issues rests upon the recognition that there are many different childhoods and, by implication, many different experiences of sexuality during childhood. Sexuality is often seen as a universal, biological norm, yet sexual acts and behaviour do not carry the same meanings cross-culturally. The appropriateness of children's sexuality is dependent upon a range of social and cultural factors such as gender, social class, ethnicity and indeed the age of the child in question. Additionally, we point to the ways in which children's sexuality is regulated and repressed in the West, often leading to a denial that children are sexually knowledgeable or experienced; a situation not found at other times or in other places. Using examples from the historical, anthropological and sociological record, we will look at the ways in which children's sexuality is socially and culturally constructed. We do not attempt to give a comprehensive view of children's sexualities in all times and places (or to identify historical trends in understanding children's sexualities); rather, by use of selective examples we aim to show that the notion that sexuality is biologically and universally driven is untenable.

Historical attitudes to children's sexuality

Attitudes towards children's sexuality are profoundly influenced by time and place, and must be seen as a product of the particular cultural or historical setting in which they take place. This section will look at various examples from western history and ethnography, examining how children's sexuality has been constructed at particular times and in particular places.

Historically in Europe, the custom of early marriage for the upper classes meant that some children would have sex at what are in contemporary understandings very young ages. The medieval European royal families regularly married children young and girls of 12 and 13 (such as the wives of Henry IV and Henry VII of England) conceived and gave birth to children at this age. Although for the rest of the population marriage tended to be delayed until they were in their twenties, the Church and common law allowed girls aged 12 and boys aged 14 to marry, assuming that at this age they were sexually mature and able to consummate their marriages (Orme 2001). However, appropriate sexuality was closely tied to ideas about reproduction and marriage. Medieval strictures against masturbation suggest that while children's sexuality was obliquely recognized, unless it was channelled into marriage, it was unacceptable. However, as this applied to both adults and children, it seems that children's sexuality was not of particular concern. Indeed, Nicholas Orme, in his study of the lives of medieval children, claims 'The Church, by excusing children from its rules about confession, implied that childish sexual play and invective, imperfectly understood and incapable of fulfilment, were matters not worth its attention' (Orme 2001: 328).

Such examples show not only the social construction of ideas about sexuality but also ideas about childhood. As long as ideas about childhood are contested and changeable, then so too are ideas about sexuality.

One of the most striking documents concerning children's sexuality and the differences between contemporary and historical sensibilities is the diary of Héroad, the physician of Henri IV of France. He kept a diary of the daily life of the king's son, the future Louis XIII, detailing his behaviour, his upbringing and the reactions of the court to him. It shows a court which is extraordinarily tolerant of children's sexuality and which, indeed, appears to focus on a very young child's sexual behaviour. Quotes from the diary are given at length in Phillipe Ariès' *Centuries of Childhood*:

> [When] Louis XIII was not yet one year old: 'He laughed uproarishly when his nanny waggled his cock with her fingers'. An amusing trick which the child soon copied. Calling a page 'he shouted "Hey there!" and pulled up his robe, showing him his cock'.

He was one year old: 'In high spirits', notes Héroad, 'he made everybody kiss his cock'. This amused them all [the court] . . .

When he was just over a year old he was engaged to the Infanta of Spain; his attendants explained to him what this meant, and he understood them fairly well. 'They asked him: "Where is the Infanta's darling?" He put his hand on his cock.

During his first three years nobody showed any reluctance or saw any harm in jokingly touching the child's sexual parts. 'The Marquise [de Verneuil] often put her hand under his coat; he got his nanny to lay him on her bed where she played with him, putting her hand under his coat' . . . The Queen, his mother, made the same sort of joke: 'The Queen, touching his cock, said "Son, I am holding your spout". Even more astonishing is this passage: "He was undressed and Madame too [his sister], and they were placed naked in bed with the King, where they kissed and twittered and gave great amusement to the King. The King asked him: Son, where is the Infanta's bundle?" He showed it to him, saying: "there is no bone in it, Papa." Then, as it was slightly distended, he added: "there is now, there it is sometimes" . . .

After 1608 this kind of joke disappeared: he had become a little man – attaining the fateful age of seven – and at this age he had to be taught decency in language and behaviour. When he was asked how children were born, he would reply . . . 'through the ear'. Mme de Montglat [his governess] scolded him when he 'showed his cock to the little Ventelet girl' . . .

. . . at the age of fourteen years two months he was put almost by force into his wife's bed. After the ceremony he 'retired and had supper in bed at a quarter to seven . . . he was put to bed beside the Queen his wife, in the presence of the Queen his mother; at a quarter past ten he returned after sleeping for about an hour and performing twice, according to what he told us; he arrived with his cock all red.'

(Ariès [1960] 1986: 100–3)

Louis XIII was in a unique position. As the heir to the throne and the future of the monarchy, it may not be surprising that so much attention was paid to his sexuality and his future potency. Certainly, there is no evidence to suggest that all children were treated in such a highly sexualized way or even that this was common among children of the upper classes in France at that time. There is also the suggestion that such behaviour is acceptable only because of his special position and that because he is so young this can all be dismissed as childish play, the joke being on the boy; that while he has been taught what to say and do sexually, he is not mature enough to do anything about it. The fact he was expected to behave in a totally different way once he reached 7 indicates that when the fear of actual sexual experience became real he was quickly expected to change his behaviour. Nevertheless, the openness with which Héroad discusses his genitals and the sexual banter surrounding Louis does point to a very different construction of childhood. In this construction children are expected, and encouraged, to be interested in sexual matters. It also implies a certain type of sexual knowledge, deemed appropriate to a child like Louis. He was taught to identify sex at an early age as a source of pleasure, in reproductive terms and also in dynastic terms.

Ariès' interpretation of this passage as evidence of a very different understanding of child sexuality has been challenged by others. Héroad's diary is not verified by other sources and we do not know how reliable a witness he actually is. Historian Lloyd de Mause (1976) has seen in this passage a description of child sexual abuse and a projection of adult fantasies rather than an objective account of a child's growing sexual awareness. In the famous opening sentence of his book, he states: 'The history of childhood is a nightmare from which we are only recently begun to awaken. The further back in history one goes, the lower the level of child care, and the more likely children are to be killed, abandoned, beaten, terrorised, and sexually abused' (p. 1). However, this interpretation is informed by contemporary ideas about the appropriate expression of children's sexuality and by a high awareness and disapproval of child sexual abuse. Clearly, Héroad did not think that what he was witnessing and detailing was abusive or even inappropriate in its highly specific context. Although not necessarily relevant for all children at the time, the importance of Héroad's diaries is that they show remarkably different ideas about certain children's sexuality and sexual awareness. The diaries also show the difficulties for a modern reader in understanding children's experiences and expressions of sexuality in cultures far removed from our own. It is difficult to read such an account leaving aside our own understandings of what is appropriate sexual experience for children, and what damages them and can be considered abusive. The issue of abuse is at the centre of notions about child sexuality. One of the reasons that the passage from Héroad's diaries sounds so shocking is because of Louis' very young age. Even his experience of sex within marriage at 14 and the phrase, 'he was put almost by force into his wife's bed' suggests to a modern reader an unacceptable level of coercion. Yet the question of when a child is able to consent to sex is fraught and one that has changed throughout history, as adults have tried to distinguish between children's increasing sexual maturity and the need to protect them.

Age of consent legislation in the UK has been much fought over as adults have attempted to draw this line. As we have seen, the earliest common and Church laws ruled that girls could marry at 12 and boys at 14, based on the belief that boys developed less faster physically than girls and reached puberty later. These laws thus recognized a link between sexual maturity, the ability to reproduce and the legal sanction of sexual activity. As marriage was the only socially sanctioned way to experience sex and to reproduce, as soon as children were able to become pregnant or impregnate each other, then marriage was legal.

The age of 12 remained constant in the UK until 1885 when ideas about sexual purity in women and young girls, along with an idealization of the sexual innocence of girls reached their height. Child sexuality was both forbidden and yet deeply fascinating and this ambivalence is apparent throughout the Victorian era. On the one hand, there was the image of the pure unsullied girl which was sentimentalized in art and fiction, while on the other hand, the interest in child prostitutes and young 'fallen' women (in the paintings of Dante Gabriel Rosetti, for example) show a deep interest in, and implicit acknowledgement of, children's sexuality. A similar acknowledgement can also be seen in attitudes towards masturbation. While the ideal was of the sexually innocent and unknowing child, the varieties of injunctions and instruments used by Victorian middle-class parents to prevent their children's possible masturbation has been well documented, from devices to ensure that children could not reach their genitals to warnings that masturbation caused blindness and insanity. Despite the ideal therefore, there was an implicit recognition that children were inherently sexual and would masturbate unless controlled.

This ambivalence surrounding sexuality is apparent in the concern over child prostitutes. The age of consent up to 1885 was 12 and undoubtedly many women between the ages of 12 and 18 worked as prostitutes in the UK during this time. Some were tricked into prostitution or forced into it by poverty but for the majority of poor, working-class women and girls, prostitution was a way to make money to enable them to survive in a society which offered little in the way of suitable employment. Yet child prostitution became something of a *cause célèbre* in the 1870s, and became the subject of vigorous campaigns to eradicate it. To this end, lurid tales were told of abduction, white slavery and abandonment in brothels in Belgium. Campaigners such as Josephine Butler spoke of 'Infamous houses in Brussels [where] there are immured little children, English girls of from ten to fourteen years of age, who have been stolen, kidnapped, betrayed, carried off from English country villages by every artifice and sold to these human shambles' (Butler 1910: 221).

In a famous exposé, William Stead of the *Pall Mall Gazette* showed how easy it was to procure a child for sex with the full consent of her parents (Stead 1885). Although some cases such as this were documented, for the vast majority of child prostitutes in London, prostitution was not about being kidnapped and taken off to a foreign brothel. Rather, it was about the lack of other opportunities for poor girls. Rarely did campaigners look at the social conditions that made prostitution an option for certain women, preferring to concentrate on an atypical minority in a way that combined prurience, pathos and passionate outrage in equal parts.

Concern about child prostitution therefore became a way of discussing children's sexuality in an oblique way. Child prostitutes exercised both fascination and repulsion and the demand for details about what happened to them in the brothels suggests that concern with their plight was tinged with prurient curiosity about their sexual behaviour. An important class distinction was also noted by Butler and her supporters who argued that while middle- and upper-class girls were protected and kept sexually innocent, their working-class counterparts were not. This point was forcefully brought home by a discussion in the House of Lords in 1884 about raising the age of consent. One peer stood up and said, 'Very few of their Lordships . . . had not, when young men, been guilty of immorality. He hoped they would pause before passing a clause within the range of which their sons might come' (quoted in Gorman 1978: 367).

In other words, construction of girls' sexuality was dependent on class, with sexual purity reserved for middle- and upper-class girls. Working-class girls were expected to be sexually active and sexually available to socially higher men. Campaigns against child prostitution led eventually to the 1885 Criminal Law Amendment Act, which raised the age of consent for girls from 12 to 16 (although it did not apply to boys). It was argued that raising the age would give some protection to younger girls and would criminalize sex between older men and pubescent girls. Whether or not it has better protected girls from older men is very debatable but it did succeed in breaking the link between puberty and sexual experience. Until this point, once a child was physically mature, it was accepted that they could and would have sex. By raising the age to 16, girls could be sexually and physically mature for several years before they were legally allowed to have sex.

The examples discussed in this section have pointed to the ways that ideas about children's sexuality have differed across time and how intertwined they are with ideas about gender, class and social status. There has never been a unitary view on children's sexuality, and constructions of children as sexual or asexual have depended on the gender of the child under discussion as well as their class. What is acceptable and appropriate for middle-class girls is very different to that for working-class boys. Children's sexuality therefore has rarely been seen as unproblematic or uncomplicated and has been regularly policed and controlled by adults.

Ethnographies of children and sexuality

If historical evidence warns us against using modern standards to judge previous eras, so anthropology gives us further insight into the variety of sexualities found among children. This raises questions about the nature of childhood and the nature of sexuality. Despite the assumption common in western societies that sexuality is, at its base, biologically determined, the ethnographic record shows clearly that sexuality is a matter of interpretation in both adults and children: 'Because a sexual act does not carry with it a universal social meaning, it follows that the relationship between sexual acts and sexual meanings is not fixed, and it is projected from the observer's time and place at great peril' (Vance 1991: 878).

To look at children's experiences of sexuality in other cultures, it is necessary to rethink much of our own cultural conditioning and to understand that acts which are sexual in western culture may not be so elsewhere. Understanding children's experiences of sexuality means following Vance's warnings and refraining from projecting our own understandings onto other people's behaviours and attitudes. It also makes it necessary to examine the various components of children's experiences of sexuality, distinguishing between sexual knowledge, sexual activity and the accepted cultural norms of their society regarding sexual behaviour. This means looking at certain acts and considering whether or not they are universally considered as sexual.

This is advice that anthropologists themselves have not always followed. The most famous example is Margaret Mead and her studies of children and adolescents in Samoa. In her book *Coming of Age in Samoa*, she analysed the daily lives of Samoan girls from infancy through early childhood until adolescence. The aim of her research was to make explicit comparisons between the USA and Samoa, looking at how adolescence, and in particular the effects of puberty, were managed differently in the two societies. Her findings showed that the stresses of adolescent life for American teenagers focused in part on the denial and disapproval surrounding adolescent sexuality, pressures that were unknown in Samoan society. According to her research, the girls whose lives she studied had several lovers, beginning just after puberty. Usually a girl's lover would be a boy some years older than herself or a much older man, and before her marriage she would expect to have many lovers or casual sexual partners. As Mead ([1928] 1972: 129) writes:

> Adolescence represented no period of crisis or stress, but was instead an orderly developing of a set of slowly maturing interests and activities. The girls' minds were perplexed by no conflicts, troubled by no philosophical queries, beset by no remote ambitions. To live as a girl with many lovers as long as possible and then to marry in one's own village, near one's own relatives, and to have many children, these were uniform and satisfying ambitions.

The tendency to see sexuality among 'primitive' people as more straightforward, guilt-free and characterized by having more partners is deeply questionable. Nevertheless, it is apparent that the range of sexual behaviours among children is very broad cross-culturally. However, Mead's interpretation of these girls' sexuality has been much questioned recently, with writers such as Freeman (1999) arguing that in looking for contrasts with the USA, Mead overlooked many of the sources of conflict in Samoan society and that girls' sexuality was not as unproblematic as she claimed. Freeman further claims that Mead's informants hoaxed her, telling her what she wanted to hear rather than giving her accounts of their actual behaviour and beliefs. Mead's work shows the difficulties of writing about children's and teenagers' sexuality with an agenda. Nevertheless, she was one of the first anthropological writers to take children's experiences of sex seriously and to understand them in their own terms, and without negative comparison to western ideals. It is very apparent that teenagers (and sometimes children) throughout the world have sex, and that this is not always disapproved of socially. However, as Mead also suggests, whether or not this is constituted as a problem depends heavily on context and the mores of the society under discussion. We know, for example, that sexual experience as a teenager is common throughout the world and this is supported by the high rates of teenage pregnancy throughout Africa and Asia. Yet it need not be problematic. Even in societies that place a strong emphasis on female chastity, early sexual experience is not necessarily a problem as long as it takes place within the confines of marriage. It is the social constraints surrounding sexuality rather than sexuality itself that cause problems.

This, however, is largely understandable to a western audience. If we accept that childhoods are different in time and place and that puberty, rather than a set age of 16 or 18, is the socially sanctioned age at which children are permitted to marry or to have sex, then discussing children's sexual experiences while teenagers is unproblematic. However, it becomes more difficult when looking at younger children's sexuality and sexual experiences. Yet, in many societies, young children are very knowledgeable about sex and it is part of their daily lives. In communities where privacy is not prized, children are likely to grow up hearing adults talking about sex, seeing and even watching their parents and other adults having sex. Hence, the mechanics of sex are no great mystery to them. Thomas Gregor has written extensively about the sexual behaviour and sexuality of an Amerindian group living in Central Brazil called the Mehinaku. He writes of parents openly attributing sexual motivation to very young children, joking about it and viewing it with amusement: 'As toddlers play and tussle in a promiscuous huddle on the floor, parents make broad jokes about their sexual relations: "Look! Glipe is having sex with Pairuma's daughter"' (Gregor 1985: 29).

In this environment, an 8-year-old boy told Gregor, 'I haven't had sex yet, but in a few years I will' (Gregor 1985: 29). Sexual knowledge, and the open acknowledgement of sexuality by children, is not uncommon. However, this does not mean that children's sexuality is always viewed as unproblematic or that Mehinaku society does not distinguish between acceptable and unacceptable behaviours. While little attention is paid to children's sexual experimentation, children are expected to do this discreetly and away from the community. If children are caught, they are teased by their parents and the rest of the community and taught that public displays of sexuality are not welcomed. The situation also changes as children get older and boys in particular are subject to strictures once they reach the age of 12 or 13. The Mehinaku believe that boys do not mature and grow into men naturally and that this process must be brought on through medicine and through sexual abstinence. Around the age of 12 therefore, boys are secluded at one end of the communal house, behind a palm-wood barrier. Here a boy must take medicine, follow certain dietary rules, speak softly and above all avoid any sexual contact with women. Appropriate sexual behaviour therefore changes as children get older. Once a girl reaches puberty she becomes dangerous to boys and her menstrual blood and vaginal secretions can cause sickness in boys who must be protected from her.

This brief exploration of children's sexuality among the Mehinaku points to the complexities of studying children's sexuality in a non-western context. It is impossible to understand children's sexuality without looking at the world views of their culture and without tying discussions to much wider issues of gender roles, reproduction, marriage rules and even cosmology. In other instances this becomes even more complicated when sexual acts carry very different meanings cross-culturally. The clearest example here is from Papua New Guinea, where certain communities practise a form of 'ritualized homosexuality'. In his work with the Sambia (a pseudonym), Gilbert Herdt studied this form of homosexuality. From the age of 7, boys are gradually initiated into manhood by a series of rituals in six stages that involve fellating or being fellated by other men of the tribe. Herdt explains:

> Sambia practice secret homosexual fellation, which is taught and instituted in first-stage initiation. Boys learn to ingest semen from older youths through oral sexual contacts. First and second stage initiates may only serve as fellators; they are forbidden to reverse erotic roles with older partners. Third stage pubescent bachelors and older youths thus act as fellateds, inseminating prepubescent boys. All males pass through both erotic stages, being first fellators, then fellateds: there are no exceptions since all Sambia males are initiated and pressured to engage in homosexual fellation.
>
> (Herdt 1993: 173)

On reading this passage, it is difficult to see anything other than sexual activity, and possibly sexual abuse going on. Yet it is arguable whether these initiations and ritual have anything to do with sex at all. To understand what is happening here involves looking at gender roles in Sambian culture and the cultural meanings placed on semen. Sambian society is rigidly split into male and female with women being seen as inferior men. In order to turn boys into men, they must be taken away from their mothers, whose milk they have drunk in their early years, and turned into men through the ingestion of semen. Semen is the essence of manhood and it cannot be produced by boys alone. Younger boys therefore have to take semen into their bodies from older partners and once they have reached a certain stage of maturity they will then pass semen on to others in turn. Herdt claims that initially boys are reluctant to take part in these rituals but come to enjoy them later on. As they become older, boys become betrothed to a preadolescent girl and enter a bisexual phase. When the girl is mature, her husband will give up the homosexual rituals of his youth and become exclusively heterosexual.

The case of the Sambia is an important one because it focuses attention away from girls' sexuality, which is often given much greater prominence than boys, and also because it calls into question the nature of sexual activity. In this instance, what is seen as a sexual practice in western terms becomes something very different when looked at in Sambian terms. The expectations on boys to perform fellatio and the cultural meanings given to semen mean that boys cannot become men without being initiated and initiating others in turn. It is possible to argue that these initiation practices have very little to do with sexual acts. Yet, Herdt writes that after an initial reluctance, the boys come to enjoy these activities and there does seem to be some element of sexual gratification in them. The role of ritualized homosexuality in Sambian culture is extremely complex but this brief example sheds light on understandings of sexual behaviour and sexuality among children. Ideas about children's sexuality based on notions of universal, biological norms are clearly inadequate in dealing with such cases, making it imperative to view sexuality among children as a cultural construct, dependent on context and related to different world views.

The Sambia are a small group and such behaviour is an extreme example of different understandings of childhood sexuality. Yet they are not unique and in other instances and among other communities interpreting children's sexuality involves understanding profoundly different world views about the nature of sex, the body and indeed childhood. The Canela, an Amerindian group living in Brazil, like many societies, have no taboos on premarital sex and children are encouraged to have frequent and early sexual experience. Amongst the Canela, it is considered necessary and desirable for both boys and girls to begin experimenting sexually from a young age (around 6), both before their marriage (which takes place for girls between the ages of approximately 11 and 13) and after (Crocker and Crocker 1994). Sexual generosity is important in this community and is viewed as an ancestral custom. Girls also have 'sequential sex' where they take on multiple partners at once and girls who show any reluctance to do this are described as 'stingy' and scolded by their female relatives:

> Children up to 6 or 7 grow up watching and hearing adults being open about extramarital trysts and sequential sex and learn how their role models enjoy these activities. Extramarital sex thus becomes a valued expectation of these young people. Experiences continue to enhance this expectation for both sexes into adolescence, when young people become thoroughly involved in extramarital sex themselves. The general atmosphere of joy and fun surrounding extramarital sex may be the principal factor which influences young people to accept and enjoy sequential sex.
>
> (Crocker and Crocker 1994: 166)

However, this is not simply a society where girls experience great sexual freedom or where they are able to control their sexuality, but is one with very different ideas about the body and the nature of sex. The Canela believe that once a woman becomes pregnant, any further semen she receives from other men becomes a biological part of the growing baby. Therefore children have several fathers, known as co-fathers or contributing fathers. To outsiders, these practices may seem bizarre and even repugnant, yet Crocker and Crocker point out that there are strictly observed rules about who can have sex with whom and that child abuse, as it is understood in the West, is very infrequent in this society:

> Our concept of child abuse includes the destruction of the child's trust in kin and others who are supposed to be her or his protectors. We also think of such abuse as involving pain and physical damage to the sexually immature child. The experience of pain in first sex is not part of Canela sexual lore. Although some girls had some anxiety before their first sequential sex, I never heard any discussion of painful experiences. Here again, cultural expectations heavily influence the physical experience.
>
> (Crocker and Crocker 1994: 166–7)

The Sambia and the Canela, although small, isolated groups, show us that it is not possible to see children's sexuality as a natural, biological fact, or that sexuality is necessarily seen as dangerous or abusive for children. They have been looked at here in order to argue that children's experiences of sexuality vary markedly between cultures and also to discuss how ideas about children's sexuality are closely tied to ideas about the body, about gender relationships and about the culturally sanctioned expression of sexuality.

Childhood sexuality as a contested concept

It was apparent in our discussions of Victorian views on children that ideas about sexuality are heavily contested and that often children's sexuality is seen as highly disruptive. We return to these themes in this section, arguing that the privileging of innocence as a central feature of childhood often involve adults in a denial of childhood sexuality. Furthermore, we illustrate the ways in which issues of sexuality have the power to disrupt adult conceptualizations of childhood and to challenge notions of what a child is and can be.

In the British context, Stevi Jackson (1982) has commented on the way in which discussions of children and sex remain controversial. Her analysis suggests that children are defined by adults as a 'special category of people', deserving of our sympathy and protection. At the same time, sexuality is usually defined as a 'special area of life' that is the preserve of adults. Hence, Jackson points to the formation of a powerful social taboo – that children and sex should be kept apart. Supporting much of the anthropological evidence presented here, she writes: 'Our feelings about children and sex are not a natural response to people of a particular age but result from the way childhood is defined in our society' (Jackson 1982: 22).

Jackson emphasizes the social taboo against children having sex. In contrast, some psychologists continue to follow Sigmund Freud (1856–1939) who popularized the notion of the innately sexual child and positioned sexuality as part of the natural developmental process. Freud's views on infantile sexuality argued that:

> It is part of a popular belief about the sexual impulse that it is absent in childhood and that it first appears in the period of life known as puberty. This, though an obvious error, is a serious one in its consequences and is chiefly due to our present ignorance of the fundamental principles of sexual life . . . No author has to my knowledge recognised the lawfulness of the sexual impulse in childhood, and in the numerous writings on the development of the child the chapter on 'Sexual development' is usually passed over.
>
> (Freud [1909] 1965: 247–8)

For Freud, childhood activities such as thumb-sucking or touching of the genitals had to be seen in their sexual context, as part of a child's growing sexual nature which the adult world would aim to bring under control and repress. The important point to note here is that Freud did not believe that childhood sexuality was a social construct but a biological given. Rather than viewing children as inherently innocent, he saw them as innately sexual. He claimed that the period between birth and puberty was sexual, if seemingly latent at the time, and that puberty was not the beginning of sexual feelings and activity. His views were intensely shocking to his contemporaries and have been much debated ever since. However, they do point to the confusion surrounding adult discussions of children's sexuality and innocence. Is a child who plays with his or her genitals, realizing that this gives pleasure, innocent or knowing? Is sexual experience a natural part of a child's development or an aberration? What sort of sexuality and sexual behaviour is normal in children and what is not? Are children sexually active and aware, and repressed by adults, or are they sexually innocent, in the sense that they know nothing about sex?

Contemporary writing indicates that children are sexually aware and that adults ignore it. In the following example, Patrick White, an Australian novelist, writes a fictionalized account of his boyhood in Sydney and his friendship with Hilary, a local boy of the same age.

> We saw a lot of each other as young boys. Hilary was welcome at our house, after school, and for weekends. We cut up a frog in the bath to watch its heart movement, we smoked a cheroot under the buhl table in the hall, and we masturbated together in bed. We were quick to tidy up and it seemed to me at the time my parents were unaware of any of these activities. They must have been. For the friendship was brought to an abrupt end. It filtered back to me through maids' chatter and innuendo from the masters that my friend was an unhealthy influence.
>
> (White 1986: 11)

In this recollection, masturbation is mentioned routinely alongside other boyish activities such as smoking and cutting up frogs. The boys' speed to tidy up suggests that they were aware of the social taboo that is promptly acted upon by adults. Many western parents may implicitly recognize that their children masturbate but social taboos against revelation still exist. The notion of childhood innocence is closely associated with sexual ignorance and this in itself becomes a rationale for keeping sex away from children. Within contemporary western constructions of childhood, adults generally assume that children do not know about sex and if they do then there is something wrong. However, as we have illustrated, there is ample evidence to suggest that children are sexually aware from an early age and, in some cases, sexually active.

On some levels, protection is obviously beneficial. It could be argued that children often do need protection from predatory adults and do need the law to look after their interests. On the other hand, this places sex in a very special position in relation to childhood. Though the age of consent may vary, sex remains unlawful for children in western societies. The argument for sexual prohibition is usually couched in terms of children's immaturity, their vulnerability and their levels of understanding. Although there is a strong developmental aspect to this, there is no consensus on what children are able to understand and cope with at what ages. Those who argue that children should be empowered through knowledge, for example through sex education, often face accusations that they are encroaching on childhood, telling children things that they do not need to know as yet and do not have the experience to cope with. This argument is countered by writers such as Jenny Kitzinger, who suggests that 'the twin concepts of innocence and ignorance are vehicles for adult double standards: a child is ignorant if she doesn't know what adults want her to know, but innocent if she doesn't know what adults don't want her to know' (1990: 169).

The issue of sexuality and control has been taken up in particular by the philosopher Michel Foucault. His book, *The History of Sexuality* (1976) specifically refers to the sexuality of children as a key feature in the development of educational provision and social policy in western Europe. Foucault presents a counter argument to the Freudian view that the sexuality of children is overlooked or repressed:

> It would be less than exact to say that the pedagogical institution has imposed a ponderous silence on the sex of children and adolescents. On the contrary, since the eighteenth century it has multiplied the forms of discourse on the subject; it has established various points of implantation for sex; it has coded contents and qualified speakers . . . [t]he sex of children and adolescents has become an important area of contention around which innumerable institutional devices and discursive strategies have been deployed.
>
> (Foucault 1976: 29–30)

Modern sexuality, from a Foucaultian perspective, can be understood as a historical construct; the product of particular ways of speaking and thinking which are articulated within relations of power. Foucault refers to these ways of thinking and speaking as *discourses*. The development of discourses to talk about sex in fields such as religion, medicine, criminal justice and education was underpinned by a notion that sexuality was a thing to be known and spoken about in the 'public interest'. From this perspective, the sexual conduct of a population becomes an object of classification, administration and regulation. Foucault suggests that sexual categories such as the hysterical woman, the homosexual, the masturbating child and the sex worker can be viewed as actively generated by discourses of sexuality. In the modern era, discourses of sexuality offer a complex means of policing the person, whereby individuals can be defined by their sexual activity rather than by any other aspect of their lives.

In a site where large numbers of young people interact, their sexual conduct becomes a matter for surveillance and intervention. Foucault outlines the ways in which schooling in the eighteenth century was preoccupied with sex, as displayed in the architectural layout of the buildings, disciplinary procedures and organizational structures. Here, the sexuality of children was addressed directly: '[t]he internal discourse of the institution – the one it employed to address itself, and which circulated among those that made it function – was largely based on the assumption that this sexuality existed, that it was precocious, active and ever present' (Foucault 1976: 28).

In particular, Foucault suggests, the sex of schoolboys was regarded as a public problem requiring vigilance, moral guidance and medical intervention. The proliferation of discourses aimed at sex and specifically the sexuality of adolescents, although aimed at restriction and confinement, can be seen to increase awareness of sexual matters and thereby serve as a further incentive to talk about sex.

The eroticization of the child

So far we have tried to explore and question the concept of childhood innocence. This has included a recognition that children may not, in fact, *be* innocent. They may be inherently sexual, as Freud suggests, or they may have been involved in sexual practices as Patrick White describes. These examples illustrate that innocence is not necessarily a given of childhood and cannot be seen as a key feature of children or childhood. So why is childhood commonly connected with ideas of innocence? It would be possible to suggest that childhood innocence is an adult ideal, something which adults would like childhood to be. This ideal can be seen to gain currency through discourses of childhood, in speech, text and popular images, in ways that can be subsequently projected onto embodied children. But what about children who are not seen as innocent? Valerie Walkerdine invites us to think about the ways in which children may be eroticized in western cultures:

> Consider then the threat to the natural child posed by the eroticised child, the little Lolita, the girl who presents as a little woman, but not of the nurturant kind, but the seductress, the unsanitised whore to the good girl's virgin. It is my contention that popular culture lets this figure into the sanitised space of natural childhood, a space from which it must be guarded and kept at all costs.
>
> (Walkerdine 1998: 256)

Walkerdine's analysis proposes that the eroticization of children (particularly girls) has a historical trajectory in the West which can be traced through cinematic portrayals in films such as those starring Mary Pickford or Shirley Temple, or those like *The Wizard of Oz* and *Gigi and Annie*. In these popular narratives, little girls have a charm and appeal, particularly to older men. The allure of such girls lies in their ability to appear simultaneously as innocent and sexually knowing – a combination that positions them as erotic in the eyes of older men. The template for such a girl is 'the little Lolita' Walkerdine refers to. A novel by Vladimir Nabokov, *Lolita* describes an older man's obsession with a 12-year-old girl, his seduction of her and their subsequent affair. The eroticization of young girls is created through the narrator of the novel, Humbert. We see them through his eyes and therefore gain an insight into the sexual allure of little girls for older men. Many of the scenes are described with a great deal of humour in which the narrator demonstrates an acute awareness of his proclivities and the ways in which these may be perceived by others. Humbert is sexually aroused by the presence of young girls and his responses from burning desire to consummate pleasure are documented in hilariously unrestrained detail. For Humbert, the gestures and behaviour of young girls manage to be innocent and erotic at the same time. He notices details of clothing and manner that draw his attention to the prepubescent body of such girls. Their childlike femininity fuels Humbert's desire and in different moments he refers to these girls as 'nymphets', 'demons' and 'darlings'.

Since the publication of *Lolita* in 1955, the name has become synonymous with the eroticization of young girls and specifically the sexual potential of girls and the desires of older men. To return to Valerie Walkerdine's analysis of this phenomenon, she points to two different ways of making sense of *Lolita*: first as a problem of innocent girls abused by older men and second as a problem inherent to some girls who are sexually precocious. Both ways of looking apportion blame to individuals and thereby overlook the pervasive presence of the sexualized girl in representations of children and in popular culture more generally. Patricia Holland (1992: 127) discussed the phenomenon of the sexualized girl in the following way: 'As a child, sexuality is forbidden to her, and it is that very ignorance that makes her the most perfect object of male desire, the inexperienced woman. Thus the fascinating exchange between knowledge and ignorance reaches beyond the boundary between girl and woman and towards the forbidden attraction of innocence itself'. As Walkerdine and Holland indicate, the eroticization of girls is a complex and contradictory issue.

One of the reasons that a novel such as *Lolita* is so unsettling is that the issue of abuse is very close to the surface but is never fully articulated. It is very difficult for a contemporary western reader, with a consciousness of child sexual abuse, to feel entirely comfortable reading *Lolita*. Humbert sees Lolita as sexualized and indeed she may well be sexually aware (later in the novel it turns out that she was already sexually active). However, she is also legally still a child and in need of protection from an older man's fantasy about her sexuality. However, the key point is that she is constructed as sexual by Humbert; he chooses to interpret her attitudes and behaviour as sexual whether they are or not. What is considered sexually innocent changes over time and depends on the standpoint of the person looking at an image or reading a text. The innocence of childhood is largely seen through the eye of the adult beholder (Ennew 1986).

An obvious example is Lewis Carroll's pictures of Alice Liddell (his model for *Alice in Wonderland*), taken in the 1870s and 1880s. Some of these pictures show semi-naked and naked children and although in no way pornographic they contain images such as a naked child reclining alluringly on a *chaise longue*. As ever it is difficult to know the intention behind these pictures or whether Carroll meant them to be erotic. It can be argued that they reflect a belief in the inherent sexual innocence of young girls, so that even when naked they are not sexual. On the other hand, they can also be seen as fulfilling a desire for prepubescent girls, eroticizing their bodies and drawing attention to their sexuality. If it is hard to access sexuality in other times and places, it is doubly hard to understand individual motivation 150 years later. Carroll is now widely regarded with suspicion as having paedophilic tendencies and yet this is judging him by contemporary standards. The images of Alice and the other children were published during his lifetime and did not cause offence. Today, however they are problematic and unsettling. It is impossible to know Carroll's intentions and yet the differences between how they were perceived in the 1880s and how they are seen today say something important about adults' changing images and expectations of innocence. Another example – Graham Greene's review of a film starring Shirley Temple – again brings some of these issues to the fore.

In 1937, the novelist Graham Greene was working as a film critic for the magazine *Night and Day* and in that year he published an article entitled 'Sex and Shirley Temple?'. Shirley Temple was the 9-year-old child actress who had appeared in countless films in the 1930s. She was golden-haired, very cute and the personification of wholesomeness. She regularly appeared as an orphan without parental protection who charmed everyone around her (especially older men). In his review of the film *Wee Willie Winkie*, Greene commented on the inappropriateness of this image and implicitly questioned the sexual motivation behind her appearance. As a result, Twentieth-Century Fox joined Temple's parents in suing the magazine, claiming that 'Green had in effect accused the company of procuring [Shirley] "for immoral purposes"'. At the subsequent trial, the magazine was denounced as a 'beastly publication' and the article as libellous and a 'gross outrage'. Damages were awarded against the magazine and against Greene personally (Temple Black 1988).

The review caused outrage because Greene was suggesting a collusion between the supposedly innocent Temple and the film company, Fox, who were both exploiting her sexuality in order to make money. Such an implication is hardly surprising nowadays and studios would rarely be given the benefit of the doubt. But in 1939, to suggest a child was knowingly sexual was outrageous, especially when that child was an icon like Shirley Temple. What the examples of Alice, Lolita or Shirley illustrate is that whether they were innocent or not is not the issue. There was nothing innate to Shirley herself that was either innocent or corrupt – it is the gaze fixed on her that labels her as either/or. What adults view as innocent says very much more about adults than it reveals about childhood.

Conclusion

This chapter has explored several meanings of children's innocence. Innocence and childhood are strongly linked in contemporary western constructions of childhood, although historical and cross-cultural evidence indicates that this is not a universally shared assumption across time and place. In the West, ideas about children's innocence come from many sources and it has only been possible to touch upon a few examples. In these examples, however, complex and contradictory ideas about children's innocence are apparent and these can have a direct impact upon children's lives. The link between innocence and loss of innocence is an unstable one, shown clearly in discussions of children and sexuality. It is an association that is also highly dependent upon social and cultural context – an idea that has recurred throughout this chapter.

PART 2
Sociocultural Approaches to Childhood

5 Constructing childhood sociologically

Chris Jenks

This chapter will outline and discuss sociological endeavours to realize the child as constituted socially, as a status of person which is comprised through a series of often heterogeneous images, representations, codes and constructs. This is an increasingly popular perspective within contemporary childhood studies (Jenks 1982, 1992; James and Prout 1990; Stainton Rogers *et al.* 1991; Qvortrup 1993). In contemporary studies of childhood, sociologists have been concerned to problematize the very idea of the child rather than treat it as a practical and pre-stated being with a relatively determined trajectory.

Sociology is burgeoning with innovative work in relation to children and is finding its way towards a concerted sociology of childhood that still leaves a degree of exciting work to do. A major contribution consolidating such research has been provided by James and Prout (1990) in a work which attempted to establish a new paradigm in our thinking. It is worthy of consideration here and can act as a manifesto in our subsequent considerations of the significance and relevance of sociological theory in our approach to development. James and Prout (1990: 8–9) identify the key features of the paradigm as:

1 Childhood is understood as a social construction. As such it provides an interpretive frame for contextualizing the early years of human life. Childhood, as distinct from biological immaturity, is neither a natural nor a universal feature of human groups but appears as a specific structural and cultural component of many societies.

2 Childhood is a variable of social analysis. It can never be entirely divorced from other variables such as class, gender and ethnicity. Comparative and cross-cultural analysis reveals a variety of childhoods rather than a single or universal phenomenon.

3 Children's social relationships and cultures are worthy of study in their own right, independent of the perspective and concern of adults.

4   Children are and must be seen as active in the construction and determination of their own social lives, the lives of those around them and of the societies in which they live. Children are not just passive subjects of social structures and processes.

5   Ethnography is a particularly useful methodology for the study of childhood. It allows children a more direct voice and participation in the production of sociological data than is possible through experimental or survey styles of research.

6   Childhood is a phenomenon in relation to which the double hermeneutic of the social sciences is acutely present. That is to say, to proclaim a new paradigm of childhood sociology is also to engage in and respond to the process of reconstructing childhood.

Such an approach, in this context, displays a variety of purpose. First, an attempt to displace the overwhelming claim made on childhood by the realm of common-sense reasoning – not that such reasoning is inferior nor unsystematic but it is conventional rather than disciplined (Schutz 1964; Garfinkel 1967). Common-sense reasoning serves to 'naturalize' the child in each and any epoch: it treats children as both natural and universal and it thus inhibits our understanding of the child's particularity and cultural difference within a particular historical context. Children, quite simply, are not always and everywhere the same thing, they are socially constructed and understood contextually, and sociologists attend to this process of construction and also to this contextualization. Second, the approach indicates that the child, like other forms of being within our culture, is presenced through a variety of forms of discourse. These discourses are not necessarily competitive but neither is their complementarity inherent and a holistic view of the child does not arise from a liberal sense of varieties of interpretation or multiple realities. Rather, the identity of children or of a particular child varies within the political contexts of those forms of discourse. Hence, the different kinds of 'knowledge' of mother, teacher, paediatrician, social worker, educational psychologist or juvenile magistrate, for example, do not live suspended in an egalitarian harmony. Hendrick (1990) has produced an instructive account of childhood constructions in Britain since 1800, through the analysis of a series of dominant forms of discourse in which he includes the 'romantic', 'evangelical', 'factory', 'delinquent', 'schooled', 'psycho-medical', 'welfare', 'psychological' and 'family' as opposed to the 'public' child – these languages have all provided for different modern lives of children. Third, the approach intends to work out the parameters within which sociology, and thus its relation to understanding childhood, must originate – therefore, I shall attempt to show sociology's conceptual limitations, and also its possibilities, as one form of discourse about childhood and the world. However, before I address sociology's conceptual base and therefore its different approach to the child, let me firmly establish its difference from developmental psychology.

The developmental psychology paradigm

In the everyday world, the category of childhood is a totalizing concept – it concretely describes a community that at some time has everybody as its member. This is a community which is therefore relatively stable and wholly predictable in its structure but by definition only fleeting in its particular membership. Beyond this, the category signifies a primary experience in the existential biography of each individual and thus inescapably derives its common-sense meanings, relevance and relation not only from what it might currently *be* as a social status but also from how each and every individual, at some time, must *have been*. It is the only truly common experience of being human, and infant mortality is no disqualification. Perhaps because of this seemingly all-encompassing character of the phenomenon as a social status and because of the essentially personal character of its particular articulation, common-sense thinking and everyday language in contemporary society are rife with notions concerning childhood. Being a child, having been a child, having children and having to continuously relate to children are all experiences which contrive to render the category as 'normal' and readily transform our attribution of it to the realm of the 'natural' (as used to be the case with sex and race). Such understandings, within the collective awareness, are organized around the single most compelling metaphor of contemporary culture, that of 'growth'. Stemming from this, the physical signs of anatomical change that accompany childhood are taken to be indicators of a social transition, so that the conflation of the realms of the 'natural' and the 'social' is perpetually reinforced.

Developmental psychology is wholly predicated on the notion of childhood's 'naturalness' and on the necessity, normality and desirability of development and constructive change through 'growth'. Children are thus routinely constructed as partially rational – that is, in the process of becoming rational. Perhaps the irony of the exclusion of the child through partial formulations of rationality is nowhere more fundamentally encountered than in the formative body of work generated by Piaget. It was Piaget who defined developmental psychology as follows:

> Developmental psychology can be described as the study of the development of mental functions, in as much as this development can provide an explanation, or at least a complete description, of their mechanisms in the finished state. In other words, developmental

> psychology consists of making use of child psychology in order to find the solution to general psychological problems.
>
> (Piaget 1972: 32)

However, as Burman has pointed out:

> Nowadays the status of developmental psychology is not clear. Some say that it is a perspective or an approach to investigating general psychological problems, rather than a particular domain or sub-discipline. According to this view we can address all major areas of psychology, such as memory, cognition, etc., from this perspective. The unit of development under investigation is also variable. We could be concerned with the development of a process, or a mechanism, rather than an individual. This is in marked contrast with the popular representations of developmental psychology which equate it with the practicalities of child development or, more recently, human development.
>
> (Burman 1994: 9)

Piaget's work on intelligence and child development has had a global impact on paediatric care and practice. Piaget's 'genetic epistemology' seeks to provide a description of the structuring of thought and finally the rational principle of nature itself, all through a theory of learning. As such, Piaget's overall project represents a significant contribution to philosophy as well. Following within the neo-Kantian tradition his ideas endeavour to conciliate the divergent epistemologies of empiricism and rationalism; the former conceiving of reality as being available in the form of synthetic truths discoverable through direct experience, and the latter viewing reality analytically through the action of pure reason alone. Kant, in his time, had transcended this dichotomy through the invocation of 'synthetic *a priori* truths' that are the immanent conditions of understanding, not simply amenable to logical analysis. Piaget's categories of understanding in his scheme of conceptual development may be treated as being of the same order. His work meticulously constitutes a particular system of scientific rationality and presents it as being both natural and universal. However, as Archard (1993: 65–6) stated:

> Piaget suggested that all children acquire cognitive competencies according to a universal sequence. Nevertheless, he has been criticized on two grounds . . . First, his ideal of adult cognitive competence is a peculiarly Western philosophical one. The goal of cognitive development is an ability to think about the world with the concepts and principles of Western logic. In particular Piaget was concerned to understand how the adult human comes to acquire the Kantian

categories of space, time and causality. If adult cognitive competence is conceived in this way then there is no reason to think it conforms to the everyday abilities of even Western adults. Second, children arguably possess some crucial competencies long before Piaget says they do.

Within Piaget's system, each stage of intellectual growth is characterized by a specific 'schema' or well-defined pattern and sequence of physical and mental actions governing the child's orientation to the world. Thus the system has a rhythm and a calender too. The development and transition from figurative to operative thought, through a sequence of stages, contains an achievement ethic. That is to say that the sequencing depends upon the child's mastery and transcendence of the schemata at each stage. This implies a change in the child's relation to the world. This transition, the compulsive passage through schemata, is what Piaget refers to as a 'decentring'. The decentring of the child demonstrates a cumulative series of transformations: a change from solipsistic subjectivism to a realistic objectivity; a change from affective response to cognitive evaluation; and a movement from the disparate realm of value to the absolute realm of fact. The successful outcome of this developmental process is latterly typified and celebrated as 'scientific rationality'. This is the stage at which the child, now adult, becomes at one with the logical structure of the cosmos. At this point, where the child's matured thought provides membership of the 'circle of science', the project of 'genetic epistemology' has reached fruition, it is complete.

Concretely, scientific rationality for Piaget is displayed through abstraction, generalization, logico-deductive process, mathematization and cognitive operations. At the analytic level, however, this rationality reveals the intentional character of Piaget's theorizing and grounds his system in the same manner as did Parsons' (1964) transcendent 'cultural values'. Within Piaget's genetic epistemology, the process of socialization can be exposed as the analytic device by and through which the child is wrenched from the possibility of difference within the realm of value and integrated into the consensus that comprises the tyrannical realm of fact. Scientific rationality or adult intelligence is thus the recognition of difference grounded in unquestioned collectivity – we are returned to the irony contained within the original ontological question; the child is, once more, abandoned in theory. Real, historically-located children are subjected to the violence of a contemporary mode of scientific rationality that reproduces itself, at the expense of their difference, beyond the context of situated social life. The 'fact' of natural process overcomes the 'value' of real social worlds. And the normality of actual children becomes scrutinized in terms of the norms predicted by developmental psychology. Rose (1990: 142), commenting on the historical context of this oppressive tendency, stated:

Developmental psychology was made possible by the clinic and the nursery school. Such institutions had a vital role, for they enabled the observation of numbers of children of the same age, and of children of a number of different ages, by skilled psychological experts under controlled experimental, almost laboratory, conditions. Thus they simultaneously allowed for standardization and normalization – the collection of comparable information on a large number of subjects and its analysis in such a way as to construct norms. A developmental norm was a standard based upon the average abilities or performances of children of a certain age in a particular task or a specified activity. It thus not only presented a picture of what was *normal* for children of such an age, but also enabled the normality of any child to be assessed by comparison with this norm.

Within Piaget's demonstrations of adult scientific rationality, the child is deemed to have appropriately adapted to the environment when he or she has achieved a balance between accommodation and assimilation. It would seem that juggling with homeostasis is forever the child's burden! However, although from a critical analytic stance accommodation might be regarded as the source of the child's integration into the consensus reality, within the parameters of the original theory the process is treated as the locus of creativity and innovation – it is that aspect of the structuring of thought and being which is to be most highly valued. In contradistinction, Piaget regards children's play as a non-serious, trivial activity in as much as it displays an emphasis on assimilation over accommodation. Play is merely diverting fun or fantasy, it deflects the child from his or her true destiny and logical purpose within the scheme of rationality. The problem is that the criteria for what constitutes play need not equate with the rigorous, factual demands of reality. In treating play in this manner (that is, from the perspective of the rational and 'serious' adult), Piaget is specifically undervaluing what might represent an important aspect of the expressive practices of the child and her or his world. Following Denzin (1982) and Stone (1965) I would argue that play is indeed an important component of the child's work as a social member. And I would argue further that play is instrumental in what Speier (1970) has designated the child's 'acquisition of interactional competencies'. Genetic epistemology wilfully disregards, or perhaps just pays insufficient attention to, play in its urge to mathematize and thus render formal the 'rational' cognitive practices of adult individuals in their collective lives.

By treating the growth process of the child's cognition as if it were impelled towards a prestated structure of adult rationality, Piaget is driven to concur with Levi-Bruhl's concept of the 'primitive mentality' of the savage, but in this instance in relation to the 'pre-logical' thought of the child. A further consequence of Piaget's conceptualization of the rational development of the child's 'embryonic' mind as if it were a natural process is that the critical part played by language in the articulation of mind and self is very much understated. Language is treated as a symbolic vehicle that carries thought and assists in the growth of concepts and a semiotic system, but it is not regarded as having a life in excess of these referential functions. Thus language, for Piaget, is insufficient in itself to bring about the mental operations that make concept formation possible. Language, then, helps in the selection, storage and retrieval of information but it does not bring about the coordination of mental operations. This level of organization is conceptualized as taking place above language and in the domain of action. This is slightly confusing until we realize that action, for Piaget, is not action regarded as the performative conduct that generates social contexts, but rather a sense of action as that which is rationally governed within the a priori strictures of an idealist metaphysics.

Language, for Piaget, itemizes the world and acts as a purely cognitive function. This is a position demonstrably confounded by Merleau-Ponty (1967) in his work on the existential and experiential generation and use of language by children – the classic example being the child's generation of a past tense in order to express the loss of uniqueness and total parental regard following the birth of a sibling; language here is not naming a state of affairs but expressing the emotion of jealousy. Merleau-Ponty's work serves to reunite the cognitive and the affective aspects of being which are so successfully sundered by Piaget. He stated: 'I pass to the fact that appeared to me to be worthy of mention . . . the relation that can be established between the development of intelligence (in particular, the acquisition of language) and the configuration of the individual's affective environment' (Merleau-Ponty 1967: 108).

I have attempted to explicate certain of the normative assumptions at the heart of developmental psychology which have been as the orthodoxy up until recent years, and I might optimistically suggest that such conventional explanations have been successfully supplanted by feminist theories in relation to the family and what have come to be grouped as 'social constructionist' views of the child, possibly instigated by this author but subsequently titled and joined by significant company. We do not have a consensus view of the child in social theory: however, a spurious consensus is not necessarily a desirable goal. It is my intention to show that it is the different manners in which theoretical commitments are grounded that gives rise to the diversity of views of childhood. At this point let us return to the conceptual bases of sociology.

The conceptual grounds of sociological thought

Although, in its various guises, sociology emerged as a critical response to the state of its culture and traditionally adopted a radical position in relation to the material constraints wrought through the progress of modernity, it was also, in origin, epistemologically imperialistic. Durkheim (1938) delineated sociology's peculiar realm of phenomena. He marked out their identifiable characteristics and the conceptual space that they occupied and he sought to devalue all other attempts to explain 'social' reality (Hirst 1975). Thus we arrive at a kernel idea for sociology, that of the 'social structure'; it is from this concept that the discipline proceeds. Social structures appear to societal members as 'facts' and as such have real and describable characteristics: they are typical – that is, they are a series of normal or taken for granted manifestations; further, they are constraining upon the actions of members either implicitly or explicitly; and finally they are, to some greater or lesser degree, independent of individual will. As Durkheim (1982: 35) put it:

> The proposition which states that social facts must be treated as things – the proposition which is at the very basis of our method – is among those which have stirred up the most opposition. It was deemed paradoxical and scandalous for us to assimilate to the realities of the external world the realities of the social world. This was singularly to misunderstand the meaning and effect of this assimilation, the object of which was not to reduce the higher forms of being to the level of lower ones but, on the contrary, to claim for the former a degree of reality at least equal to that which everyone accords the latter. Indeed, we do not say that social facts are material things, but that they are things just as are material things, although in a different way.

The 'social structure' then becomes the supra-individual source of causality in sociological explanations, whether it is experienced by members as a cognitive, moral, political or economic orientation (Parsons 1968). All sociological worlds seek to build in and analyse a series of constraints that work upon the individual and (however the particular perspective places itself, within the debate over free will versus determinism) there tends to be a primary commitment to treat the self as an epiphenomenon of the society and thus prey to apprehension in terms of epistemological binaries (Wrong 1961; Cicourel 1964; Dawe 1970; Hollis 1977). As O'Neill put it, 'The *tabula rasa* or clean-slate individual of liberal contract theory is as much a fiction as is its counterpart fiction of the many-headed monster state, or Leviathan. Each device serves to stampede thought into those forced alternatives of the under- or over-socialized individual' (1994: 54).

So, sociology's tradition makes little claim to provide a strong theory of the individual and this holds implications for our understanding of the child. Ironically, the most contemporary sociology of the late or postmodern scene is even less secure in its explanations of self (Giddens 1991; Beck 1992). Thus, despite the apparent cult of the individual and celebration of the ego in the latter part of the twentieth century, sociological analysis appears increasingly unprepared to formulate the social identity of people, let alone the emergent identity of children.

The problems of structural causality, in relation to a study of the child, are further compounded by the fact that sociological systems of explanation are constructed in relation to the conduct of typical rational 'adult' members – children are largely theorized as states of pathology or inadequacy in relation to the prestated model of the actor. All sociologies, in their variety of forms, relate to the childhood experience through theories of socialization, whether in relation to the institutional contexts of the family, the peer group or the school. These three sites are regarded as the serious arenas wherein the child is most systematically exposed to concerted induction procedures. It is here that the child, within the social system, relates as a subordinate to the formalized strategies of constraint, control, inculcation and patterning which will serve to transform his or her status into the tangible and intelligible form of an adult competent being:

> In sociological writings characterized as normative, the term sociali-
> zation glosses the phenomenon of change from the birth of a child
> to maturity or old age. To observe that changes take place after birth
> is trivial, but the quasi-scientific use of the term socialization masks
> this triviality. In fact, the study of these changes as socialization is an
> expression of the sociologists' common sense position in the world –
> i.e. as adults. The notion of socialization leads to the theoretical
> formulations mirroring the adult view that children are incomplete
> adults.
>
> (MacKay 1973: 27)

A child's social, and ontological, purpose is therefore, it would seem, not to stay a child. Within this inexorable trajectory any signs of entrenchment or backtracking, like play for example, may be interpreted as indicators of a fail-ure to 'develop' (Piaget 1977). It is a further irony that were one to confront a sociologist with the issue of 'development' then their immediate frame of reference would be to consider the modes of transition occurring between the structures of simple and complex societies (Frank 1971). The concept of devel-opment, with relation to persons, is no part of a sociologist's vocabulary. Structures are sociologists' primary realities and the only organism that they might consider in a state of development is that, by analogy, of the society as a whole.

The sociological child

In the following sections I introduce a series of models specifically from within the sociological tradition. As ever within any overview of sociological approaches to a particular phenomenon, I need to add the caveat that the models that follow are not all part of a total mosaic, nor are they necessarily compatible. Sociological perspectives on childhood, although they share certain basic premises concerning the fundamentally 'social' and even 'social structural' character of their object of attention are nevertheless divided from the level of metatheory to the level of methodology. It is also the case that many theorists do not see these models as standing in splendid isolation and routinely combine elements across the boundaries. I shall attempt here to elucidate some of the commonality between them as well as expressing the sources of their differences.

The socially developing child

Sociologists have always been concerned with the development of the child in as much as their theories of social order, social stability and social integration depend upon a uniform and predictable standard of action from the participating members. In this sense then, they begin with a formally established concept of society and work back to the necessary inculcation of its rules into the consciousness of its potential participants – these are always children. The process of this inculcation is referred to as 'socialization'. The direction of influence is apparent; the society shapes the individual. Sociologists are not ignorant of the biological character of the human organism but are singularly committed to an explication of its development within a social context. The socially developing model of childhood does share certain chronological and incremental characteristics with the naturally developing model but it largely avoids, or indeed resists, the reduction to explanation in terms of natural propensities or dispositions. The socially developing model is not attached to what the child naturally is so much as to what the society naturally demands of the child – a major commonality between the models can be seen here in terms of the obvious essentialism that their shared positivism brings to bear.

Socialization is a concept that has been much employed by sociologists to delineate the process through which children, though in some cases adults, learn to conform to social norms (see Goslin 1969; Danziger 1971; Morrison and McIntyre 1971; Elkin and Handel 1972; Denzin 1977; White 1977). Sociology has depended upon the efficacy of socialization to ensure that societies sustain through time. The process involves, in essence, the successful transmission of culture from one generation to another. Let us look at two definitions of the process – the first from Ritchie and Kollar (1964: 117), writing solidly within the tradition of socialization theory:

> The central concept in the sociological approach to childhood is socialization. A synonym for this process may well be acculturation because this term implies that children acquire the culture of the human groupings in which they find themselves. Children are not to be viewed as individuals fully equipped to participate in a complex adult world, but as beings who have the potentials for being slowly brought into contact with human beings.

And then Speier (1970: 208) from a more critical, phenomenological stance:

> Sociology considers the social life of the child as a basic area of study in so-called institutional analyses of family and school, for example. What is classically problematic about studying children is the fact of cultural induction, as I might refer to it. That is, sociologists (and this probably goes for anthropologists and psychologists) commonly treat childhood as a stage of life that builds preparatory mechanisms into the child's behavior so that he is gradually equipped with the competence to participate in the everyday activities of his cultural partners, and eventually as a bona fide adult member himself. This classical sociological problem has been subsumed under the major heading of socialization.

The process has been conceived of in two ways. First, what we might term the 'hard' way, or what Wrong (1961) referred to as the 'oversocialized conception of man in modern sociology' where socialization is seen as the internalization of social constraints. Through this transfer from the outside to the inside the norms of society become internal to the individual, but this occurs through external regulation. The individual child's personality thus becomes continuous with the goals and means of the society itself; the individual is seen as a microcosm. The 'hard' way derives largely from structural sociology and systems theory and finds its most persuasive and influential exponent in Parsons, who defines the process as follows:

> The term socialization in its current usage in the literature refers primarily to the process of child development . . . However, there is another reason for singling out the socialization of the child. There is reason to believe that, among the learned elements of personality in certain respects the stablest and most enduring are the major value-orientation patterns and there is much evidence that these are

'laid down' in childhood and are not on a large scale subject to drastic alteration during adult life.

(Parsons 1964: 101)

What Parsons successfully achieves in his social system is a stable and uniform isomorphism, such that individual actors and their particular personalities have a homologous relation with groups, institutions, sub-systems and the society itself; they are all cut to a common pattern. What he also achieves is universality in the practice and experience of childhood, because the content of socialization is secondary to the form of socialization in each and every case. The potentiality for an expression of the child's intentionality is constrained through the limited number of choices that are made available in social inter-action, which Parsons refers to as 'pattern variables'. In this way the model achieves a very generalized sense of the child at a level of abstraction and one determined by structure rather than pronounced through the exercise of agency. As this model is also based on a developmental scheme the child is necessarily considered to be incompetent or in possession of incomplete, unformed or proto-competencies. This latter understanding ensures that any research following from such a model does not attend to the everyday world of the child nor its skills in interaction and world view, except in terms of generating a diagnosis for remedial action.

The second, and somewhat 'softer', way in which the socialization process has been conceived by sociologists is as an essential element in interaction, as a transactional negotiation that occurs when individuals strive to become group members. This is the version of socialization that stems from the symbolic interactionism of George Herbert Mead and the Chicago School and involves a social psychology of group dynamics. This is really, however, a perspective on adult socialization. The Meadian analysis of child development is much more of a thesis in materialism. The basic theory of the acquisition of language and interactional skills is based very much on an unexplicated behaviourism, and the final resolution of the matured relationship between the individual and the collective other (that is, the 'Self' and 'Other') is a thinly disguised reworking of Freud's triumph of the *super-ego* over the *id*. Symbolic interactionism has generated a wealth of sensitive ethnographic studies of small groups and communities but it begins from the baseline of adult inter-actional competence and thus shares, at this level, much with the socialization theory espoused by Parsons and structural sociology.

What is highly instructive in all manifestations of the model of the socially developing child (that is, socialization theory) as they have appeared in many forms of sociology, is that they have little or no time for children. To a large extent this accounts for sociology's long neglect of the topic of child-hood and also demonstrates why the child was only ever considered under the broadest of umbrellas, namely the sociology of the family.

The socially constructed child

What is now called social constructionism is a relatively new departure in the understanding of childhood which found three major landmarks in the works of Jenks (1982), James and Prout (1990) and Stainton Rogers *et al.* (1991). The perspective derives, in large part, from the 1970s backlash in British sociology to the stranglehold that varieties of positivism were exercising on the field. A wave of critical, deconstructing phenomenology had come into competition with the absolutist pronouncements of the structural sociologies and Marxisms that appeared to hold sway. Such theorizing also complemented the growing liberalism and relativism that were permeating the academy in the wake of the 1960s. The dominating philosophical paradigm shifted from a dogmatic materialism to an idealism inspired by the works of Husserl and Heidegger; in fact, such original phenomenology appeared rather too 'wild' for the standards of British reason and was rendered acceptable through the mediation of Schutz (1964) and Berger and Luckmann (1966).

To describe childhood, or indeed any phenomenon, as socially con-structed is to suspend a belief in or a willing reception of its taken-for-granted meanings. Thus, quite obviously with our current topic, we all know what children are and what childhood is like but this is not a knowledge that we can reliably draw upon. Such knowledge of the child and its life world depends upon the predispositions of a consciousness constituted in relation to our social, political, historical and moral context. Social constructionists have to suspend assumptions about the existence and causal powers of a social structure that makes things, like childhood, as they are; their purpose is to go back to the phenomenon in consciousness and show how it is built up. So within a socially constructed, idealist world, there are no absolutes. Childhood does not exist in a finite and identifiable form; Ariès ([1960] 1986) had already shown us this historically and Mead and Wolfenstein (1954) had made early demonstrations of this cross-culturally. This moves us to a multiple concep-tion of childhoods; what Schutz would have referred to as multiple realities. Social constructionism stresses the issue of plurality and far from this model recommending a unitary form it foregrounds diverse constructions. The model is dedicatedly hermeneutic and therefore provides scope for exciting new development, new forms and new interpretations. It also erodes the conventional standards of judgement and truth. Therefore if, for example, as many commentators have suggested, child abuse was rife in earlier times and a fully anticipated feature of adult-child relations, then how are we to say that it was bad, exploitative and harmful? Our standards of judgement are relative to our world view – therefore we cannot make universal statements of value. We can, on the other hand, attend to the socially constructed 'increase' in cases of child abuse during the 'Cleveland Affair' of 1987. What of infanticide in contemporary non-western societies? Is it an immoral and criminal act or an economic necessity? Is it an extension of the western belief in 'a woman's right to choose'? Social constructionism and cultural relativism do have an intense relationship. As a model it lends itself to a cultural studies style of analysis, or the now fashionable modes of discourse analysis – children are brought into being.

Children within this model are, clearly, unspecifiable as an ideal type and childhoods are variable and intentional but, we should note, this intentionality is the responsibility of the theorist. This model demands a level of reflexivity from its exponents. It is also the case that social constructionists, through their objections to positivist methods and assumptions, are more likely to be of the view that children are not formed by natural and social forces but rather that they inhabit a world of meaning created by themselves and through their interaction with adults. The child in this model is to be located semantically rather than causally:

> There are no hard and fast principles for defining when disagreements about how things are seen become significant enough to talk about them as different social realities ... When social constructionists look at childhood, it is to these different social realities that they turn. The interest is not just in learning about the constructions of childhood in history or in different cultures – it is also a technique that throws light on why we construct childhood as we do in our own time and society.
>
> (Stainton Rogers *et al*. 1991: 24)

Social constructionism has played an important political role in the study of childhood in that it was well situated to prise the child free of biological determinism and thus claim the phenomenon, epistemologically, within the realm of the social. While it remains important to emphasize that the model is more than a theory of the ideational (it is about the practical application of formed mental constructs and the impact that this has on the generation of reality and real consequences), it is also important not to abandon the embodied material child.

The tribal child

This model contains a quite significant alteration in thinking, and not simply in terms of the particular theoretical perspective that is to be applied to the topic. Here we witness a moral reappraisal of the stratification system and power relation that conventionally exists between adults and children, and a decision to articulate the *Weltanschauung* of what the Chicago School would have called the 'underdog' in their studies of deviance and criminality. This model sets out from a commitment to children's social worlds as real places and provinces of meaning in their own right and not as fantasies, games, poor imitations or inadequate precursors of the adult state of being. It would be claiming too much to say that this position takes children seriously, as it would suggest that previously considered models do not, however it can be argued that there is a seriousness here which attaches to the child's own view. We have a sense of what Mayall (1994) has referred to as 'children's childhoods'. Here we honour children's difference and celebrate their relative autonomy. In the manner of the enlightened anthropologist we desist from imposing our own constructs and transformations upon the actions of the child and attempt to treat children's accounts and explanations at face value. Within this model, children are not understood as 'cultural dopes' – that is, we do not begin from the premise that they have only a misguided, mythological, superficial or irrational understanding of the rules of social life. Their worlds are real locations, as are our own, and they demand to be understood in those terms.

An early and well publicized excursion into the possibilities provided by this model is to be found in the copious mass observation studies of the Opies (Opie and Opie 1959). The Opies, and other researchers following their lead, have argued for the long-overdue recognition of an autonomous community of children. The children's world is to be seen as not unaffected by but nevertheless artfully insulated from the world of adults; it is to be understood as an independent place with its own folklore, rituals, rules and normative constraints. This is the world of the schoolyard, the playground, the club and the gang.

What this model encourages is an emphasis on children's social action as structured but within a system that is unfamiliar to us and therefore to be revealed. Childhood intentionality welcomes the anthropological strangeness that has been recommended by ethnomethodology. If the tribes of childhood are to be provided with the status of social worlds then it is to be anticipated that their particularity will systematically confound our taken-for-granted knowledge of how other (adult) social worlds function. There will be homologies, but the purpose of such a model as this is to ensure that the homologies do not legislate or stand in a dictatorial relationship to the child's world. We might anticipate that ethnographies of the tribes will, and should, proliferate. Work within the model has a negative potential for generating whimsical tales – quaint fables of the tribes of childhood; the kind of anecdotal accounting so favoured by the doting parent with little generalizability and less enlightenment. This, however, should not be this model's purpose. Much is spoken in the literature on childhood about the child's ontology, but mostly as an aspiration rather than a viable construct. It is within the bounds of this model that such a form of life can begin to receive annotation. The mapping of childhood practices, self-presentations, motives and assumptions provides the very basis for an attention to the intrinsic being of childhood time, which in turn can enable both more effective communication and latterly more apposite policy measures. On the child's side of the equation, a successful and ultimately knowing intrusion into their tribal folkways inevitably brings the threat of increased strategies of control. The ever-looming panopticon vision explodes into fruition once the interior and the ontological become available.

One obvious benefit of the ethnographies that follow from within the tribal model is that they enable a sustained and long awaited concentration on children's language, language acquisition, language games and burgeoning competence. This can help us in our relations with children and in their education, but it can also advise us about the constitution of mind, as Chomsky's work on transformational grammar has done. Methodology, however, is a constant problem.

The minority group child

This model can attend to children epistemologically in any number of ways. Its binding feature is its politicization of childhood in line with previously established agendas concerning an unequal and structurally discriminatory society. Oakley (1994: 13), in a paper that explicitly attempts to demonstrate parallels between the politics of women's studies and childhood studies, states the following:

> This chapter considers the emerging field of childhood studies from the viewpoint of the established discipline of women's studies. Women and children are, of course, linked socially, but the development of these specialist academic studies also poses interesting methodological and political questions about the relationship between the status of women and children as social minority groups and their constitution as objects of the academic gaze.

The status of a minority group is a question that seeks to challenge rather than confirm an existing set of power relations and the very title 'minority' reveals a moral rather than a demographic classification that is itself intended to convey notions of relative powerlessness or victimization. Such a model of the child begins, then, not from an intrinsic interest in childhood, though this may certainly accompany the larger purpose, but instead from an indictment of a social structure and an accompanying dominant ideology which, to quote Oakley's conclusion, 'deprive[s] some people of freedom in order to give it to others' (Oakley 1994: 32).

It is certainly the case that sociology over the last 30 years has striven to convert the natural into the cultural. This has not simply been a completion of the Durkheimian endeavour to understand all phenomena as if they were primarily social. What has been occurring, and what has finally given rise to this model of the child, is a systematic move to re-democratize modern society and to disassemble all remaining covert forms of stratification. Whereas classical sociology attended primarily to the stratification wrought through social class, modern sociology has begun to address all of those areas that have been treated as 'natural' (like our critical address of developmental psychology), or 'only human nature'. Thus race, sex, sexuality, age and physical and mental ability have all come under scrutiny and have all been shown to derive their meaning and routine practices from their social context. Childhood is rather late in gaining both fashion and attention but it has finally arrived. Standpoint epistemologies are being forged on behalf of the child, never more powerfully than when linked to empirical findings from within the previous model.

The strengths of this model derive from its seeming dedication to the child's interests and purposes, though it is always important with such political processes to ensure that a group is not being driven by a hidden agenda or a political subtext. In many senses children here are regarded as essentially indistinguishable from adults, or indeed all people; it is important within such thinking not to reimport new forms of stratification. Children are therefore seen as active subjects and a sociology develops, sharing charac-teristics with action research – a sociology for children! The weaknesses of this model derive from the necessary categorical transformation of any social group into the status of a group for-itself instead of just in-itself – that is, the imposition of a uniformity that defies the differences within. Thus the universal child becomes a minority group with demands that have to be heard, but that group is fractured in its internal diversity. This is analogous to the problems found in, for example, applying the consciousness-raising of the white middle-class woman to the everyday experience of black working-class women.

The social structural child

This model contains a good deal of sound sense, if not pragmatism. It begins from a recognition of the obvious – that children are a constant feature of all social worlds. As a component of all societies children are typical, tangible, persistent and normal, indeed they demonstrate all of the characteristics of social facts. Their manifestations may vary from society to society but within each particular society they are uniform. To this degree they constitute a formative component of all social structures. This model of the child begins from such an assumption: children are not pathological or incomplete, they form a group, a body of social actors and as citizens they have needs and rights. In the model of the socially developing child we saw a social structure and a society made up of rational adults with children waiting to be processed through the particular rite of passage that socialization within that society demanded. Now the constancy of the child is acknowledged as is its essentiality. From this beginning any theorizing around this model can proceed to examine both the necessary and sufficient conditions that apply to childhood within the particular or indeed to children in general. Children are again very much a universal category and they are seen to properly emerge from the constraints that their particular social structure proffers. Children, then, are a body of subjects but their subjectivity is neither wilful nor capricious – it is determined by their society. This model concentrates not so much on the child's intentionality as on its instancing structural formation. Qvortrup's (1993) huge international survey of childhood as a social phenomenon can be more accurately understood as an analysis of the universal structural components in the recognizability and processing of childhood:

> There is . . . a more positive, and more important reason for preferring to speak about *the* childhood, namely the suggestion that children who live within a defined area – whether in terms of time, space, economics or other relevant criteria – have a number of characteristics in common. This preference in other words enables us to characterize not only childhood, but also the society in which this childhood is situated as mutually both independent and indispensable constructions; moreover it allows us to compare childhood thus characterized with other groups from the same country, perhaps most notably other age groups like youth, adulthood and old age, because they in principle are influenced by the same characterizing and formative societal parameters, although in different ways; it also permits us to ask to what extent childhood within a given area has changed historically, because – typically – continuity reigns within one country more than within any other unit of that order; and finally, it becomes possible, when the concept of childhood is used, to compare childhoods internationally and interculturally, because we are availing ourselves of the same types of parameters – e.g. economic, political, social, environmental parameters.
>
> (Qvortrup 1994: 5–6)

What such work demonstrates is the dual and non-contradictory view that children bear the same status as research subjects as adults, but that they may also have a different set of competencies, all of which are recognizable features of the social structure. Frones has shown that there are multiple dimensions to the 'social structural' child and that it always remains possible to investigate these dimensions separately, but ultimately in relation to the integrative, interrelated and functional constraints of the institutional arrangements within the overall social structure:

> Childhood may be defined as *the life period during which a human being is regarded as a child, and the cultural, social and economic characteristics of that period* . . . most of the studies on childhood concentrate on aspects that fall into one of four main categories: relations among generations, relations among children, children as an age group, and the institutional arrangements relating to children, their upbringing, and their education. Factors from one category may, of course, be important in another, as when the institutional apparatus concerned with children is significant in an analysis of child culture or child-parent relations.
>
> (Frones 1994: 148, original emphasis)

The 'social structural' child, then, has certain universal characteristics which are specifically related to the institutional structure of societies in general and are not simply subject to the changing nature of discourses about children nor the radical contingencies of the historical process.

6 Developmental psychology and the study of childhood

Valerie Walkerdine

Introduction

Over the last decade or so there has been a sea change in the study of childhood. Work coming from sociology and cultural studies (James and Prout 1997; Buckingham 2000; Lee 2001; Castenada 2002) has been quite rightly critical of the place of developmental psychology in producing explanations of children as potential subjects, whose presence is understood only in terms of their place on a path towards becoming an adult. Instead, current sociological approaches stress the importance of understanding how child subjects are produced in the present and of blurring the line between childhood as an unfinished and adulthood as a finished state (Lee 2001). It would seem from this work that sociology has displaced the psychological study of children altogether and so I want to raise some issues about how we might think about the place of psychology in the understanding of childhood and also to raise concerns about the apparent solving of a problem of psychology by shifting explanations to the other pole of individual-society dualism – sociology (Henriques *et al*. 1998).

The place of psychology in accounts of childhood

As many commentators point out, psychology has had a central place in understanding childhood. While many point to the importance of the beginning of compulsory schooling in Europe for explaining the emergence of concern about childhood as a separate state, as has been demonstrated elsewhere (Walkerdine 1984; Rose 1985), psychology has had a central role to play since its emergence at the end of the nineteenth century. This section will briefly set out the emergence of developmental psychology as part of the scientific study of children. I will argue that the idea of development assumes a rational, civilized adult as its end-point. The criticisms by sociologists of the idea of the child as a potential adult derive from developmental psychology's concern with a path towards an end-point. Since the idea of development has come to appear so commonplace and normal, it is difficult to imagine how a psychological approach to childhood could be different. I will argue that sociological studies of childhood have a tendency towards dualism – that is, they still maintain a separation between something called sociology and something called psychology and have a tendency to want to explain childhood sociologically, which has two effects. The first is to leave no room for a discussion of the 'psychological' and the other is to get rid of developmental psychology only to replace it with a set of hard 'facts' derived, for example, from cognitive neuroscience. This problem, present in a number of sociological accounts (Lee 2001) leaves no place for either a reworking of psychology nor for moving beyond dualism. I want therefore to ask what place psychology might have and what a post-developmental approach to childhood might actually look like.

The emergence of developmental psychology as the study of childhood

Many have pointed to the importance of the rise of science from the seventeenth century for understanding the emergence of psychology as a science (Venn 1984). Using a Foucaultian framework, we can be clear that developmental psychology was made possible by what Foucault calls certain 'conditions of possibility' (Foucault 1979). That is, certain historical conditions make the emergence of developmental psychology seem natural and inevitable. What we need to think about is what could produce this effect? What needs to be understood is that this idea of studying children scientifically was a new idea. As Ariès ([1960] 1986) and other historians tell us, the idea of childhood as a separate state is a modern one. Ariès puts forward a convincing case that up until the eighteenth century children were regarded simply as small adults, and he analyses in particular Velasquez's painting, *Las Meninas*, to demonstrate that the children in the painting are represented as miniature adults. These royal children were already betrothed at an early age. Among the lower orders, children also routinely worked alongside adults and were often used specifically for jobs which adults could not do – the chimney sweep in the story *Peter Pan* being perhaps the most obvious British example (a story written at a time when there was an outcry about child labour). In particular, industrialization brought with it a move away from a rural life in which small people were integrated into farming and village life, to factories which regularly employed children. As we know, in many parts of the world, child labour is still not only common but an important source of income for families. It is generally accepted that what brought about the idea of childhood as something separate was the emergence of popular and then compulsory schooling (Walkerdine 1984), established in Britain around 1880.

What were the conditions which made a national system of education seem important? While child labour was important, the poverty of the 'working classes' brought with it crime. Jones and Williamson (1979) argue that schooling was set out as the solution to two national problems: crime and pauperism (that is, becoming a burden on the state by being poor and needing poor relief). It was argued that these two conditions were moral issues, produced by the habits and life of the poor. Schooling would allow children to learn to read the Bible and therefore to lead a more moral life. Jones and Williamson said: 'the deterioration in moral character was related to a deterioration in the religious character of the population and the political threat which this posed' (1979: 67).

It was the political threat that would be abated by teaching children correct moral values through the inculcation of good habits, rather than ending poverty. Crime and pauperism in this analysis are taken to be produced by certain qualities, habits, which could be changed. This idea of habits fits absolutely with what emerged within psychology as accounts of conditioning. As Rose (1985) argues, it was a 'happy accident' that psychology had the tools to hand! Science was used to develop a system of scientific schooling in which good habits could be taught. The monitorial schools were the prime example of this. But these schools were soon found to be wanting as children would 'recite the Lord's prayer for a half penny' (Jones and Williamson 1979: 88). It is at this point that childhood as a separate aspect of psychology could be taken to enter the stage. If habits were not enough, what had to be understood and regulated was something about the specific *nature* of children. It needs to be said here that the focus of this concern was the children of the masses. The male children of the wealthy were already being educated and had been educated in schools for many hundreds of years, or had been given private tutors. These children were being equipped to enter a life of wealth, government and leadership. So, the nature that concerns us is the nature of the masses, the poor, those likely to produce the 'disturbances of the social order' (Hamilton 1981: 2). It is common to refer here to the schools set up by industrialist Robert Owen as part of his Scottish mills. Owen looked to the French Revolution for a model of progress and beyond that to the work of Rousseau. As the historian Stewart says, 'Owen's educational principles could almost be summed up as Rousseauism applied to working-class children' (1972: 35). It was the achievement of rationality that was Owen's concern, a rationality which was at the heart of liberal government. That is, an understanding of liberal government as operating without overt coercion through a process of rational decision making. To take part in this government, the masses had to be rational (or failing that, at least be reasonable). The issue then became one of how to produce rational adults out of a mob, mass or herd, an issue which was at the heart of concerns within a number of emerging branches of psychology, such as social psychology and psychoanalysis.

The search for the nature of children became an attempt to understand how to produce rational adults through education. Rousseau's concept of nature, however, was one taken out of French courtly life – the nature of shepherds and shepherdesses, not of poor peasants. Rousseau produced a fictional account of the education according to nature of two prototypical children, Emile and Sophie. To understand how this concept of nature came to stand for the 'nature of the child' we need to make reference to other debates about nature that were merging in other scientific domains. Nikolas Rose (1985) makes clear that the concept of animal versus human nature was a centre-point of post-Enlightenment thinking. He gives the example of the Wild Boy of Aveyron: a boy, named Victor, who was found in the eighteenth century in the woods in Aveyron in France, apparently having been brought up by animals. His education, to be turned from a human animal into a civilized and rational being, was seen as a test of whether human animals could become, through education, rational and civilized human beings capable of being part of liberal government. The civilizing project therefore was to take those Others – human animals, dangerous classes, savages and other colonial subjects, and turn them into rational, civilized human beings. Castenada (2002) argues that the nature of the Other was understood through an evolutionary account. The nature of those Others was simply lower down the evolutionary chain – the issue was, could they be brought up further by an education that worked with and not against their nature? For this to work, it was necessary to know what that nature was. What is significant for the story of childhood is that evolution, a science which became well-known with Darwin's work on the evolution of species, argued that human nature is not a simple bedrock but has been formed by a process of evolution – that is, of change and adaptation to an environment over long periods of prehistorical time. Darwin extended his study of evolution to the idea of ontogeny (the evolution of the species-being) copying or recapitulating phylogeny (the evolution of the species). To this end he studied his infant son (Darwin 1887). The idea of studying children in terms of an evolutionary process took off around this time, with child study societies being established around Britain. If human nature was understood as a process of evolutionary adaptation which was copied by the species-being it is not hard to understand that the evolutionary idea could be taken to relate to Others (lower classes, colonial peoples, savages, women) who were seen as lower down the evolutionary scale, and children, who were doing their own process of evolving as species-beings. Childhood in this way became a developmental process in which adaptation to the environment was understood as a natural stage-wise progression towards a rational and civilized adulthood, which was to be the basis for liberal government. Of course, the environment could be such as to inhibit full development, which kept those Others lower down the evolutionary scale.

What I have been at pains to establish then is that the idea of development is a historically specific one, which has a particular place in government in Foucault's sense. It is not natural or inevitable as a way of understanding what we have come to call childhood. Indeed, the natural itself is a very specific reading of the relation of a biology, understood evolutionarily, to a psychology. Of course it would be possible to argue that what studies in evolution demonstrated was an advance on what we knew before and so we now know scientifically that childhood is a distinct state which follows a stage-wise progression towards adulthood. My argument here is that this approach ignores the historical specificity of the introduction of the idea of development. That specific history demonstrates not a simple path of progress towards greater knowledge but a political project of liberalism which drew on scientific studies for its rationale. In this analysis, the production of the rational subject for liberalism is central (Henriques *et al.* 1998).

Childhood and developmental psychology

We have seen why a developmental account of childhood was established and we have understood its setting – the school – as the site in which the correctly developing child on a path to rationality is to be produced. Within developmental accounts there are classically aspects of human nature and those of an environment, with the human nature gradually changing and adapting to the environment. The best-known exponent of this approach is Jean Piaget. Piaget's approach to development could be described as the archetype of developmental theories in that it assumes a developmental approach to rationality or intelligence, produced out of the adaptation of structures of thinking to the structure of the physical world. Through a series of ingenious experiments, Piaget attempted to demonstrate the evolution or successive adaptation of structures of reasoning until they attained adult rationality. What we need to understand here is the status of the 'truths' supplied by this approach. When we see a child being able successfully to accomplish a Piagetian task, such as conservation of liquids, it looks like the theory must be valid and true. But there is no such necessary relation between the accomplishment of this task and something called development. The task itself is part of a theoretical framework which makes certain assumptions about the nature of mind, childhood, evolution, a pregiven subject changed through adaptation to a physical world etc. None of these things is given a priori at all. What Foucault's work allows us to understand is that the truths of Piaget's and other claims about development are not timeless and universal scientific verities but are produced at a specific historical moment as an effect of power. That is, the concerns about the production of the rational individual and the setting out of a naturalistic developmental sequence to achieve that, as well as the whole way the idea of development is put forward, are part of technologies of population management, which themselves are an aspect of how power works (Henriques *et al.* 1998). Thus, this approach is not relative – it does not say that there are a number of truths about development, all of which might have validity. Rather, it is the centrality of the relation of knowledge and power which allows us to understand how and why these particular claims to truth become enshrined as fact at any particular moment.

This is missed by many new sociological approaches to childhood, which stress a move to active childhood. The issue is rather to understand that childhood is always produced as an object in relation to power. Thus, there can be no timeless truth, sociological or psychological, about childhood. There can rather be understandings of how childhood is produced at any one time and place and an imperative to understand what kinds of childhoods we want to produce, if indeed we want childhood at all. For example, developmental psychology understands children's thinking as becoming more and more like that of adults. It figures therefore that children's thinking is assumed to be different from adult thinking and that this difference is understood as a deficiency, a natural deficiency that will be put right as the child grows up. This position is described by James and Prout (1997) as seeing children as 'human becomings' rather than human beings. However, Lee (2001) understands this position as in some ways 'throwing out the baby with the bathwater' in the sense that children are in need of supplementation. Lee asks 'how does the "being" child change if that change is not thought of as the supplementation of a natural lack? What could "growing up" mean once we have distanced ourselves from the dominant frameworks' account of socialization and development?' (Lee 2001: 54). Of course, we can also argue that supplementation and lack define aspects of that so-called stable state of adulthood. After all, old people (for example) often need supplementation as they get older. Indeed, we can understand the definition of adulthood as a stable state of being, and indeed equally as a definition of childhood as unstable, as a product of power. That is, liberal government is dependent on a notion of rights and responsibilities carried out by rational, stable beings. Any instability is often understood as childlike and as developmentally regressive. Whereas, we could understand adulthood as an unstable state too, with a fictional stability produced in the practices in which adulthood is defined and accomplished.

The other important issue to remember is that childhood as defined in terms of economic dependency on adults, access to schooling etc., is, in fact, still the norm for only a minority of the world's children. Children in many countries routinely work, and, as we know, multinationals like Nike are very dependent upon inexpensive child labour. In that sense, the modern western conception of the child exists, as Castenada (2002) argues, in circuits of exchange between the First World and the Third. In this case, for example, the situation of prosperity for adults and children in the West is directly produced by the exploitation of children in the Third World. There is no figure of the child who stands outside such circuits of exchange. In this case, the story of the developing child does something more than universalize human becom-ingness. It also means that we can only see the relation of exploitation between the First World and the Third as one in which Third-World children are being denied a childhood or are underdeveloped. If the First-World child exists, in a sense, at the expense of the Third, the complex economic relation-ality is being lost in the developmental explanation.

However, in relation to the western present, arguments have been made that globalization and neo-liberalism have produced a situation which has extended education and therefore childhood dependence well into the twenties, a period which would previously have been considered adult. Similarly, low pay and casual work have produced a situation in which people are not able to afford to leave the parental home until they are into their twenties and thirties. Lee (2001) understands this historical shift in the West as blurring the lines between adulthood and childhood and therefore presenting childhood as a shifting state. Buckingham (2000) argues that after Postman's (1983) announcement of the 'end of childhood' because of television's access to 'adult' programmes, children in the West have considerable economic power, being a prime market, even if it is their parents who actually buy the goods. These arguments, taken together, suggest a historical shift in which childhood and adulthood, being and becoming, are no longer clear and dis-tinct categories in the West, though for many adult and child Others, they have never been distinct.

Doing childhood differently

Given these arguments, developmental psychology has to be understood as a powerful technology of the social, which itself inscribes and catches up children and adults. However, as we have seen following arguments put forward by Lee and others about the present historical shifts, the economic and social position of both children and adults is changing, allowing the conditions of emergence for new regimes of power/knowledge and modes of population management. Within this context, we can rethink the place of the psychological in the study of childhood. In this section, I want to point the way to a number of possible directions that this work can take.

The first thing I want to stress is the necessity to move beyond a number of dualisms. The most obvious is the dualism of sociology and psychology. It is not helpful simply to attempt to replace interiority with exteriority, individual with social and so forth, because all that achieves is to leave the dualisms that created the problem intact. If it is clear that there is no essential state of child-hood or adulthood, what we need to understand is how people of particular ages become subjects within specific, local practices and to understand how those subject positions and practices operate within complex circuits of exchange (Castenada 2002). The theoretical framework that underpins this move is derived from a post-foundational approach to the social sciences (Henriques *et al.* 1998). In this account, the subject is not made social, but rather the social is the site for the production of discursive practices which produce the possibility of being a subject. I would argue that it is absolutely essential for a different approach to the psychological study of childhood not to understand psychology as one part of a dualistic divide. Rather, it is important to understand how those classic aspects of psychology – learning, reasoning, emotions and so forth are produced as part of social practices. I want to gesture towards some of my own work in this area and also to mention other work which presents us with the possibility of approaching the study of children in a different way.

The production of children as subjects within educational practices

Some years ago, I attempted to rethink an approach to mathematics learning as cognitive development by approaching school mathematics as a set of discursive practices and asking how children became subjects within those practices in such a way that the learning of mathematics was accomplished (Walkerdine 1989). I wanted to understand how school mathematics discourse had specific properties and how it formed a particular relation between signifier and signified. I argued that we could explore in detail how children learned mathematics through an understanding of their production as subjects within school mathematics practices. In addition to this, however, I argued that as Rotman (1980) has also argued, mathematics was 'reason's dream', a dream of mastery over the physical universe. I suggested that this meant that it embodied particular fantasies of mastery over a calculable universe which were powerful fantasies linked to an omnipotent masculinity.

Childhood in this analysis contains two key elements: difference (not all childhoods are the same) and an emotional or libidinal economy. I want to think about these issues as they relate to one kind of difference, that of gender. British discourses of childhood have tended to implicitly define the child as male. If, for example, we examine educational writings about natural childhood, they often assume attributes that are understood as masculine: activity, breaking rules, naughtiness. Girls are often defined within education as displaying characteristics of passivity, rule-following and good behaviour, which makes their status as natural children quite problematic (Walkerdine 1989). I want to explore some of the ways in which girls and girlhood figure as an Other to adult men and the way in which this produces a set of practices for the production of the girl as a subject. Castenada (2002) argues that all children can be understood as figures in complex global circuits of exchange.

With this in mind, we can think about how the relation between woman and girl, adulthood and childhood, is always a difficult one for women in the contemporary West. Are women only women when they are no longer considered sexually desirable to men? How does the idea of adult women as girls portray the girl as always and already a sexual object for a man? Women then must always strive to continue to be girls and the status of little girls with respect to sexuality is a complex one. Although there is a very clear discourse about girls as children, I have argued that there is a ubiquitous, but completely disavowed and eroticized gaze at the little girl within popular culture (Walkerdine 1997). Girls are used to sell anything from yoghurt to cars. Indeed, the adverts play on the innocence, vulnerability and hidden eroticism of the little girl. In this way the girl is never unproblematically a child. It is her production as the object of an erotic male gaze that renders her always potentially a woman. But the production of the girl as a problematic figure is made possible by the centrality of a male fantasy of conquering and deflowering innocence, projected onto the girl and the woman. The girl then is a complex figure in a circuit of exchange between men. In order to understand the practices in which girls are produced as subjects, we would need to understand just how those fantasies become embodied in the actual discourses and practices of girlhood. But more than this. We are also talking about emotions – about circuits of desire and power. The girl as object of male fantasy and desire struggles to be desirable. The relation of both the man and the girl's emotions and fantasies can be understood as both interior and exterior – that is, contained within the desires, pains and anxieties of the subjects themselves, but inseparable from the embodiment of those emotions within the discourses and practices of both girlhood and masculinity: in girls' dreams of becoming.

It is difficult to imagine becoming an adult without a place within the circuits of sexual exchange. In these practices, she is the object exchanged, while the masculine assumes the subject position of both proper child and proper adult. To illustrate this, I want to make brief mention of a debate that ensued in the press following a 1980s television series called *Minipops*, in which young children sang pop songs. What particularly caught the attention of the broadsheet press was the fact that many little girls wore quite heavy make-up, 'lashings of lipstick on mini-mouths', according to one critic. The discussion that ensued in the press was about whether the girls in particular were being stripped of their childhood by the intrusion of adult sexual fantasies. The producers of the show argued that the girls had wanted the make-up, a fact hardly difficult to imagine. On the other hand, the tabloid press compared the children to the 'kids from *Fame*' and talked about future talent, not mentioning sexuality at all. Thus it seems that childhood innocence and the intrusion of adult sexuality was a middle-class concern, fame and making it a working-class one and the desire to wear make-up another. It is not difficult to see that the actual little girls in the show were located at the intersection of all these competing discourses which not only claimed to know them but also to have their best interests at heart.

How then does any little girl herself come to understand her own desire to wear lipstick? Is she not always positioned as a human becoming? Is she not always, whatever she does, already positioned as a problem? The broadsheet critics wanted to remove her lipstick and give her a childhood, while the tabloids wanted her talent to be allowed to reach its potential. If she herself wants the lipstick, then she must be some kind of deviant. I am trying to say that any girl's desires are caught inside these complex circuits of exchange, which position her in complex and contradictory ways. Her task, it would seem, is to be able to manage those contradictory positions and to find a way through them. We could understand subjectivity as composed of just that relation between the discourses, practices and circuits of exchange and the practices of self-management through which those contradictory positions are held together and lived. This allows us to study childhood as simultaneously both exterior and interior, being and becoming, psychological and social.

Understanding the social production of children as subjects

I argue that the study of childhood must be able to understand the discourses and practices in which childhood is produced and the way that the positions within those practices are experienced and managed to produce particular configurations of subjectivity. The examples I have given above do point to some aspects of how this work might be done. However, we need to develop tools for the micro analysis of practices and their place in the positioning of subjects. I want to point finally and briefly to three approaches to this that already exist and which might be developed to assist in this work. The first is work on situated learning and apprenticeship (Cole and Scribner 1990; Haraway 1991; Lave and Wenger 1991); the second is actor network theory (Law and Moser 2002); and the third is the idea of assemblages (Deleuze and Guattari 1988; Lee 2002).

Work on the idea of learning being situated rather than general comes from two sources. The first is the work of feminist theorist Donna Haraway (1991), who questioned the idea of a 'god-trick' of large macro stories told by science as universalized accounts freed from context. The other trajectory comes from the work in the 1970s of Michael Cole and Sylvia Scribner (1990), who aimed to demonstrate that reasoning is not a generalized accomplishment but something produced in specific and local practices. This idea has been taken up by many psychologists and anthropologists in the last 30 years, perhaps the best-known of whom is Jean Lave. This body of work, known as situated cognition, has developed the study of apprenticeship (Lave and Wenger 1991) as a way of thinking about specific accomplishment of competencies without having to look to a generalized developmental model. Lave

and Wenger report a number of studies of traditional and modern apprenticeship. What they demonstrate is the way in which apprentices participate
peripherally in the practices of the craft or skill they are learning. They argue
that learning involves an inculcation into the culture of the practices being
learnt:

> From a broadly peripheral perspective, apprentices gradually assemble
> a general idea of what constitutes the practice of the community.
> This uneven sketch of the enterprise (available if there is legitimate
> access) might include who is involved; what they do; what everyday
> life is like; how masters talk, walk, work, and generally conduct their
> lives; how people who are not part of the community of practice
> interact with it, what other learners are doing; and what learners
> need to learn to become full practitioners. It includes an increasing
> understanding of how, when, and about what old-timers collaborate,
> collude and collide, and what they enjoy, dislike, respect, and admire.
> In particular it offers exemplars (which are grounds and motivation
> for learning activity), including masters, finished products, and more
> advanced apprentices in the process of becoming full practitioners.
>
> (Lave and Wenger 1991: 95)

This approach gives us a clear way of thinking about how children both
are and become outside a developmental framework. The approach does not
locate learning within the child but within the culture of practice. It is not at
all incompatible with one which draws upon an idea of the production of
children as subjects within particular practices as I discussed earlier. However,
the approach which I proposed did also stress the importance of power
in terms of understanding of the kind of subject needed by liberalism. In
addition, I stressed the importance of the complex emotional economies
which form part of the production of the child as subject within a practice.

Other approaches, which are also compatible are the reference by Lee
(2001) to Deleuze and Guattari's (1988) idea of assemblages in which, for
example, horse and rider as an assemblage manage to produce more than, or a
supplement to, what either could accomplish alone. For Lee, the child learns
by supplementation to take their place within the adult world. Finally, it is
worth also considering the work of Bruno Latour and what is often described
as actor network theory (Law and Moser 2002). Law and others have developed
Latour's approach to science studies to take in the idea that organizations work
to produce subjects in quite complex ways, so that what we might classically
think of as power and agency are distributed. So, for example, when exploring
how the subjectivity of a manager of a science laboratory is created, Law
and Moser (2002: 3) demonstrate that all actions within the organization are
joined in a complex network so that 'it is no longer easy to determine the locus

of agency, to point to one place and say with certainty that action emerges from that point rather than from somewhere else'. The manager only knows where 'he' is because his subjectivity as manager is an effect of a performance that is distributed in a network of other materials and persons, jobs and activities. It is these which produce the manager as an effect of power, power distributed in the complexities of networks, the 'intersecting performance of multiple discourses and logics' (2002: 6). Like Lee, Law and Moser propose that the manager is an assemblage. In this approach, as in the others explored, the subject (in this case the manager) is not an essential psychological being-ness. Rather it is created as a nodal point at an intersection of complex discourses and practices. Could it be that children as subjects are created as both beings and becomings through the production of them as subjects who are created in practices, through what Law *et al.* call intersecting per-formances of discourses and practices, yet also in a way which means that they are constantly apprenticed into new practices? Could we also say that the practices themselves involve complex circuits of exchange between children and between adults and children, which not only link locals to globals in Castenada's sense but also make connections within emotional economies in which, as with the case of the little girls I explored, girlhood does work for both adults and children and catches them up emotionally through the emotional investments in the contradictory positions which they enter? I am proposing that all of these approaches potentially offer us ways of approaching childhood which take us beyond development but which do not throw out the psychological, but then also attempt to go beyond a number of dualisms, thus displacing the binaries of interior and exterior, individual and social, psychology and sociology.

Childhood, within these approaches, is mobile and shifting. Yet, poten-tially, change and transformation can just as easily be studied as within the developmental approach. But we are no longer in the terrain of an essential childhood with a fixed and universalized psychology of development. Rather, the practices in which we are produced as subjects from birth to death, and the ways in which they produce our subjectivity as both being and becoming, always in relation, always at once interior and exterior, provide us with a different way of studying and understanding the many and varied childhoods in their local variants and global forms.

7 New media, new childhoods? Children's changing cultural environment in the age of digital technology

David Buckingham

Some very grand claims have been made about the impact of new media technologies on children's lives. Like the idea of childhood itself, technology is often invested with our most intense fears and fantasies. It holds out the promise of a better future, while simultaneously provoking anxieties about a fundamental break with the past. Whether for good or ill, these new media are seen to exercise an extraordinary power to mould children's consciousness, to determine their identities and to dictate the patterns of their everyday lives. Children are undoubtedly among the most significant target markets for computer games, websites, CD-ROMs, chat rooms, text messaging and other forms of interactive multimedia. Yet to what extent does this amount to a dangerous 'technologizing' of childhood, as some have alleged? Or – as others have argued – do these new media offer a form of empowerment, through which the essential creativity and spontaneity of children can be more fully realized? Are children merely passive victims of the electronic screen or are they technologically literate 'cyberkids', riding the wave of the digital revolution?

In this chapter, I begin by considering some of the more extreme positions that are often rehearsed in popular debate about these issues. While not seeking to dismiss the potential of these technologies – or indeed some of the concerns they have provoked – I argue that we need to move beyond a determinist view of the effects of media technology on children. I then go on to consider these new media and communication technologies within the context of broader changes in children's culture – changes which are characterized by a growing convergence between different cultural forms, but also by increasing commercialism and by a renewed anxiety about the need for control. I conclude by considering the implications of these arguments for future research and debate in this field. I suggest that we need to pay closer attention to the diverse ways in which children use these media in their everyday lives;

but also that we need to situate their use of new media in the context of more wide-ranging social, economic and cultural forces.

Nightmares and utopias

Public debates about the impact of new digital technologies have been marked by the kind of schizophrenia that often accompanies the advent of new cultural forms. If we look back to the early days of the cinema, or indeed to the invention of the printing press, it is possible to identify a similar mixture of hopes and fears (Luke 1989; Jowitt *et al.* 1996). On the one hand, these new forms are seen to have enormous positive potential, particularly for learning; while on the other, they are frequently seen to be harmful to those who are regarded as particularly vulnerable. In both cases, it is children – or perhaps more accurately, the *idea* of childhood – which are/is the focus for many of these aspirations and concerns.

This was certainly apparent in the early years of television. Amid current fears about the impact of television violence, it is interesting to recall that television was initially promoted to parents as an *educational* medium (Melody 1973). Likewise, in the 1950s and 1960s, television and other new electronic technologies were widely seen to embody the future of schooling (Cuban 1986). Even here, however, hopes of a utopian future were often balanced against fears of loss and cultural decline. Television was seen both as a new way of bringing the family together, and as something which would undermine natural family interaction (Spigel 1992). The notion that television might replace the teacher was powerfully asserted by some, yet it also provoked predictable anxiety and concern. The medium was extolled as a means of nurturing children's emotional and educational development, and simultaneously condemned for taking them away from more wholesome or worthwhile activities (Oswell 2002).

This kind of schizophrenia is also apparent in contemporary responses to digital technology. On the one hand, there is a form of visionary utopianism, particularly among educationists. Seymour Papert, the inventor of 'logo' programming language, for example, argues that computers bring about new forms of learning which transcend the limitations of older, 'linear' methods such as print and television (Papert 1993). It is children who are seen to be most responsive to these new approaches: the computer somehow spontaneously releases their natural creativity and desire to learn, which are apparently blocked and frustrated by old-fashioned methods. According to Papert, the computer is 'the children's machine'. Meanwhile, the creative potential offered by these technologies is often seen to render formal training in artistic techniques redundant: the computer, it is argued, will make artists of us all. Far from destroying 'natural' human relationships and forms of learning, digital technology will liberate children's innate spontaneity and imagination (see Sefton-Green and Buckingham 1996).

Such utopianism often has a distinctly political edge. Writers like Richard Lanham (1993: 200), for example, argue that digital technology will bring about a new form of democratic literacy. It will bring the means of expression and communication within everyone's reach, and thereby 'enfranchise the public imagination in genuinely new ways'. Likewise, Jon Katz (1997: 173–4) regards the internet almost as a means of children's liberation: it provides children with opportunities to escape from adult control and to create their own cultures and communities. 'For the first time', he argues, 'children can reach past the suffocating boundaries of social convention, past their elders' rigid notions of what is good for them.' It is children, according to Katz, who will 'lead the revolution'.

In many instances, this advocacy is based on an opposition between 'old' and 'new' media, and between the generations with which they are identified. Don Tapscott (1998), for example, sets up a direct opposition between television and the internet. Television is seen as passive, while the net is active; television 'dumbs down' its users, while the net raises their intelligence; television broadcasts a singular view of the world, while the net is democratic and interactive; television isolates, while the net builds communities; and so on. Just as television is the antithesis of the net, so the 'television generation' is the antithesis of the 'net generation'. Like the technology they now control, the values of the television generation are increasingly conservative, hierarchical, inflexible and centralized. By contrast, the members of the 'net generation' are 'hungry for expression, discovery and their own self-development': they are savvy, self-reliant, analytical, creative, inquisitive, accepting of diversity, socially conscious, globally-oriented – all, it would seem, because of their intuitive relationship with technology.

There are interesting parallels between the utopianism of some academic (and quasi-academic) writing about digital media and the rhetoric of the sales pitch. This is very much reflected in advertising for computers, particularly that aimed at parents and teachers (Nixon 1998). Ads for Apple Macs or Microsoft, for example, work hard to counter popular views of technology as somehow unnatural or inhuman, and therefore threatening. They focus not on the scientific specifications but on the magical promise of the technology: the computer is represented here as a window onto new worlds, a way of developing children's intuitive sense of wonder and their thirst for knowledge. 'Where,' they ask, 'do you want to go today?' This tone is also increasingly adopted by politicians and policy makers, who are keen to represent information and communication technology as the solution to all the problems of contemporary schooling.

On the other hand, however, there is a much more negative account of the impact of digital technologies on children's lives. This account focuses not on their *educational* potential, but on their role as a medium of *entertainment*. Some of the anxieties that are regularly rehearsed in relation to television now appear to have been carried over to this new medium. This is readily apparent in contemporary 'moral panics' about the influence of computer games or chat rooms, or the availability of computer pornography; yet it is also evident in some academic writing. Neil Postman, for example, whose reputation as a latter-day defender of print culture was established in his polemical critiques of television, offers a dystopian vision of contemporary America as a 'Technopoly' (Postman 1992). Explicitly acknowledging his debt to the Luddites, Postman accuses technology of dehumanizing, of destroying natural forms of culture and human communication in favour of a mechanistic bureaucracy.

As with television, the range of concerns that are evoked here is very broad. Thus, digital media are frequently seen to be a bad influence on children's behaviour – and particularly to cause imitative violence. Events like the shootings at Columbine High School in Colorado, USA, in 1999 are routinely blamed on violent computer games or on children's access to 'hate sites' on the worldwide web. The more 'realistic' graphic effects in computer games become, it is argued, the more likely they are to encourage 'copycat' behaviour (Provenzo 1991). These technologies are also seen to be bad for your brain – and indeed for your body. There is now a growing collection of clinical and laboratory studies on phenomena such as 'Nintendo elbow' and epileptic fits allegedly caused by computer games, through to research on 'internet addiction' and the effects of radiation from computer screens (Griffiths 1996). Such technologies are also seen to be bad for your social life: they apparently cause young people to become antisocial, destroying normal human interaction and family togetherness. The phenomenon of the 'Otaku' or 'stay-at-home tribe' in Japan is seen as emblematic of the ways in which young people come to prefer the distance and anonymity of virtual communication to the reality of face-to-face interaction (Tobin 1998). Meanwhile, games playing is seen as a highly gendered activity, which reinforces traditional stereotypes and negative role models (e.g. Alloway and Gilbert 1998); there is a rising tide of concern about the availability of pornography on the internet and its tendency to corrupt the young (Wallace and Mangan 1996); and children are seen to be particularly at risk from the paedophiles who lurk anonymously in online chat rooms, seeking to lure them away from the apparent safety of the home.

While there are undoubtedly some important and genuine concerns here, the empirical evidence for many of these assertions remains decidedly limited (Buckingham 2002a). As with arguments about the effects of television, they often involve a form of scapegoating. Like television, the game console or the home computer becomes a convenient bad object onto which we can dump our worries and frustrations – whether they are about violence or immorality or commercialism or sexism or the demise of traditional notions of childhood and family life. As with other screen-based media, at least some of this concern is expressed in the call for stricter legislation; although it also leads to the view that parents and teachers should be exercising greater control in order to protect children from such corrupting influences.

Despite their obvious differences, these apparently contrasting positions share similar weaknesses. As with debates about television, both positive and negative arguments draw upon more general beliefs about childhood – indeed, a *mythology* about childhood. On the one hand, children are seen to possess a natural, spontaneous creativity, which is somehow released by the machine; while on the other, children are seen as vulnerable, innocent and in need of protection. Ultimately, both positions are symptomatic of the chronic senti-mentality with which our society views children – of the very limited and limiting ways in which we construct the meaning of childhood, and thereby constrain the lives of children (Buckingham 2000).

At the same time, both positions seem to be characterized by a kind of technological determinism – that is, a belief that technology will bring about social changes in and of itself (see Williams 1974). Whether we regard these changes as good or bad, they are seen to follow inexorably from the imple-mentation or availability of the technology. Technology is seen to have 'effects' irrespective of the ways in which it is used, and of the social contexts and processes into which it enters. Thus, computers are believed to produce fundamental shifts in the way we create and experience human identity (Turkle 1995). Through their encounters with new media, it is argued, con-temporary children have become 'aliens': they represent a 'postmodern generation' whose subjectivity has been formed through the all-encompassing electronic habitat in which they live (Green and Bigum 1993).

Yet however overstated these arguments may appear, it would also be a mistake to conclude that we have seen it all before, and that nothing is new. As I shall argue in the following sections of this chapter, there are several broader changes in children's cultural environment that are currently underway – changes that in turn reflect the changing social and economic position of children. We need to consider new media in relation to 'older' media, and in the context of children's everyday lives; and we also need to locate children's uses of these media in relation to broader social, economic and political forces.

Convergence

The history of innovation suggests that new media do not necessarily replace older media, so much as add to the range of options that are available. In the process, they may alter the reasons why people use existing media, the kinds of people who use them, or the contexts in which they do so. But at least in the sphere of culture and communications, technologies complement each other in complex and sometimes unforeseen ways. Television, for example, has not replaced the book, just as the book did not replace earlier forms of oral storytelling or communication – even if the purposes for which people use these different forms may have changed (Ong 1982).

On present showing, it seems likely that the same will be true of the digital technologies of computers and multimedia. Of course, there may be an element of displacement here: statistics show that children in homes with computers and game consoles do spend less time watching television, and there is a perceptible decline in overall viewing hours. In fact, however, this change has been far from dramatic. Likewise, despite the increasing pro-liferation of electronic media, there is little evidence that children's reading of print has actually declined; although they may well be reading for different reasons, or in different ways (Neuman 1995). As in the case of television and reading, what is notable is that children are increasingly able to combine different activities – to chat on the computer as they watch TV and listen to CDs and do their homework (or so they will frequently allege). While some see this as evidence of a form of postmodern distraction, others see it as a manifestation of children's selective and autonomous relationships with contemporary communications media.

As this implies, the current context is not so much one of displacement as of *convergence*. Thus, it is argued, we are witnessing a blurring of boundaries, a coming together of previously distinct technologies, cultural forms and practices, both at the point of production and of reception. To be sure, this convergence is partly a result of changes in technology. The possibility of 'digitizing' a whole range of different forms of communication (not just writing, but visual and moving images, music, sound and speech) transforms the computer into much more than a calculator or a typewriter with a mem-ory. It becomes a means of delivering and producing not just written texts, but texts in a variety of media; and it has led critics to talk in terms of the 'teleputer' – the notion that the digital screen will become the focus of a whole range of entertainment, information and communication options.

However, this convergence of media is driven not only by technological change, but also by commercial imperatives. Over the past decade, for example, television programmes have become increasingly linked with movies, books, comics, computer games, CD-ROMs, toys, clothes and other merchandise. This has been particularly the case with children's media – from Disney to Harry Potter – although it is by no means only confined to it. Con-temporary children's 'crazes' – of which Pokémon is the most striking recent example – typically entail a high degree of 'interactivity', not just in the texts themselves (such as computer games) but also in the communication that takes place as children move between one cultural form and another, from the TV series to the card game to the books and the toys. In the process, the gathering of specialist knowledge – much of it impenetrable to adults, of course – becomes inextricably entailed in the purchase and collecting of commodities (Buckingham and Sefton-Green 2002). In this form of 'integrated marketing', each medium has become bound up with other media, in what Marsha Kinder (1991) has aptly called the 'supersystem' of 'transmedia intertextuality' – a development which, as she acknowledges, is fundamentally driven by profit.

At the same time, we can point to a convergence of *forms* of communication. The advent of video, desktop publishing and modems has helped to break down the distinction between interpersonal communication and mass communication. At least potentially, such equipment enables consumers to become producers, as it becomes possible to reproduce and to publish using technologies that were formerly the preserve of small elites. More and more teenagers have home computers in their bedrooms that can be used to create music, to manipulate images or to edit video to a relatively professional standard. These technologies also permit a highly conscious and potentially subversive manipulation of commercially-produced media texts – for example, through sampling and re-editing found material, alongside 'original' creative production. Likewise, the internet is both a public and a private medium, which allows new forms of interpersonal communication as well as new forms of 'publishing'. Its essential anonymity – for example, in the case of chat rooms – permits a degree of fluidity or experimentation with alternative identities; although this can clearly be seen as a source of risk as well as a means of liberation from constraint.

At the same time, what remains striking about many of these new media technologies is how much they rely on the forms and conventions of old technologies. Just as a great deal of television is in some sense literary or conventionally dramatic, so many CD-ROMs implicitly use the book as the model for structuring the ways in which readers get access to information; and the internet, of course, is heavily reliant on print, and on conventional verbal literacy – as indeed are many computer games.

Nevertheless, this convergence of technologies and cultural forms has been greeted by many critics as reflecting a breakdown of established cultural and social hierarchies. Thus, it is argued, these new cultural forms both express and create new forms of social identity in which hitherto marginalized groups come to be represented, and to represent themselves. In the case of children and young people, these new forms do offer new possibilities for self-expression and communication. The internet, for example, provides *some* children with the opportunity for their voices to be heard, in ways that transcend hitherto insurmountable barriers of geographical distance or social difference (Sefton-Green 1998). Even within the protected space of mainstream broadcasting, the paternalism which characterized the public service tradition has been steadily undermined and abandoned: to the distress of many adults, children's media culture is increasingly characterized by a kind of pleasurable anarchy and sensuality which is very different from the sedate and often patronizing approach of earlier decades (Wagg 1992; Holland 1996; Buckingham 2002b). Whether we see this as a corruption of childhood or as a means of cultural liberation for children clearly depends upon how we conceive of childhood in the first place.

Commerce

Certainly, there are several reasons to be more cautious about this broadly optimistic scenario. As I have noted, many of these developments are economically driven: they are part of a much more general move towards a market-led media system in which the maximizing of profit takes precedence over any public service imperatives. The new era is one of vertical integration and globalization in the cultural and communications industries, as producers attempt to exploit successes across a much wider range of media. Having 'invented' the teenager in the 1950s, capitalism's inexorable drive to find new markets has increasingly come to focus on children: while they do not generate disposable income of their own, they have been seen to exercise increasing control over that of their parents (see Kline 1993; Seiter 1993).

In the 1980s, much of the debate here centred on the emergence of '30-minute commercials' – animated programmes produced or commissioned by toy manufacturers with the express intention of advertising toys and related merchandise (Engelhardt 1986). While 'exploitation' of this kind can be traced back at least to the earliest days of Disney, the concern was that merchandising had begun to drive the production of media for children, rather than the other way round. Since that time, the boundaries between these different activities have become almost imperceptible: every text has become an advertisement for other texts. After watching the latest Disney movie, for example, it is now possible not only to buy the toys, the clothes, the books and the spin-off videos from the Disney shop in your local mall, or to watch further episodes on the Disney Channel, but also to visit the website, play the computer game and obtain the CD-ROM.

While such tendencies have been more pronounced in the USA, children's media in Britain – even in the public service sector – are rapidly moving in the same direction. Children's TV magazine shows, for example, construct a self-referential world where the guests are pop stars or actors from soaps, the games and the pop videos are ads for other commodities and the prizes are other media artefacts (Wagg 1992). Meanwhile, the programmes themselves are a kind of extended advertisement for a range of spin-off products, such as magazines and websites. Similar issues are beginning to surface in relation to the internet – as they already have in the USA. For all its potentially liberating decentralization, the internet provides advertisers with very accurate ways of reaching particular kinds of consumers, and gathering detailed information about their consumption habits and preferences. Not least in relation to children, it represents a highly effective means of 'niche marketing' (Center for Media Education 1997).

Of course, this is not to posit some kind of golden age where culture was somehow uncontaminated by commerce; nor indeed is it to imply that commercialism is somehow incompatible with creativity or with genuine communication. Discussion of these issues – particularly in relation to children – is often characterized by a form of Puritanism, in which children's leisure time is expected to be occupied with activities which adults define as 'educational' and 'improving'. The notion that children should be somehow shielded from the influence of the market, in a 'pure', non-commercial sphere, is not only utopian; it also fails to provide a basis for equipping them to deal with the challenges of an increasingly market-oriented culture.

Nevertheless, there are some difficult and perhaps rather traditional questions to be asked about these developments. We need to decide how far we want our public discourse to be dominated by what in the USA is called 'commercial speech' – in other words, by the imperatives of selling. As the BBC, for example, becomes increasingly commercialized, does it still make sense to talk about notions of public service, or about the cultural functions of broadcasting – or do we simply trust in the market to 'give people what they want'? Clearly, this is not an either/or debate. There is a long history of paternalism within public service broadcasting, which has been strangely resistant to taking much notice of the public it is purporting to serve. Some critics of this tradition have argued that a market system ensures a degree of accountability that has historically been lacking from state-supported cultural provision: the market must remain dynamic and responsive to consumers' needs if products are to sell. On the other hand, it is clear that not all needs are equally served by the market – and that some needs may not be served at all. Many critics would argue that, at least in the sphere of culture, the market has proven to be a conservative force: material which is more risky, which serves more specialized audiences, or for whatever reason is perceived to be less likely to make a profit, is bound to be squeezed out (Buckingham *et al.* 1999).

This leads on to questions about access. Although the range of media available is currently proliferating, most of these media cost money. Family expenditure on entertainment media (both software and hardware) has been increasing exponentially over the past decade, both as a global figure and as a proportion of household income. However, these new technologies are differentially distributed: there are significantly more PCs, video recorders and camcorders in middle-class homes than in working-class homes (Livingstone 2002). As a result, different social groups increasingly live in very different cultural worlds. Furthermore, these differences are not simply to do with access to technology: they are also to do with access to the intellectual or cultural capital that is needed to use that technology in effective and creative ways. Put simply, middle-class children are not only likely to have better quality computers and software; they are also likely to have much more informed support in using them from parents and other adults, and greater access to social networks which will provide them with a sense of motivation and purpose in using such technology in the first place (Sefton-Green and Buckingham 1996).

Control

While some have argued that these new technologies are 'empowering' for children, others are becoming very alarmed at this prospect. As with older technologies, there is now a growing anxiety about the need for control, which has come to play a significant part in policy making. The argument here is that children are an especially vulnerable audience – easily influenced and exploited, at risk from all sorts of grubby commercial interests, and particularly from those who peddle violence and pornography. As with television, digital technology is being held responsible for the wholesale destruction of childhood as we know it (Sanders 1995). One of the boundaries that is being blurred here, we are told, is that between adults and children: the problem with these new technologies is that they give children access to things which used to be kept hidden from them, and which they really ought not to know.

The notion that children are turning on their computers and being confronted by a barrage of graphic pornography is, to say the least, somewhat of an exaggeration. Nevertheless, many of these technologies do enable people to bypass centralized systems of control. For the moralists, it is as though the sacred space of the home has been invaded. In earlier times, children may have tried to sneak into the cinema to see what were quaintly termed X-films; but it is now significantly easier to get hold of them on video. Likewise, material which used to be only available to those over the age of majority can (at least in theory) be obtained by anyone with access to the internet and some means of payment. Centralized control – and even parental control – is becoming significantly harder to exert, as growing numbers of children have unsupervised access to these technologies in their bedrooms (Livingstone 2002).

This has led to an increasingly desperate search for alternatives. In recent years, attention has shifted to the possibility of a 'technological fix' which will provide the control that parents are seen to be unable or unwilling to exercise. The V-chip, a means to 'filter out' violent content which has been compulsory on all new TV sets manufactured in the USA since 1998, is a typical example; although it is a technology which UK policy makers seem to have realized is doomed to fail. In the case of the internet, regulators are increasingly looking to 'blocking software' – programs with symptomatic titles such as 'Net Nanny' and 'Cybersitter'; although here too, it is likely that the producers of internet sites, or those who use them, will be able to find ways of defeating this, and that more sophisticated measures will be required (Waltermann and Machill 2000).

While other countries are steadily abandoning censorship, the USA and the UK seem to be moving in the opposite direction. Here, we have seen the strengthening of the censor's powers through the Video Recordings Act (1984) and the Criminal Justice Act (1994); although in the USA, the Communications Decency Act, which attempted to outlaw 'obscenity' on the internet, was ruled to be contrary to the First Amendment. Nevertheless, there seems to be a growing recognition that simply increasing censorship is unlikely to have the desired effect – and indeed, that technological developments have to a large extent made it a lost cause. Regulatory bodies such as the British Board of Film Classification seem to be increasingly looking to education as an alternative – although there is some criticism of the notion that education might function as a surrogate form of censorship (Buckingham and Sefton-Green 1997).

Here again, there are much wider issues at stake. Current concerns about censorship and media regulation are merely part of a wider sense of crisis about the changing relationships of power and authority between adults and children. The debate around the James Bulger case in the early 1990s was perhaps the most obvious example of this process in recent times – and one which symptomatically came to focus on the media, as though (yet again) 'bad media' were the sole explanation of the problem (see Buckingham 1996; Franklin and Petley 1996). In the context of this growing 'moral panic' about childhood, it has become increasingly difficult to sustain a rational debate. Youth crime has become an increasingly salient issue in political debate over the past five years, in which the two main parties have attempted to outdo each other in offering ever more authoritarian solutions, irrespective of evidence about their effectiveness (Newburn 1996). In this context, control of the media has a crucial *symbolic* significance for politicians and others who are seeking to demonstrate their moral authority and responsibility.

Technology in everyday life

Much of this debate about childhood, and specifically about children's uses of new communication technologies, has been conducted over the heads of children themselves. We still know very little about how children perceive, interpret and use these new media. As in the case of television, most of the research has been preoccupied with the search for evidence of negative effects; and much of it has been based on implicitly behaviourist assumptions. There has been very little attention to the social contexts in which the technology is used, or to the social relationships of which it forms a part. Children are typically seen here as isolated individuals, who are powerless to resist the negative influences of the media upon them. If anything, the specific properties of digital technologies appear to have accentuated this approach. Computer games and the internet, for example, are often seen to involve (and indeed to produce) social isolation. The phenomenon of 'interactivity' is widely seen to increase the power of the media, rather than to reduce it: game players, for example, are seen to 'identify' with characters much more intensely than television viewers, and hence to be more likely to copy their behaviour. And, as we have seen, the difficulty of exercising centralized control over these new media has led to renewed concerns about the potential impact of representations of sex and violence.

Within the broader field of media research, a rather different approach has begun to emerge in recent years. Researchers are increasingly seeing children as 'active' readers, not as passive consumers. Children, it is argued, are *already* sophisticated, discriminating, even critical users of media (see e.g. Hodge and Tripp 1986; Buckingham 1993a, 2000; Tobin 2000). In the context of recurrent 'moral panics' about the effects of the media on children, this kind of argument is still a necessary one, although it can also sanction a kind of complacency. The image of the 'media-wise' child is in many ways just as sentimental as the image of the vulnerable innocent it has sought to replace. To celebrate children's 'activity' and 'sophistication' may be to neglect some important limitations and constraints on their uses of the media, both in terms of the nature of media texts themselves and in terms of the social contexts in which they are read and used.

Research on children's uses of new media is still in its infancy (see Buckingham 2002a). As in the case of television, much of the research has been preoccupied with the search for evidence of negative effects; and much of it has been based on implicitly behaviourist assumptions. Nevertheless, there is a growing body of work that analyses the ways in which media use is embedded within children's daily lives, rather than seeing it as an extraneous influence that impacts upon them from outside. This work effectively refutes both the alarmist claims about the dangers of new media and the optimistic celebration of children as 'cyberkids'.

For example, research strongly refutes the popular idea that computer games-playing is an antisocial activity (Buckingham 1993b; Jenkins 1993; Jessen 1999; Livingstone 2002). While the actual playing of games is sometimes an individual, isolated pursuit, it is also often collaborative, and the focus of a great deal of talk and interaction. Furthermore, the culture surrounding the games is an important means of establishing and sustaining interpersonal relationships – from the swapping of games, advice and 'cheats', through to participation in the more public culture of games shops, arcades, magazines and TV shows. The culture of games-playing involves an ongoing social construction of an 'interpretive community' – and in this respect, as Jessen (1999) argues, it may be better suited to the pattern of children's play than older media such as books, which one is alone in consuming.

At the same time, this social process is mediated by the operations of the market. Much of children's discussion is about what you can buy, what you have bought, or what you are going to buy – and this is a discussion in which children are not all equal. Furthermore, this surrounding culture is an arena for the 'border work' that characterizes children's gender relationships (Thorne 1993): it frequently serves to mark the boundaries between boys and girls, and thereby to prevent girls gaining access to technology or to the knowledge that is required to use it (Orr Vered 1998). Through such processes, children are actively constructing and defining themselves, both as consumers and as gendered subjects.

Likewise, research on domestic uses of educational computing suggests that much depends on the 'social envelope' – that is, on the sets of expectations, contexts and social practices – that surrounds it. Growing numbers of researchers are suggesting that the educational promise of this technology has been largely unfulfilled (e.g. Giacquinta et al. 1993; Cupitt and Stockbridge 1996; Sefton-Green and Buckingham 1996; Facer et al. 2001). While parents are likely to invest in computers and software with educational benefits in mind, children generally prefer to use them for playing games, and resist overtly 'educational' activities. Many parents also lack the time and expertise to support their children's use of computers; while the uses of computers in schools are frequently limited, and there is often little dialogue between parents and teachers on the issue. Males are generally the major users and decision makers in relation to home computing, while females (particularly mothers) are often defined as incompetent; and since mothers are generally the primary caregivers, this further reduces the potential for parental support. For many children, using computers – like watching television – seems to be regarded as a way of filling in time when they are bored, and when other, more attractive activities are not available. Nevertheless, we need to know much more about how both groups perceive and balance out the 'educational' and 'entertainment' aspects of these new media – and indeed, the extent to which these distinctions are still possible to sustain.

As this implies, the meaning and use of technology is mediated by social relationships. We need to analyse how technology enters into the peer group and the family, how children get access to it, how they learn about it, and how its use is regulated and controlled (for instance by parents). Certain combinations of technology and social relationships bring about particular uses, but they also prevent others. In the process, technology comes to be defined as (for example) 'male' or 'female', 'educational' or 'entertaining', in ways which systematically favour access among particular social groups. As with television, people use the technology to construct social relationships and to define their social identities – although the resources which are available to them mean that they do not have infinite choice in how they do this.

At the same time, the forms of new media may challenge some of the accepted terms and categories of media analysis. For example, analysing the ways in which children 'read' digital texts (CD-ROMs, computer games, the internet) raises important questions about what a 'text' actually is. It may not make sense to talk about a computer game or a CD-ROM as a 'text' in the same way as one would talk about a book or a movie. The narrative of a computer game depends very much on the person who is playing it – most obviously in terms of how long it lasts, but also in terms of its complexity, what one needs to remember, the choices one makes and so on. At the same time, it is false to suggest that such choices are infinite, or that the player somehow 'creates' the text. Indeed, there is often a spurious form of 'interactivity' here, in which one is confined simply to following paths that have already been laid down, while enjoying the illusion of choice.

In this area, as in many other aspects of childhood studies, the fundamental challenge is to find ways of connecting the 'micro' and the 'macro'. We need to situate children's relationships with the media in the texture of their everyday lives and relationships; and yet we also need to take account of the broader economic and political forces that are at stake. While not denying the active, interpretive dimensions of children's uses of media, we also need to look at the economic, institutional and social dynamics that characterize specific forms of media consumption. In both respects, we need to move beyond the individualistic construction of childhood, and work towards a broader social analysis.

Beyond technology

In writing this chapter, I have been distinctly uneasy about some of the key terms of my argument. I have slipped between 'technology' in the singular and 'technologies' in the plural; between 'technology', 'media' and 'cultural forms'; and between 'digital technologies', 'media technologies' and 'communication technologies'. The word processor may have erased some of these uncertainties, but it cannot erase all of them. Indeed, I would argue that they are probably unavoidable.

Ultimately, I want to resist any reduction of the phenomena I have been describing to a label like 'information technology'. This is not simply a matter of *information*. It is about entertainment, art and culture; it is about literacy and communication. We urgently need to extend our definitions of these things if we are to develop adequate responses to the challenge of these new technologies. Equally, these phenomena are not simply a matter of *technology*.

We need to see digital media in the context of the convergence of previously distinct media and cultural forms; and in terms of wider economic, social and political forces. Despite their 'newness', these technologies force us to go on asking some very traditional questions about access, about control and about public culture.

As I have argued, we need to move beyond the idea that technology has consequences in and of itself. There may indeed be great creative, educational and democratic potential here; but whether that potential is realized depends upon how the technology is used, and on the social relationships that are constructed around it. We need to think creatively about the new forms of educational practice, and the new forms of community, which can make this happen. Technology in itself will not make children creative, nor will it motivate or enable them to learn. Children need to develop specific skills both in using software and hardware, and in more 'traditional' areas of literacy and artistic expression, if the potential is to be realized. We need to abandon the idea that these 'new' and 'old' forms of literacy are mutually exclusive alternatives; or that the 'new' literacies are simply routes towards the 'old'.

Perhaps most crucially, we need to ensure that the use of technology is a collaborative, social process, rather than a privatized, individualized one. We need to construct new kinds of public spheres in which *all* children can work collaboratively with media technology, share what they produce and communicate with a wider audience. If this does not happen, it is likely that the creative, educational and communicative benefits of these technologies will only ever be realized by a small elite.

Acknowledgement

This chapter incorporates some material previously published in Buckingham, D. (2002a) The electronic generation? Children and new media, in L. Lievrouw and S. Livingstone (eds) *Handbook of New Media*. London: Sage.

PART 3
Policy Perspectives on Childhood

8   Promoting better childhoods: constructions of child concern

Wendy Stainton Rogers

Zadie is 14, going on 25. Teetering on the brink between childhood and adulthood, like many girls of her age, she works hard at coming across as 'grown up' and, to look at her, it's hard to tell she is still 'a child'. As for her behaviour – well, it depends where and when you look. At school her teachers describe her behaviour as 'bordering on the infantile sometimes'. Zadie herself is contemptuous about her teachers – indeed, school, she says, bores her and she can't wait to leave. She says they treat her like she's stupid, and most of the stuff they teach is irrelevant to her.

Yet at home Zadie shows a maturity well beyond what we expect of someone her age. Her dad left when she was 11 and, since then, she's looked after her mum, who is wheelchair-bound, and her little sister Sally. Every morning Zadie makes Sally her breakfast and gets her ready for school before helping her mum to dress herself. She usually shops on the way home and then she gets tea for them all, tidies the house and does some washing or ironing. Then she puts Sally to bed and reads her a story. Her boyfriend Luke usually comes round about then. He's 19, and he tells his mates that Zadie is 'no innocent flower – she's a real looker and a real goer'.

Other people pop in and out. There's a home help two mornings a week, and someone from social services who comes to visit Zadie's mum every couple of months. 'They usually ignore me,' Zadie says, with a shrug, 'I'm just the dogsbody to them – they know I'm the one who mainly looks after Mum and Sally, but they hardly talk to me at all and just expect me to get on with it.'

Introduction

In Chapter 10 you will be introduced to the complexities of deciding, in legal terms, 'What is in the best interests of the child?' In this chapter I will explore the practical implications of answering this question in different ways. I will examine how different perceptions and understandings of children – of their needs, their rights, their value for and position in society – lead to different kinds of social policy towards them, and different ways for professionals to approach their care and welfare. In general I will restrict my analysis to social policy in England and Wales, though sometimes I will also mention other systems where the contrast is a helpful aid to putting this in context. Thus here I will examine the impact of different constructions of children and childhood upon the way children are treated within the state policy of England and Wales (such as the services that are and are not offered to them), its institutions (such as welfare, health and education) and the people who work for these agencies (such as health visitors and teachers). In particular I will focus on the extent to which children get any say in what is done to and for them, what services they get and how these are provided.

Take Zadie – what is in her 'best interests'? What sort of social policies and provision would best promote her welfare? She herself thinks she gets a decidedly poor deal. School, she says, has nothing to offer her. The social workers supporting her mum seem to forget that she has any needs of her own and treat her as a drudge. And when she asked her GP to prescribe the contraceptive pill for her, she said he treated her like a 'naughty little girl', even though going to see him took a lot of courage and she thought she was being responsible.

The social construction of child concern

When considering social policy and welfare provision for children, like others in this book my analysis is informed by social constructionism. Such an approach holds that our beliefs about and attitudes towards children – like all of our beliefs, attitudes, expectations, understandings and so on; the ways we see and make sense of the world – are socially constructed. By this I am arguing that the 'realities' that we take for granted about children – the things we 'know' about them and how they are positioned in families, in society, by the media, and so on – are not what they seem to be: self-evident truths about what children and childhood are. Rather they are always the products of human meaning-making.

Social constructionism means more than simply recognizing that there are different ways in which people may understand what is in a child's 'best interest'. It looks beneath the different perspectives to consider 'where they come from' – the moral and political values and beliefs that underpin them. Crucially, it also highlights the practical consequences for children of different viewpoints and world views and specifically it alerts us to, and sensitizes us to, issues, for example, of power. It makes us ask questions like:

- Who is gaining what, and who is losing what, if we attach *this* meaning to *this* set of events or *this* social phenomenon in relation to children?
- What ideology, world view or political position is being promoted?
- What behaviour or action is being justified and what behaviour or action is being prohibited or judged as bad or unacceptable?

Discourses of child concern

Both the social construction of childhood/children and the notion of alternative discourses on the child should be familiar to you from other chapters in this book. In this one I will be looking specifically at what I have termed 'discourses of child concern' – that is, those that frame social policy and welfare provision in relation to different answers to what is in a child's 'best interests'. By 'discourse' I mean a whole set of interconnected ideas that work together in a self-contained way, ideas that are held together by a particular ideology or view of the world. Different discourses are constructed through different sources of knowledge. Each works from a particular set of assumptions, and, crucially, each is founded on a particular set of values and ethical standpoints. From these bases they inform the actions that can be taken – in this case towards children – at different levels, ranging from how professionals (like teachers and social workers) act towards children, to how social and economic policies define children's needs and entitlements at local, national and international levels.

I think that currently operating in the West in the early twenty-first century there are three main discourses of concern towards children informing policy and practice:

- a *'needs' discourse*, that seeks to identify children's basic needs, and where action is directed to ensuring that those needs are met;
- a *'rights' discourse*, that seeks to establish children's rights and entitlements, and where action is directed to promoting these rights;
- a *'quality of life' discourse*, that seeks to determine what constitutes, for children, a 'good' quality of life, where action is directed to improving the quality of children's lives.

The 'children's needs' discourse

With the establishment in England and Wales in the 1940s of a welfare state, services for children were set up to explicitly meet their needs. This reflected a growing conviction among policy makers that children – as children – have particular needs *because* they are children, and that states have a responsibility to ensure those needs are met, encapsulated in the United Nations *Declaration on the Rights of the Child* (UNDRC) (United Nations 1959). While billed as about children's rights, the text of the document itself is firmly couched within a 'needs' discourse. For example:

> The child, for the full and harmonious development of his personality, *needs* love and understanding. He shall, wherever possible, grow up in the care and under the responsibility of his parents, and in any case in an atmosphere of affection and moral and material security; a child of tender years shall not, save in exceptional circumstances, be separated from his mother.
>
> (United Nations 1959: 17, emphasis added)

To put this into context, the declaration was prepared in the wake of World War II, when many children had been refugees or (as was the case in the UK) were evacuated to rural areas to keep them safe from bombardment. An influential theorist at that time, Mia Kellmer Pringle, identified four 'basic needs' of children – for love and security, for new experiences, for praise and recognition and for responsibility (Kellmer Pringle 1974).

The influence of psychological theories about child development

Notice what is going on here. The 'needs' identified – both by the UNDRC and by Kellmer Pringle – are not material needs (such as for food or for shelter) but *psychological* needs. It is clear that the 'needs' discourse I am talking about arises from developmental psychology. In Chapter 6 Valerie Walkerdine explored with you the way in which developmental psychology constructs childhood as a 'becoming' rather a 'being'. It positions children as having 'needs' particular to their status as developing persons – 'needs' determined by the desired end-state of a 'full and harmonious development'. In other words, the 'needs discourse' of child concern is heavily predicated on developmental psychology's theories. This depiction of the child arises from three main theoretical frameworks that constitute child development. All have their basis in biological theories of development.

The first framework consists of theories of *evolutionary development*, based on the assumption that human behaviour arises from the same evolutionary forces that have moulded animal behaviour. In evolutionary developmental theory, comparisons are made with animal species where the young have 'critical periods', usually occurring soon after birth, when the young animal goes through a process of attachment. In their critical period baby ducks, for example, attach (in a psychological sense) to and will subsequently follow whatever moving object they observe at this point. Usually this is the mother duck, but Konrad Lorenz, an animal behaviourist, was able to get baby ducks to follow him by swimming around them at the crucial moment.

Psychologists (such as John Bowlby 1969, 1980) proposed that human babies also have a critical period during which they normally attach to their mother. Bowlby argued that children's development is impaired if this process of attachment is compromised. If children do not have sufficient close contact with their mothers during the critical early stage of their development, he contended, then they are likely to grow up into a dysfunctional adult, prone to criminality, unable to form close relationships and incapable of functioning as a well-adjusted member of society.

The second framework consists of theories of *psychodynamic development*, based upon the work of Sigmund Freud. Freud also assumed a biological basis for human behaviour, whereby childhood consists of a sequence of bio-logically pre-programmed unfolding stages, each of which had to be properly accomplished and resolved in order to move on to the next. Only by success-fully completing each stage can a child develop into a fully mature adult. Problems at any stage can leave the developing individual 'fixated' and there-fore lacking the capacity to become well adjusted in adulthood. For instance, a child who does not properly achieve the transition from the 'anal' stage will, according to this theory, develop a dysfunctional 'anal' personality.

The third theoretical category is that of *cognitive development*, usually attributed to the work of Jean Piaget. Here the stages through which a child has to pass are to do with their thinking ability – the ways in which they make sense of and understand the world. Piaget regarded children as 'cognitive aliens' (although the term is not his) – as thinking in profoundly different ways from adults. Children, in this context, are seen as incapable of under-standing ideas and concepts that adults deploy with such ease that they simply take them for granted. A good example is a cognitive theory of moral development, proposed by Kohlberg. In it, small children, for example, see an act's rightness or wrongness in terms of its consequences, not the intentions of the person committing it. So, for instance, if somebody gets hurt, then small children assume that the act was 'naughty' or 'bad', irrespective of whether the person doing it did so on purpose or by accident.

What all of these developmental theories have in common is that they position children as:

- lacking adult capacities – of autonomy, rationality and responsibility;
- psychologically and emotionally dependent and vulnerable;
- 'needy' for particular experiences and opportunities which, if not provided, will undermine the child's proper development.

Clearly babies – and even small children to some degree – are incapable, vulnerable and needy in a strictly biological sense. But animals in the wild do not remain dependent for long. Equally, children throughout the world can and do live autonomously at very young ages. In parts of Africa children as young as 8 have become heads of households, looking after their brothers and sisters when their parents have died of AIDS. As we have seen in Zadie's case, the same is sometimes true in the UK too. She is 14, but again, children as young as 8 can take on this role.

Nevertheless, in the modern western world in which psychology so profoundly informs our thinking, the 'needs' discourse is applied as much to adolescents as it is to smaller children. Indeed, Christine Griffin (1993) argues that when applied to young people, this discourse is profoundly one of 'problematization'. It construes young people as not so much lacking and vulnerable as inherently 'problematic' – as both 'troubled' and as 'troublesome' – and hence always ever 'in need' of adult surveillance, intervention and control. We can observe this prejudice at work in relation to the way Zadie is treated. While at home she is expected to take on heavy responsibilities; at school she is seen as 'trouble'. And despite her evident capability in caring for her mother and little sister, social workers fail to consult and negotiate with her as they would with an adult carer. Thus, while the 'children's needs' discourse is undoubtedly well intentioned – motivated by a desire to improve children's welfare and make sure that state policies and welfare services take their well-being seriously – it has another (almost certainly unintentioned) consequence. By positioning children and young people as 'in need' it sets up an expectation that we (the adult world) should view children in terms of their needs and seek to meet them. It demands, in effect, that we must provide 'solutions' to the 'problems' that are posed by the needs of children and young people. What this does, in effect, is turn children and young people *themselves* into 'problems' that need to be 'solved'.

The warranting function of discourses

Discourses are like this. They do not merely 'describe', they also carry moral invectives. They prescribe action (what should be done) and agency (attribute responsibility for action) – a term that is increasingly used is to refer to the 'warranting function' of discourses (see e.g. O'Dell 1998; Stainton Rogers and Stainton Rogers 2001). A particular instance is what O'Dell calls 'harm warranting' – that is, where intervention is based upon the warrant that it is necessary in order to protect a child from harm. O'Dell was writing in relation to child sexual abuse, a 'social problem' that from the late twentieth century has become a matter of extreme concern in the English-speaking world. Children who are exposed to almost any level of sexual engagement with an adult are seen to be in danger of suffering extreme emotional and psychological harm. Even where no actual contact occurs – where, for example, children are engaged in sexually charged conversations – there is still the

Issue	Warrant	Prescribed action
Child sexual abuse	is inevitably and seriously harmful	so adults must intervene to prevent it and stop it

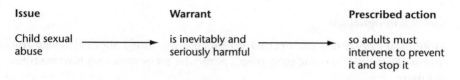

Figure 8.1   Harm warranting

view that this can cause severe and long-lasting damage to their psychological development and emotional well-being. The underlying logic of this 'harm warranting' is show in Figure 8.1.

An extreme case of such intervention was when, in response to concerns about ritual abuse, a number of children were forcibly removed from their homes in 'dawn raids' and kept in isolation from any contact with each other and their families. This was done in order to 'protect' any possible evidence they might give, in pursuit of a prosecution against their suspected abusers. One of the children involved complained afterwards that this treatment was far more punitive than would have been meted out if he had been accused of murder.

Most cases are nowhere near as brutal as this. But the fear of abuse has had a pervasive impact on virtually all children in the western world, contributing to the present situation where today children are seldom allowed out of parental sight. Whereas in the 1970s a majority of children over the age of 8 walked to school unaccompanied by an adult, today few parents would be comfortable with this.

Children's worlds have profoundly changed as a result of this 'harm warrant'. Social welfare services for children – in the UK in particular and the English-speaking world generally – have become dominated by concerns to protect children from abuse (Parton 1991; Pringle 1998). Again we can see this manifested in the way Zadie is treated by her doctor. When she tried to get him to prescribe contraception, he treated her like a naughty child – or this is how Zadie saw it, anyway. But it is probable that the doctor was not so much making a judgement about Zadie's behaviour as protecting himself from the accusation of colluding with Zadie being 'sexually abused' (which is how, in English law, having sex with her boyfriend at the age of 14 would be regarded). In this way the 'needs' discourse can lead to a very partial and distorted concern – to protect a child from abuse at virtually any cost. This renders invisible all other concerns about other 'needs' the child may have (such as access to information) and, indeed, about their fundamental human rights (such as not being held incommunicado against their will).

Cultural imperialism

Woodhead (1997: 63) has opened up broader questions about the way the 'needs' discourse has come to impose a particular set of values on how we treat children:

> Conceptualizing childhood in terms of 'needs' reflects the distinctive status accorded to young humanity in twentieth century western societies. It is widely regarded as a progressive and enlightened framework for working with children ... But ... this seemingly innocuous and benign four-letter word conceals in practice a complex of latent assumptions about children.

Woodhead thus highlights another problem with the 'needs' discourse's warrants – their cultural imperialism, that imposes the specifically western values that are enmeshed within developmental psychology. To claim (as developmental psychology does) that children *need* 'praise and recognition' implies that without these, children will be harmed – will grow up psychologically stunted and lacking in self-esteem. But at other times and in other places, other conceptions of adult maturity are valued more and given greater priority. In most religious communities, for instance, a high priority is placed on the need to be 'saved' – a salvation that can only be achieved through obeying God's word. In such contexts children will be seen to have quite different 'needs' from 'praise and recognition'. Harm warranting predicated upon a developmental perspective of childhood thus imposes a particularly western world view on how we construe children's needs. Crucially, it adopts the western prioritization of the individual self, and of individual autonomy and freedom. Viewing the child as in transit towards becoming an autonomous, independent individual focuses our attention on what children 'need' in order to achieve this goal. But what if a different sort of adulthood is aspired to – one that values connectedness, mutuality and interdependence?

Authentic personhood and values

Evidence is growing that there is wide cultural variation in what is regarded as desirable adult authentic personhood – what are seen to be the traits and qualities to which childrearing is directed. Yet, as the psychologist Mansur Lalljee points out, this is by no means a universal perception of what an authentic person should be:

> In the West the person is though of as an autonomous unit, consisting of a set of core attributes, that are carried with the person through time and context . . . In Japan, India and most parts of the world other

Table 8.1 Hofstede's (1980) cross-cultural study of values

High value placed on individualism	High value placed on collectivism
USA, Australia, UK, Canada and the Netherlands	Latin America and Asia

Low value placed on deference	High value placed on deference
Australia, Israel, Denmark, New Zealand and Ireland	Malaysia, Panama, Guatemala, the Philippines and Venezuela

than 'the West', people are seen in terms of their roles and relationships, in terms of their activities and interests, because of the interconnected networks in these societies. For people living in such societies, the self integrally includes social relationships and social context.

(Lalljee 2000: 133)

Psychological studies on values indicate that there is a strong divide between those cultures that value individualism and autonomy (i.e. resisting deference to elders and authority figures), and those that prize collectivism and respect for elders and people in authority. Hofstede's (1980) cross-cultural study of values illustrates this well, as shown in Table 8.1

Schwartz's (e.g. Schwartz *et al.* 2000) more recent studies of cross-cultural values pick out a cluster of collectivist values that tend to be prioritized in countries such as Malaya, Taiwan, Turkey and Poland. These do not just place strong value on collectivism – valuing relatedness, reciprocity and community cohesion – they also include respect for tradition, honouring parents, obedience, self-discipline and politeness. It is not hard to see how such values will construct a very different perception of what constitute children's 'needs'. In these societies a child's needs are to learn to comply with the moral codes and/or religious doctrines with which they will be expected, as authentic adults, to comply. These very different goals for childhood that are espoused by collectivist cultures cannot be reconciled with the 'needs' discourse based upon developmental psychology. The contrast powerfully highlights the extent to which developmental psychology is, indeed, based upon a particular complex of latent assumptions about children (Woodhead 1997). The 'needs' discourse for children's welfare is revealed for what it is – as culturally contingent and far from universally applicable.

The 'children's rights' discourse

Since about the 1970s sociologists of childhood (such as James and Prout 1997) and policy makers have argued that children are not just a bundle of 'needs' that must be met. They are people in their own right, with their own concerns, priorities and aspirations.

This position is the basis of a 'children's rights' discourse. It views children, above all, as *citizens* who have rights *as* citizens. So it encourages us to go further than just doing things for children simply because they are 'good for them' – which is often the way adults treat them. For example, think of children's play. If you read textbooks about the crucial functions served by children's play – helping them to learn, helping them to develop social skills like taking turns and sharing, and so on – then it can be easy to lose sight of an alternative set of ideas about the function of play: to delight in having fun and getting pleasure. Adult entertainment and leisure pursuits are not viewed in terms of simply 'being good for them'. Rather they are recognized as things an adult is entitled to do for their own sake, simply because they are enjoyable. Equally, even if we accept that children cannot thrive and flourish unless they have warm and caring relationships – this is not *all* that intimate relationships mean to a child. Adults don't regard being loved and cared about as just about having their 'needs' met. Neither do children. For a child, being loved is profoundly meaningful and valuable in itself.

Crucially, a move from a 'needs' discourse to one of 'rights' treats children as *social actors* – able to act on their own behalf and both capable of and entitled to have a say in what is done to and for them. This discourse proposes that while it is true that childhood may be a time of greater physical growth and intellectual maturation than adulthood, this does not mean that in some way children are 'incomplete'. Certainly it does not mean we can treat them as 'lesser mortals' – as not deserving the same rights and respect as adults. Woodhead expresses this well: 'Children are not incomplete human beings to be shaped into society's mould. They have needs and aspirations of their own, and rights which must be respected' (Woodhead 1996: 12). This is not just a matter of semantics: it has powerful practical consequences. Advocates of the 'children's rights' discourse point out that the paternalism of the 'children's needs' discourse allows adults to abuse the power it gives them. Within the 'needs' discourse, they contend, concepts like 'children's welfare' and 'the best interests of the child' warrant actions towards children that, in fact, serve adult interests. Gerison Lansdown (2001: 89) makes the point explicitly: 'During the course of the twentieth century adults with responsibility for children across the professional spectrum have been responsible for decisions, policies and actions that have been inappropriate for, if not actively harmful to, children while claiming to be acting to promote their welfare'. She then goes on to list a long string of such abuses. These include social policies of evacuating children in wars, putting children in institutions and isolating them in hospitals. Lansdown also lists examples of where parents' rights are prioritized over the welfare of children – such as legally prohibiting children from being told about their biological parentage in cases of assisted reproduction. An even more extreme example is where children have been born with genetic disorders that mean their genitals are ambiguous (i.e. it is unclear whether they have a clitoris or a penis). In such cases children have been subjected to surgery to 'regularize' their gender, not just at birth but repeatedly in childhood, without being able to give consent and frequently being lied to about what the surgery is for (Simmonds 2003). One case is described where a pubescent girl was told the surgery she was having was for ovarian cancer, when, in fact, it was to reduce the size of her clitoris (Moreno 1998). It has been suggested (Kitzinger in press) that in such cases the surgery is performed in the name of 'child welfare' when, in fact, it is being done either to ameliorate parental embarrassment or to conform to medical constructions of what constitutes 'normality'. The child's body is reconstructed, without the child's knowledge or consent, in order to meet the needs and expectations of adults.

What are children's rights?

Such abuses of children in the pursuit of 'meeting their needs' have provided a strong case for according children 'rights'. The United Nations Convention on the Rights of the Child (UNCRC) was instituted in 1991 to specifically counter such abuses. It identifies three main forms of rights for children, often called the 'three Ps' – rights to:

- *provision* of appropriate support and services for their healthy development;
- *protection* from exploitation and abuse;
- *participation* in decisions made about their upbringing and care.

Within a 'children's rights' approach, the intention is to devise and deliver social welfare policies and services for children in ways that promote these rights. A good example is that the 1989 England and Wales Children Act explicitly specifies that a child's 'wishes and feelings' should be ascertained and must be taken into account in court rulings about her or his future (such as following parental divorce). It also gives older children the potential to challenge their parents' decisions by seeking a court order – for example, to go and live with a relative rather than remain in the family home.

Problems with the children's rights discourse

But, as a number of commentators have noted (e.g. Roche 1992), the 'three Ps' do not always sit easily together. Action to protect children may mean having to limit their participation in decision making. As you will see in Chapter 9, criticisms have also been made about the ethnocentricity of the formulation of rights built into the UNCRC and problems with applying it in certain situations. Montgomery (2001) argues, for instance, that in regard to child prostitutes, the response to the UNCRC by the Thai government – taking such children from their families – is not only contrary to what the children want. While protecting these children from the specific harm of sexual exploitation entailed in prostitution, Montgomery asserts that the Thai government's policy of placing them in institutions cuts them off from their families and communities in ways that are highly detrimental to their welfare. Moreover, the children's rights discourse is not immune to being appropriated by adults for their own purposes. For instance, one of the forms of 'exploitation' from which children are seen as in need of 'protection' is paid employment. From a western perspective, children should be in school, receiving their entitlement to education. But it is worth noting that Trade Unions are key players in the movement to stop child labour. It does not require much cynicism to suggest that their motivation may have more to do with protecting adults' jobs and rates of pay than promoting children's rights.

When parental rights conflict with children's rights

However, the greatest antagonism towards children's rights is often in situations where they are seen to directly challenge parental rights. When the 1989 Children Act was introduced, its provisions allowing children to challenge aspects of parental upbringing received a very hostile press. In an article headlined 'Pocket money rise or it's divorce', the journalist Polly Ghazi argued:

> Parents who turn up their noses when their children bury themselves in *Viz*, *Smash Hits* or *Just 17* may be making a big mistake. The magazines may soon contain advertisements for a booklet entitled *Your Say in Court*, which could have a significant effect on family relationships. Aimed at 10- to 16-year-olds, it provides a step-by-step guide on how to 'divorce' parents.
>
> (*Observer*, 25 July 1993)

The rest of the article is somewhat more measured in tone and explains that the booklet is produced by the Children's Legal Centre, not to incite childish rebellion, but to inform children about their rights, and that it is endorsed by the National Society for the Prevention of Cruelty to Children (NSPCC). But the article nonetheless conveys the erroneous message that children can 'divorce' their parents at will, for trivial reasons. In actuality, it is very difficult for a child to contest her or his parent's views about where she or he should live. It would only be ordered by a court if the child could make a compelling case that living with a relative, say, is better for them than living with their parent(s).

It remains that the concept of 'children's rights' can touch a very raw nerve when it puts adult decisions and actions to the test – are they *really* 'in the best interests of the child'? Yet it is in this, I believe, that the power of a children's rights discourse lies. The point is that while most parents, most of the time, act in their children's best interests, some do not. And all parents are capable of sometimes allowing other considerations to cloud their judgement, or get in the way of doing what is best for their children. Parents are not saints. They get angry, they have divided loyalties, they sometimes loose their tempers. Parents, especially when in conflict with each other or with outside agencies, can and do sometimes use their children to work out problems or ambitions of their own. Equally, professionals have their own concerns, their own battles to fight, their own needs, and can and do justify self-serving actions by claiming that they are 'in the child's best interests'. Thus the main purpose of identifying children's rights and seeking to promote them is to acknowledge that adults do not always know best, and may not always act in the most honourable ways, and to recognize therefore that there must be some limits on adult power over children. According to its advocates, the UNCRC is not intended to undermine adults' ability to care about and care for children, and to protect them and to promote their welfare. Rather it can provide an essential counter to the *misuse* of adult power.

The 'quality of life' discourse

An alternative to both the 'needs' and 'rights' discourses has recently been posed by a 'children's quality of life' discourse. Its proponents argue that the concept of quality of life – because it specifically acknowledges the variability of value systems – allows us to move beyond the ethnocentric concerns of the needs and rights discourses. It also acknowledges, in a way that the other discourse fail to address, that children's welfare is always contextual. It cannot be fostered in isolation, but has to take into account the concerns, values, resources and limitations of the families and communities in which children are reared and cared for. The most usual situation in which this concept is used is in health care settings. It is defined by the World Health Organization as follows:

> An individual's perception of their position in life in the context of the culture and value systems in which they live and in relation to their goals, expectations, standards and concerns. It is a broad ranging concept affected in a complex way by the person's physical health, psychological state, level of independence, social relationships and their relationships to salient features in their environment.
>
> (WHO 1993: 30)

Usually in health care settings it is used as a measure to decide how to apportion services, in situations where people are suffering from chronic conditions that cannot be cured, including services for people who are dying. The impact of the service is not measured in terms of its ability to 'cure', but rather in terms of its contribution to improving the patient's quality of life.

The application of the concept of quality of life to childhood has been developed, in particular, by Ferran Casas (1998, 2000). He draws upon a general shift in theorizing that began in the 1960s where a number of social policy theorists began to argue that welfare should not be understood merely in terms of material conditions (such as decent housing and sufficient income) but more in relation to how people *experience* their lives and what they see as giving them 'quality' (see e.g. Campbell *et el*. 1976).

Casas proposes that the concept of quality of life is useful in considering children's welfare because it acknowledges that children's satisfaction with their lives and their general state of happiness do not narrowly depend on meeting their 'developmental needs' or even on fostering their 'rights'. We must also take account of more culturally mediated factors, such as children's role and status in their families and communities. Crucially, Casas argues that when we focus on how to improve children's quality of life, then this has a significant impact upon how we think about what children are entitled to receive from society and the social policies and services provided for them. The basis of his contention is that social policy based upon children's rights – particularly to protection and provision of services – may seem to be an improvement upon one based upon meeting children's needs. But, in fact, it is still preoccupied with the problems that children face in *negative* circumstances. It leads to an approach of identifying 'risk factors' – circumstances where children may need professionals to intervene to redress the disadvantages they face (such as inadequate parenting, social exclusion or poverty) and/or to protect them from harm. Casas contrasts this with his belief that what is needed is a 'pro-activity to ensure that children's living conditions should improve' (Casas 2000: 8). We should, he says, turn our attention away from what harms children and instead concentrate upon what we can do to help children overcome difficult situations and to thrive in adversity.

Promoting resilience

A key concept here is that of resilience, which has been defined as *'normal development under difficult conditions'* (Fonagy *et al*. 1994, original emphasis). Resilient children are those who somehow manage to grow up healthy, happy and 'together' despite having had to face major setbacks and difficulties in their childhoods: 'Whether such experiences crush or strengthen an individual child depends, in part, on his or her resilience. Resilience is important because it is the human capacity to face, overcome and be strengthened by or even transformed by the adversities of life' (Grotberg 1995: 10).

According to Fonagy *et al*., focusing on promoting children's resilience not only has direct benefits in enabling them to overcome adversity in itself, but it also helps to overcome the stigmatization faced by children from 'problem families' or with impoverished backgrounds. In particular it helps individuals to challenge the assumption often made that a 'bad childhood' inevitably means growing up into an incompetent adult and, especially, a 'bad parent': 'history is not destiny. Clinical and epidemiological data both show that the majority of parents who in their childhood faced brutality, desertion, poverty and death imperil neither their bond to their child, nor their child's bond to them' (Fonagy *et al*. 1994: 234).

Grotberg makes a number of suggestions about how parents and others can promote resilience in children, including encouraging children to become 'autonomous, independent, responsible, empathetic and altruistic' and helping children to learn how to 'communicate with others, solve problems, and successfully handle negative thoughts, feelings and behaviours'. Crucially, she argues, with such treatments 'children themselves become active in promoting their own resilience' (Grotberg 1995: 3). More recently, Ungar (2003) has proposed that 'resilience' offers a productive way to understand how troubled young people explain their productive behaviours. By nurturing their resilience, he argues, they can be helped to tackle the problems that they face.

Seeking children's views

A second critical element of quality of life is that its evaluation must include the views of those whose well-being is at stake. Roche (2001) gives as an example the way parents and children might judge a school. What may matter to parents are things like its physical environment and its position in the 'league tables'. But children may be more concerned about how they are treated by teachers and other pupils – whether they are treated with respect or humiliated and bullied. This example highlights the importance of taking into account how children, as *users* of services provided for them, evaluate those services. However good the service may be judged against other criteria,

if it fails to take account of the concerns and priorities of its intended bene-
ficiaries then it can hardly be seen as unequivocally in children's best interests.
Hill (1999) notes that only recently have there been attempts to discover the
views of parents, as service users, of the services provided for their children.
And, he points out, it is rarer still for children to be consulted. Yet children are
key stakeholders in the services and care provided for them, and if quality
services are to be offered to them this cannot be done without finding out
about *their* priorities and concerns – what, to them, constitutes 'quality care'.
Hill argues that we should not expect children's views to be the same as
parents'. For example he reports research about the worries of primary-school
age children and their parents. It indicates that parents' concerns about their
children focused on external threats like traffic, being snatched by strangers
and violence on the streets, whereas children's anxieties were much more
about problems in their immediate relationships. They worried about tensions
and conflicts with their peers – falling out with friends, bullying, insults
and 'slagging'; about loss – from the illness or death of relatives or parental
separation; about resentments – broken promises, parental conflicts and so on.
Clearly what matters to children can be quite different from what matters to
parents. Hill also reports on children's views of the adults who care for them.
Two concerns emerged as very important. First, they felt they were not listened
to – that parents and others caring for them were often so preoccupied they
did not attend to children when they wanted to talk about things that were
upsetting them. Second, children felt that adults did not take their concerns
seriously. Their attempts to seek help were often met with false reassurance –
'Don't worry' – when what they wanted were opportunities to express their
feelings and to have someone to mediate in the conflicts and resentments they
faced. In other words, for children a crucial element of quality in their care is
that adults listen to them and take what they have to say seriously.

If we view 'quality of life' as being about the factors in children's life
circumstances and life worlds that give them satisfaction and meaning – that
make life worth living – then we have to go beyond just 'meeting their needs'
and positively promote their well-being. This also entails helping them to
achieve their potential – giving them opportunities to flourish and achieve
their life goals. It requires us to consult them, to find out their opinions about
what matters to them, and to involve them in the plans and decisions that are
made. Crucially, it makes us acknowledge that while some children's
expectations may be limited by their life circumstances, we cannot simply
set lower standards for them. Rather we need to concentrate on how their
capabilities can be enhanced – how can we counter the disadvantage they face,
and how can they be helped to survive and overcome adversity?

The shift to looking at how children's quality of life can be fostered has
three main benefits to our understanding of the needs and rights of children
and our ability to meet them. First, this discourse sets a positive agenda.

Instead of focusing on children's vulnerabilities and incapacities (and those of their families and communities) it emphasizes their strengths and capabilities. I would argue that many of the problems that families face in caring for and bringing up their children cannot be solved by individual workers or organizations. They are deeply entrenched social problems – such as poverty, racism and social exclusion – that can only be tackled by society as a whole. To make any real inroads into solving problems like poverty or racism requires major *political* changes. For example, doing something about child poverty requires improvements to be made in the money and support that the government provides to help poor families.

When Casas writes about the way some previous approaches have tended to focus on 'risk factors', these were generally the kinds of problem he was talking about. He thinks we need a new approach because describing things like racist prejudice or poverty as 'risk factors' tends to locate the problem in families. It *individualizes* problems that are better seen as problems of social, political and economic systems. When a family is exposed to racism, for example, this is not the family's fault – it's not *their* problem. The problem lies in the racism of society, in people's attitudes and in institutional racism. Equally, the poverty that many families in Britain face cannot simply be seen as the fault of parents who are poor. We know this because in other countries there are far fewer children growing up in poverty. In terms of well-being, Britain is currently the worst place in Europe to be a child. A recent UNICEF report (Piachaud and Sutherland 2000) has concluded that the UK rates lowest of all European Union countries on seven specific indicators of child well-being. It reports that child poverty in Britain has trebled in the last 20 years, and 40 per cent of children in the UK are now born into low-income house-holds. Compare this with Denmark, where only 5 per cent of children are born into poverty, and it is clear that political, social and economic forces have a profound impact.

Baldwin *et al.* (1990) have also contested the individualizing of problems. They illustrated this by looking at the assertion that 'social class . . . is an important risk variable'. They point out that belonging to the disadvantaged social class is not, in itself, what undermines children's healthy development. Rather it is the circumstances that tend to go along with being in the lowest social class – parents who are unemployed or have such a badly paid job that they have to work very long hours; inadequate housing; living in neighbourhoods with few resources and high crime rates, and so on. Baldwin and his colleagues then go on to argue:

> At one time we thought, somewhat naively, that knowing the major risk factors would point the way to intervention, because removing risk factors might prevent the development of problem behaviour. It is clear, however, that without a social revolution we are not going to

> remove the risk factors of lower SES [socioeconomic status], divorce
> and minority prejudice . . . We must help these families and their
> children to cope with the risks in their environment, rather than
> attempting the futile task of removing the large-scale risk factors
> themselves.
>
> (Baldwin *et al.* 1990: 278)

This is not to say that we should ignore problems like racism or poverty. Tackling these is crucial to enhancing children's lives and opening up their opportunities. But this takes time and resources. Individual workers and organizations can only do so much to counter poverty, racism and social exclusion – though there are some things they can do, such as establishing anti-discriminatory practice. The point here is that in the meanwhile, by finding out what makes children and families more able to cope with adversity, we can devise practical strategies for helping and supporting them.

Focusing on the notion of quality of life thus helps to challenge the 'problematizing' of children, young people and, indeed, their families. If we look, instead, at the *positive* qualities that families may possess – things like having good relationships, emotional warmth and people who will support and stick by them at times of crisis – then we get a different picture. Instead of marking out certain families as 'problems', it encourages us to look for what is potentially good in nearly all families. Even in the poorest and most deprived families there are usually very powerful bonds of love between parents and children, with (most of the time) enormous emotional warmth. Lone parents are usually prepared to go through a lot to 'stick by' their children through thick and thin. Most children have grandparents, aunts and uncles, brothers and sisters or neighbours and friends who can make all the difference to whether they can get through tough times. Of course, there are exceptions – it cannot be denied that there are extreme cases where parents are so inadequate or cruel (or both) that they cause their children harm. But the point here is that these really are quite unusual circumstances. Avoiding problematization is not about claiming that every family can function effectively if they are given sufficient support. There will always be some parents who cannot care for their children properly however much help they are given. It is about recognizing that *most* parents who experience difficulties looking after their children have strengths that can be built upon to help them cope with their problems. It is also about recognizing that in those rare cases where children have to be removed from their parents in order to keep them safe, the care provided for them needs to draw upon similar kinds of support and benefits. And this should, wherever possible, include *still* maintaining family bonds, *still* encouraging emotional warmth from their parents, recognizing that just because their parents cannot care for their children, this does not mean they do not care *about* them.

Conclusions

It should be obvious by now where I stand – as an advocate of the 'quality of life' discourse. Not only does it offer a more positive agenda than either the 'needs' or the 'rights' discourse, it is also more holistic. The 'rights' and 'needs' discourses are taxonomic, in that they set out lists of what is seen to be required. But in both cases there can be conflicts between them. A quality of life analysis looks at a child's life experience, circumstances, values and priorities *as a whole*, and recognizes that there can be considerable variation in what matters to a particular child, family, group or community. The quality of life discourse is also less vulnerable to ideological bias – in the way that, say, formulations of children's rights have been accused of being. In focusing on the child's values and priorities (alongside those of the families, communities and cultures within which they live) it is more respectful of social, cultural and religious variation. There is a risk here – that this may lead to lower standards being applied to children in economically disadvantaged countries. Or worse, it could be used to condone the exploitation of children (economic as well as sexual) in countries made poor by the actions of richer countries. But this risk should not prevent us from seeking greater respect for cultural diversity.

Finally I would argue that in policy terms, this discourse is also more likely to be effective. Attempts to reduce the 'risk factors' that make children vulnerable have largely been unsuccessful. Moreover, they frequently add to the problems that children face, since they are stigmatizing and, for instance, can exacerbate social exclusion. By directing action towards what matters for particular children, families and communities (i.e. what *they regard* as crucial to a child's quality of life), any action taken is more likely to gain the cooperation of the children concerned, their families and communities. Action can thus be collaborative and participatory – with recipients taking an active part in what is done, rather than being the passive receivers of services. Looking, instead, to how resilience can be actively promoted can be much more effective. It is a strategy that can work on a small scale, and can enable the poorest and most disadvantaged families and communities to deliver real benefits to improve the quality of life of their children. A child like Zadie, in my mind, illustrates the utility of the quality of life discourse. There are no simple solutions from either the 'needs' or 'rights' discourses to the hardships she faces and the sacrifices she makes to keep her family together. Focusing on her 'needs' is highly problematic, since they cannot easily be reconciled. She 'needs' her mother look after her and yet her mother is, instead, highly dependent on her. Meeting Zadie's needs for parenting (which could be met by, say, being placed in foster care) would mean separating her from her mother. Focusing on Zadie's 'rights' also poses irreconcilable conflicts – between her right to a 'normal childhood' and her right to determine for herself how she wants to spend her childhood. She is hardly going to agree to deserting her mother and sister to make her own life easier and more 'normal'. A quality of life discourse turns the focus away from the problems Zadie's family faces, and concentrates instead on their strengths. It acknowledges that whatever Zadie may be losing out on in being a young carer, it will also be giving her great satisfaction and fostering her self-esteem. It persuades us to explore how the incredible resilience she shows in holding her family together could be better supported by the professionals responsible for her mother, and marshalled at school so that Zadie gets more out of her education. It enjoins us to respect the courage and responsibility she shows in seeking contraception. It encourages us to look differently at her boyfriend and recognize that he is the only person who is actually giving Zadie any real support (emotional and probably practical). In other words, it makes us look at Zadie and her family in a completely different light – as resilient, strong and, above all, functional. It makes us see them as deserving of a great deal more help than they are getting – not as a 'solution' to a set of 'problems', but as an investment in a family who are winning out against the odds.

9 Children's rights: international policy and lived practice

Rachel Burr

Introduction

In this chapter we look at the children's rights movements and examine some of the ways in which child rights are being interpreted and applied both internationally and very locally among children living in Vietnam. Some of the work presented here is based on research carried out when I spent two years from 1996 to 1998 living in Hanoi, the capital of Vietnam, doing ethnographic-based fieldwork informed by participatory observation to explore the impact of the United Nations Convention on the Rights of the Child (UNCRC) on the work of aid agencies and the children they worked among. The children I did fieldwork among fitted the United Nations Children's Fund (UNICEF) category of children in need of special protection measures and as such were often the focus of international aid agency support. The children referred to here either worked on the streets selling postcards or shining shoes or were serving a two-year sentence in a reform school after getting into trouble with the police. I chose to work in Vietnam because in 1990 it became the first country in Asia to ratify the UNCRC and this meant that some of the aid agencies were particularly interested in applying a rights-based approach when working with children. In this chapter I start by providing a brief history of the UNCRC and give some examples of how the rights movement is meant to improve children's lives. In the second half of the chapter I move on to discuss some of the ways in which the UNCRC is beginning to be applied in Vietnam with direct reference to the experiences of the children among whom I did fieldwork.

History and background of the UNCRC

The idea that children should be rights-bearing citizens of their countries is grounded in and supported by the UNCRC. In November 1989 the United

Nations formally adopted 54 principles that make up this convention – from the rights of a child to a nationality and name, to the right to education and play and special protection for children going into care or being put up for adoption. On the face of it this child-focused convention has achieved unprecedented international recognition. During the first four years post-1989, 128 countries became signatories, making it the most swiftly signed human rights convention to date. Today 191 of the world's 193 countries have ratified the UNCRC, making themselves legally bound to comply with its obligations, the only exceptions being the USA and Somalia.

The intentions set down in the UNCRC on the face of it indicate a genuine will to avoid past and contemporary situations in which children become victims of man-made and natural difficulties, as Archbishop Desmond Tutu makes clear in his introduction to a UNICEF published children's book on the UNCRC:

> In this book you will see many pictures of children as they should be – happy, healthy, laughing, learning, holding securely to adults they could trust, who would protect and uphold their inalienable rights – the rights formally laid out in the UNCRC ... There have been pictures to appal us, showing children as they should not be, hollow eyed and pot bellied, as victims of malnutrition, famine and disease ... We have seen children benumbed after witnessing the mass killings of relatives ... children abused and raped ... Let us commit ourselves to outlaw the conditions that have made the second kind of pictures possible.
>
> (Fogelman 2000)

But the UNCRC is not only designed to deal with such extreme childhood experiences. Its advocates intend that it also be used to give children rights that impact upon everyday life experiences. In doing so they embrace a particular view of what childhood should be like: for example under the UNCRC all children are expected to receive a formal education at primary level, and children should as much as is possible reside in a family home with adults to support them. The UNCRC also marks a shift in focus away from a purely protectionist understanding of childhood to one in which children are also given participatory rights. This shift away from purely protectionist support to a legal and internationally ratified document that supports children's participatory rights has been a long time in the making and marks a fundamental change in how children are now expected to be treated at every level within the confines of their member state. Such participatory rights are meant to ensure that children participate in decisions and, depending on their age and maturity, are able to have their opinions taken seriously.

The preoccupations and interests of western democracies are apparent in previous laws that predate and inform development of the UNCRC. The Universal Declaration of Human Rights is one of a number of laws that informs the human rights angle taken in the UNCRC. Susan Waltz argues that 'It would be foolish to deny a connection between western philosophy and the modern notion of human rights: philosophical writings in support of human rights are easily located in the larger body of Western thought' (2002: 442).

The development of human rights specifically relating to children also links children's rights with women's rights. It was the International Labour Organization (ILO) that pioneered the establishment of international standards on women's work and child labour through a series of conventions and recommendations. The ILO's concern with regulating child labour commenced with their 1919 Convention restricting children doing night work. The early laws encouraged states to protect women and children from exploitation but in doing so still treated both women and children as vulnerable members of society in need of protection rather than as members of society with full rights to participate in any decision making affecting them. The fifth assembly of the League of Nations adopted The Declaration on Children's Rights (also known as the declaration of Geneva) in 1924 well before the concern with fundamental human rights had been articulated in the Universal Declaration of Human Rights (1948). The drafting of this declaration came about through the efforts of the British children's activist Eglantyne Jebb, founder of the Save the Children Fund.

In 1959, building on the 1924 Declaration on Children's Rights, the United Nations developed the Declaration on the Rights of the Child at the international level. Here the focus was on children as people entitled to rights in their own capacity. However, the document was criticized for not providing a clearly articulated framework of rights: rights which the 1989 Convention was later intended to properly address. The 1959 Declaration was followed by several initiatives from the Hague Conference on Private International Law. These dealt with international issues involving matters such as child custody and maintenance. This was quickly followed by a summit of world leaders in 1990. This summit adopted a World Declaration on the Survival, Protection and Development of Children, and a plan of action for implementing this declaration. Thus the UNCRC was fleshed out within an action plan that can be used to develop actual programmes in countries and stimulate more than political rhetoric at the international level.

The procedure of national ratification also dictates that state legislatures examine their laws and bring them in line with the UNCRC. Article 3 of the UNCRC requires them to fulfil a commitment that the different components of the legal system – legislative bodies, courts of law and administrative agencies – will make the best interests of the child a primary concern. A monitoring committee was also set up to follow the performance of each state signed to the UNCRC. The committee is empowered to obtain from state parties periodic reports, initially after two years and then after every five years, on their steps taken to realize their commitments under the UNCRC. Countries are also given the option of opting out of certain articles that they feel they are not as yet able to comply with.

Vietnam's move towards a child rights approach

Vietnam signed the UNCRC in 1989. From the end of the America-Vietnam War until 1987 Vietnam considered its strongest allies to be the Soviet Union and very few of its people travelled outside Eastern Bloc countries. In 1987 under legislation known as *Doi Moi* or 'renovation', the Vietnamese government began to move away from Marxist-grounded communism to a socialist-orientated market economy. For the first time in two decades the government of Vietnam licensed a substantial number of modern businesses to enter the country and establish working relations deriving from western capitalist and non-communist philosophy. This also meant that soon after 1987, leading inter-governmental organizations such as UNICEF established stronger relations with Vietnam. To date the only other human rights document that Vietnam has signed is the United Nations Convention on the Elimination of all Forms of Discrimination Against Women, which was ratified on 17 February 1982.

Thus, in the space of three years Vietnam witnessed the 1989 collapse of the Soviet Union, subsequently significantly loosened its ties with Russia, began to re-establish relations with the West and subsequently signed the UNCRC. Vietnam was among the first three nations to report to the Committee on the Rights of the Child, set up under Article 43 of the UNCRC to monitor its provision. In 1990 Vietnam became the first country in Asia to ratify the UNCRC and during the same period non-government organizations such as members of the Save the Children Alliance and PLAN International set up headquarters in Hanoi and began to develop children's rights projects.

Vietnam publicly prides itself on having been the first country in Asia to ratify the UNCRC (Khanh 1996). However, while the Vietnamese media frequently refers to the country's ratification of the UNCRC as an unprecedented success for the welfare of its children (Khanh 1996), my research findings and also those of Bond (1996) indicate that much of what the UNCRC stands for is alien to Vietnamese treatment of children. My findings raise questions about whether any preliminary groundwork should have been done prior to ratification of the UNCRC into the extent to which local cultural practices might influence how the UNCRC was received and understood in that context. One of the significant problems that emerged out of my fieldwork findings was that different child-focused organizations (and also the individuals working within those organizations, whether they be Vietnamese or expatriate), worked towards their own quite personal, and therefore highly varied, interpretation of what the UNCRC stands for.

To some extent contradictory practices are to be expected because the UNCRC is considered to offer countries an ideal of what childhood should be like that they can gradually move towards. However, as I became more familiar with local cultural practices the more sceptical I was about the level to which the UNCRC could ever be properly supported in that context. During fieldwork I interviewed both expatriate and Vietnamese aid workers working for ten child-focused aid agencies based in Hanoi. One Vietnamese woman called Huong, who worked for an international aid agency that conducted child rights training in villages in the north told me:

> I consider the UNCRC is 'good' if society is developed. But for us we have many customs which prevent us raising children to say what they think to their elders. They [the international aid workers] say children should not work . . . but for many this is an impossibility. Many of us aid workers know this and there is a difference between ours and the foreigners' approach, but we do not voice this. We know our country is not ready for many of the changes.

Huong felt unable to voice her concerns about the relevance of the UNCRC to local child care practices in part because she did not want to challenge her expatriate director's authority. Vietnamese society is organized in a hierarchy and because of this people in general find it difficult to speak their mind to those they consider to be superior to themselves. Under such circumstances it is common for workers to at least pay lip-service to an idea voiced by their next in command even though they may have no intention of following the idea through. As an outsider, unfamiliar with this way of working, it understandably takes time to grasp that resistance to an idea is expressed not in direct discussion but over time, by a kind of passive inertia to a proposal. During my first week in Hanoi I was invited to attend a meeting to which a freelance expatriate worker had invited representatives from numerous aid agencies to discuss the setting up of a centralized social-work school. On the face of it people seemed supportive of the proposal. But one year later the ideas suggested and discussed at the committee's monthly meetings had still not led to any concrete developments. There could be only one conclusion: for whatever reason the idea was not supported from within the Vietnamese aid community. As for most outsiders it took me almost a year to understand the exact nature of how people were most likely to communicate in the Vietnamese context: and it was crucial that I did so if I was to be effective in that context. This was even more the case for aid agency directors wielding large sums of aid funding towards the development of particular aid projects. Yet, as is the nature of employment in the aid world, most were working in Vietnam on short-term contracts of two to three years leaving them little time to become familiar with local cultural practices before they were likely to be sent off to work in another country. While there was an opportunity to extend contracts, during the period that I was living in Hanoi there was a high turnover of directors in some of the most prominent child rights aid agencies.

The Vietnamese government's treatment of its children

Confusion exists at every level regarding the extent to which the child rights movement is having an impact in Vietnam. But by looking beyond the rhetoric directly at child care practice one gets a clearer measure of Vietnam's actual level of commitment to the UNCRC. From an outsider's perspective the Vietnamese government is, on the face of it, actively encouraging both government and non-government organizations (such as international and domestic aid agencies) to introduce and apply the child rights agenda to their work. For example, Vietnamese government organizations such as the Committee for Protection and Care of Children (CPCC) now refer to the UNCRC in their training of outreach workers to work with children who make their living on the streets. However, as I have already suggested the situation is more complex than it might at first appear: other government practices coexist alongside their child rights work that raise questions about Vietnam's true level of commitment to the UNCRC. For example, one year after Vietnam ratified the UNCRC the Vietnamese government developed the *National Law on Child Protection, Care and Education* that laid out different expectations for its children. Article 13 reads: 'Children shall have the following obligations: To show love, respect and piety towards grandparents and parents, politeness towards adults, affection towards the younger ones and solidarity with friends' (National Assembly of the Socialist Republic of Vietnam 1991).

Thus under national law, Vietnamese children are expected to show deferential respect towards their elders. While this reflects the dominant value system within the local environment it directly opposes two of the central intentions of the UNCRC: first that children should be given individual rights and second that children should not be required to be deferential. The Vietnamese dichotomy is not unusual. African human rights lawyers have also written extensively about modern western individual human rights and southern ideas of communal responsibilities (Ncube 1998). Much of what they argue about the need for communal rights to be recognized is reflected in the regional human rights document drawn up by the Organization of African

Unity which, in response to the UNCRC, developed its own charter for children in November 1999. The African Charter, just like the Vietnamese law for children, refers to child *rights* as per the UNCRC but also to childhood *responsibilities*. For example, Article 31 reads that:

> Every child shall have responsibilities towards his family and society, the State and other legally recognized communities and the inter-national community. The child, subject to his age and ability, and such limitations as may be contained in the present Charter, shall have the duty:
>
> (a)   to work for the cohesion of the family, to respect his parents, superiors and elders at all times and to assist them in case of need.

Both the Vietnamese national law and the African Charter were written in response to the UNCRC. This clearly shows that the UNCRC model for supporting children is not universally applicable even though the United Nations claims in the preamble that it is a universally applicable document. Under the Vietnamese national law children are required to be filial towards their elders while under the UNCRC they are not. At present these two legal frameworks coexist uneasily, and while this is the case social policy towards children in the Vietnamese context is likely to be confused, but is more likely to lean towards local traditional practices than the much more recent expectations introduced via the UNCRC.

The individual's experience

Central government policies towards children who work on the streets also fail to adhere to basic human rights principles as supported through the United Nations. During fieldwork in Hanoi I got to know a group of boys who worked on the streets. Because street work is considered illegal in Vietnam, the children were subjected to random arrests but by paying the police a retainer of ten dollars a month their presence on the streets was overlooked. However, when children did not have the money to bribe the police they were liable to be arrested. In one group of ten children ranging in age from 8 to 16, every child was arrested without trial during my first year in Hanoi and placed in a re-education centre until they could raise the money to pay off their warders. Two of the older boys, Phuc and Ly, told me that without the money to bribe their way out, their stay in the centres could be over a year. I was already doing fieldwork in a reform school that housed children whose whole families lived in the city, but the Vietnamese authorities were reluctant to give foreigners access to the centre that these children were sent to. On three occasions during fieldwork I witnessed children like Phuc and Ly working on the streets and being rounded up by the police and sent off to the reform centre.

The UNCRC and the individual self

Local people may parrot the Convention's rhetoric, it does not follow that they fully support it or understand that the UNCRC upholds that individual children have particular rights, perhaps because in many contexts children are most likely to be valued as part of the family collective and not as autonomous individuals holding independent positions in society (Bond 1996; Goodman 2000). In Asia and other parts of the South, as well as among some communities living in the West a significant number of societies recognize the family as more important than the individuals that make up parts of that whole (Alston 1994).

The impact of Confucianism

It is widely acknowledged among historians such as Barton (1988), that Confucianism has been a fundamental influence over the Chinese and Vietnamese attitude towards the individual in relation to their family and friends. As Dutton points out 'an intricate web of relations, based ultimately upon the family . . . succeeded in maintaining social harmony for most of the dynastic period' (1992: 3). For countries like China and Vietnam the philosophy of Confucius still influences how people behave. Confucius stated that the greatest level of responsibility should reside within the family unit, rather than among its individual members. This philosophy, which was originally developed by the Chinese (Barton 1988), directs that people should respect their elders, and in doing so show filial piety. It also gives men higher social standing than women and children. I believe that it is partly because of the dominance of these long-held traditions of Confucius that there is increasing resistance from many quarters in Vietnam to the UNCRC's message, which fundamentally conflicts with these Confucian norms.

The UNCRC is based on an idealized western concept of the self. It is 'I' who has rights; it is the 'individual' child who needs protection and support. Locke and Scheper-Hughes (1997: 7) have said that 'We may reasonably assume that all people share at least some intuitive sense of the embodied self as existing apart from other individual bodies'. But they also state that the way in which the 'body- mind, matter, psyche, soul, self . . . is received . . . is highly variable' (p. 7). They refer to John Locke's work in the seventeenth century as being the first written record in which the individual self was referred to, and they subsequently argue that 'the modern conception of the individual self is of recent historical origin, even in the West' (1997: 14).

It is the idealized western sense of self which is referred to and made universally applicable in the international discourse on childhood and therefore within United Nations' reports. However, as I discovered in many parts of the world, the self is not viewed in this way (Alston 1994). For example, Eber's work in China undermines any assumption that the UNCRC can be universally applicable in its decision to bestow rights on the individual child: 'the West has always emphasized the individual and the state. Individual development is extolled, and the single human being regarded as central and as an atom of society. Unlike westerners, the Chinese have given greater weight to family and mankind. The consciousness of the individual is contained in the family' (Eber in Dutton 1992: 37). This argument is not only relevant to China but to countries such as Vietnam and many others throughout Africa where emphasis is placed on the value of the family as a collective rather than the individuals that make up that whole.

Fieldwork examples

In January 1998, I was invited to attend a workshop on child participation organized by the Save the Children Consortium for Vietnamese aid workers. During the workshop we ran a session in which Vietnamese project workers were given an opportunity to express what they understood child partici-patory rights to mean. In general there was confusion about what it meant to give children rights, but one woman stood up as spokesperson for a group of six people and said:

> I go to the village and tell local people about child rights because that is what my aid agency works on, but here in Vietnam we do things differently, and children must respect their elders and do as they are told. So in my own family I expect my children to do as they are told and not question or participate in decisions made on their behalf. Child rights does not exist in my household.
>
> (Fieldnotes, January 1997)

This woman was confidently expressing a fundamentally divergent child-rearing philosophy to any based on treating children as individuals whose opinions should be respected. Clearly she, like a number of others taking part in the workshop, did not view children as individuals with rights, but as members of a hierarchy in which individual rights are subordinated to the greater good agreed on and supported by their elders.

The facilitators of the workshop were British and American expatriates who expressed their surprise to me once the session had drawn to a close. One of them said he was now concerned that some of the people working for him were not being open about their attitudes towards children. So I reasoned with him that he should understand that the hierarchy in which children operated was the same one in which their parents were also positioned. It was this hierarchy that made it difficult for women to be considered equal to men and which led to workers hiding their opinions from those people they considered their superiors. Such views had also been initially withheld from me because of my status as a foreign visitor. For example, Huong was very reserved with me and did not voice her true feelings until I had known her for over a year and we had begun to spend time together outside of her workplace. Perhaps I ultimately was given this alternative response to child participation and child rights in general because of my low position in the societal hierarchy as a female research student.

Hiep's story

When I first arrived in Hanoi I used to cycle down to the centre of town after my language class at the university and sit by the lake where I would read over my lesson. Kids who sold postcards or made a living cleaning people's shoes worked in the area, and as time went by I became a familiar face to some of them. A group of five, led by a young boy called Hiep, started to take an interest in me and Hiep and I began to meet up for him to practise speaking English and me to speak Vietnamese. On one such occasion we had just sat down on a bench when without warning police rode up on motorbikes and all the working kids in our vicinity began to shout and run off in different directions. Hiep, whose shoe-cleaning box was by his feet, reacted by first standing up and then pausing as he began to gauge which direction was best to run in. By this point the police were everywhere and if he had set off in any direction he would have drawn unwanted attention to himself. As he looked helplessly on at policemen chasing children in all directions I grabbed his box from under his arm, threw it in my bicycle basket, covered it with my sweater and yanked him down onto the bench and whispered that we should act as if we were still deep in study. On this occasion Hiep was not arrested even though some of the police who were familiar with the area would have known that he usually worked around where we were sitting.

Once the police had disappeared Hiep flung down the book and we grinned accomplice's smiles at each other. It was then that he started telling me about his experiences of being arrested. He was a constant target for monthly police bribes and was arrested if he was unable to pay up or the police were having an official crackdown on street work. Hiep told me that he was arrested about twice a year and that on such occasions was usually sent to a centre specifically for kids who worked on the streets. From Hiep's description the centre's objective was to contain and force children off the streets and back to the rural areas from where they came. But as Hiep, who always tried to return to the lakeside, told me: 'I have worked and had my freedom for so long that I would not want to live with adults telling me what to do. My life is better this way because I can come and go as I please and I have my friends who I consider to be my family'.

Hiep's determination to shape his future

At the time that I met Hiep he was 14. His views on family and the independent lifestyle he chose to pursue raise questions about different societies' expectations of children. To what extent and at what point in a child's life should we consider them capable of participating fully in making decisions that directly shape how their lives should be led? In our conversations Hiep was adamant that by working on the streets he was maximizing his opportunities and those of his family.

As time went on and I spent more time becoming familiar with Vietnamese society and the very different opportunities available to people from different social backgrounds I found Hiep's arguments increasingly convincing. If he had stayed in the countryside he would have added to his family's financial costs. His family could not have afforded for him to attend school and so by working on the streets he certainly was not jeopardizing his chances of receiving an education.

In reality the greatest threat to his existence came from official sources, from those adults who in their capacity as police officers locked him up, ostensibly for his own good to stop him from working on the streets, but in reality to gain financially from the bribes he was forced to pay them. Paradoxically the other threat to his lifestyle came from internationally-led child rights advocates, some of whom (like the Vietnam director of an aid agency within the Save the Children consortium) spoke to me of wanting to give 'street children' a full-time education and permanent homes in boarding-school type accommodation. Yet for someone like Hiep, who had chosen to keep adult contact to a minimum and to live independently, this was the exact opposite of what he wanted. Kids who work on the streets often send money home to their families. Rather than feel abandoned, some of the children spoke with pride about the contribution their earnings made to their families and of the pride that their parents felt towards them. It was telling that during *Tet* (the Vietnamese New Year and most important national holiday) most of the children working on the streets had returned home to the countryside to be with their relatives.

Thus child rights advocates such as the director working with Save the Children were informed by a protectionist understanding of childhood in which the working child is automatically assumed to be disadvantaged and children are still best supported living inside adult-led family units. Proper implementation of the UNCRC would also mean that children such as Hiep fully participate in the development of interventions designed to support them. Yet, as my fieldwork indicates, many kids feel they have little choice but to work and to move away from their family in order to do so. Thus for most of the kids I knew, the international child rights agenda had no real impact or relevance to their lives. Most of them continued to work in between bouts in reform schools or detention centres, or periods when they returned to visit or live with their families.

Support from Western aid agencies

In a chapter on the construction of childhood in Western culture, Patricia Holland (1992) points out that Southern children are often viewed as vulnerable and in need of rescuing, which reflects the welfarist protectionist approach. But they are also to be offered child rights not by their own people, but by outsiders assumed to be better equipped to offer such support. The countries of the modern West thus set themselves up as sole caregivers and also paradoxically as defenders of southern children's rights. This confused and contradictory approach and the problems it can lead to are demonstrated by the following examples in which different types of aid agency adopted different approaches for dealing with the same group of children.

When I was in Hanoi, there were three quite distinct forms of aid agency working with children: those which focused on the child rights discourse grounded in the UNCRC; smaller international organizations which received money from private (sometimes religious) sources; and local Vietnamese run and funded organizations. The groups rarely came into contact with each other and held very different agendas and working practices.

During interviews I was particularly struck by the work of two Christian-based American aid agencies that worked with children sentenced to live in a reform school for two years, usually after having been arrested and taken off the streets. By working directly in the school the director developed close relationships with boys there and frequently asked them what type of support they needed to improve their lives. A number of the boys said that their biggest fear was being put in a position where they would have to return to their previous ways of earning a living once their sentences came to an end. At the request of these children, most of whom had never had a formal education, he set up skills training programmes in motorbike mechanics and air-conditioning repair.

The reform school attracted a great deal of interest from within the international aid community and the director often welcomed visitors to what he proudly felt was a model school. On one occasion when UNICEF staff visited the workshop and saw children working on motorbikes a member of the group accused the director of the school of practising child labour. The same UNICEF staff member accused the aid agency of starting up a project that contravened the children's rights to schooling. She stated that the circumstances under which the children worked contravened the UNCRC. (In fact the UNCRC does not address child labour. Moreover, Article 28 asks that state parties recognize the right of a child to an education and in that context stipulates that vocational training should also be available.) At the end of the training two boys went on to work in garages; as one of them explained to me and the director of the charity, this would give him an opportunity to experience a better lifestyle than any he had before. It would also mean that he was able to afford to rent a room and study in the evenings.

Participatory rights

As this fieldwork example indicates, a central problem with the UNCRC and the child rights rhetoric is that it marks a fundamental shift in how adults are expected to respond to children. Geraldine Van Bueren who, as a lawyer, was instrumental in the drafting of the UNCRC concedes that participatory rights are still viewed as the most problematic and contentious area of the UNCRC (personal communication). In a discussion I had with her, she pointed out that participatory rights are still those which are most likely to be ignored or addressed ineffectually. During my time in Vietnam I met Vietnamese aid workers who viewed child participatory rights as a western invention and yet the UNICEF spokesperson visiting the reform school had likewise failed to recognize that child participation in an aid project design had led to the development of a skilled training programme.

This understanding of childhood suggests that while being 'adult' is considered whole, being a child is considered incomplete or immature (Qvortrup 1994). This perception of childhood renders children, their individual experience and concerns, invisible. Over-romanticism adds to the view of children existing in a world without responsibilities so that they are forever 'becoming' rather than 'being' (Qvortrup 1994). This understanding of childhood ignores the possibility supported under the child rights discourse that children can be treated as autonomous individuals, and that while they may benefit from adult-led protection they are capable of making informed choices for themselves. Article 12 of the UNCRC states that: 'State parties shall assure to the child who is capable of forming his or her own views the right to express those views freely in all matters affecting the child, the views of the child being given due weight in accordance with the age and maturity of the child'.

While this is a commendable intention, Article 12 runs into difficulties because it is so broadly based and open to too broad an interpretation. Contemporary childhood is still on the one hand understood in the West from within a more traditional welfarist approach, while on the other hand it is informed by local cultural practices that do not recognize the rights of the individual. Only rarely are children recognized as subjects of individual rights with particular viewpoints that should be respected. Ironically, in the Vietnamese context, I found that it was the small religious aid agencies that did not support or refer to the UNCRC that demonstrated a genuine commitment to child participation.

Application of the UNCRC out of context

While I was working with one of the aid organizations within Save the Children, the director told me that it was one of her missions, supported by Article 7 of the UNCRC, to have all children who worked on the street registered so that they could be eligible to receive a formal education and health care. Article 7 states that a child shall be registered immediately after birth and shall have the right to acquire a nationality and, as far as possible, the right to know and be cared for by his or her parents. In Vietnam, some people choose to actively avoid formal registration. This is because a person's registration determines whether they are allowed to officially live in the countryside or in an urban setting. Most of the children with whom I came into contact had illegally migrated to Hanoi either with their families or alone. If they were to be registered then this would alert the authorities to their whereabouts and would result in enforced repatriation to the countryside. The boys I knew who worked on the streets told me that they had all emigrated from the countryside and were able to avoid being transported back because no records existed to show that they lived in the city. On one occasion during my second year of fieldwork, boys serving sentences in the reform school went into a state of panic when the guards discussed the possibility of insisting upon each boy registering his details with their nearest commune before they could return home. Thang, one of the boys I knew quite well, explained that registration would expose not only his illegal status but also those of other family members living with him. For a couple of weeks children at the school were quite anxious about the possibility of being registered but soon after the plan was dropped from the policemen's discussion and was not put into practice. Not being registered meant not being able to access local services, such as health-care and education, but despite this, for all these children being anonymous meant that they could at least stay in the city and on balance this was more important to them. During my discussion with the director I explained that registering children would lead to their disappearance to the countryside and would not, as she presumed, allow them to gain access to urban-based services, but she rejected my argument, insisting that this would contravene the UNCRC. I often heard expatriate staff complain about the lack of understanding local staff had concerning the work they were doing. However, as Justice (1986: 151) argues, and my examples show, the reality may be more complicated than that: 'International planners often attribute failures to the fact that cultural influences can lead people to reject programs. But the bureaucrats have their own culture too. One that may obstruct their views of other cultures, resulting in programs that are destined to fail'.

Conclusion

When attention centres on the rights-based approach of the UNCRC, what Boyden (1990) refers to as a global model of an acceptable childhood takes precedence over local understanding. One of the problems I encountered in Vietnam was that the UNCRC's strongest advocates were expatriate members of international aid agencies. Some of these organisations assumed an educational role in Vietnam while ignoring local childhood experiences and assuming that their western-informed experiences under the child rights umbrella were superior to local methods of treating children. I found that people working within these agencies were also most likely to criticize the conditions in which Vietnamese children lived but that these criticisms were often based on fragmented knowledge of the country and culturally insensitive ideas about how children should be treated. In this context the religious-based aid agencies that did not uphold the UNCRC children's rights agenda were most likely to be respectful towards children and to support children's wishes. The different philosophy from the UNCRC of childhood responsibility espoused both by the African Charter and the Vietnamese national law on children undermines the United Nations' claim that the UNCRC is universally applicable. In reality the UNCRC is not having its intended impact in Vietnam because local attitudes towards children are still just as likely to inform the direction that social policy takes even where the UNCRC has been ratified.

10 Childhood and the law: in whose 'best interests'?

Daniel Monk

Introduction

When non-lawyers think about law, whether they be professionals who work with children or parents and young people themselves, two assumptions or images often come to mind. The first is that law is a highly specialist and technical language, frequently unintelligible to the uninitiated. The second is that law is concerned primarily with rules and regulations that tell individuals and authorities what they must, may or cannot do (in law-speak: rights, prohibitions, powers and duties).

There is of course much truth in these assumptions. Legal materials sometimes use obscure Latin expressions and even when everyday terms are used, in a legal context they frequently have quite distinct meanings. Moreover, the inaccessibility of law is reflected and upheld by the elite status, professional interests and social composition of lawyers themselves. Yet at the same time, and particularly in modern western societies, law has become an unavoidable aspect of daily practice for many professionals working with children. This is particularly true for the police, probation officers and social workers, but also for those in health and education, and as a result law is now frequently included in professional training. The increasing impact and importance of law reflects the 'juridification' of liberal democratic western societies more generally. Consequently, while the material focus of this chapter is primarily the law of England and Wales, the analysis of law and adult-child relations applies equally to other western societies.

The common assumptions about law, informed and confirmed by professional demarcations and everyday experiences, combine to paint a picture of law as an institution and practice which is necessary and important, but, at the same time, complex, rather dry and, depending on the circumstances, a burden or a source of protection. The aim of this chapter is not to counter these assumptions but, rather, to suggest alternative ways of engaging with and thinking about law.

In particular it will attempt to demonstrate that while the law relating to children does indeed provide a code of behaviour or 'rule book' that tells us what children can do at particular ages and how adults (parents, professionals and 'the state') should behave towards them, it is simultaneously implicated and plays an increasingly important role in the construction and legitimation of contemporary knowledge about childhood. In other words it is not simply functional but productive. This perspective on the relationship between law and childhood requires us to think of law not simply as 'rules' but as a continually shifting cultural and social text. Significantly, this approach to 'reading' law challenges traditional legal scholarship as well as the preconceptions of non-lawyers. Within the traditional approach, which is sometimes referred to as 'legal positivism' or 'black-letter' law, analyses of judicial decisions and interpretations of statutes are made primarily, and often solely, by recourse to the language and texts of law. Critical, feminist and socio-legal scholars have for many years now criticized this approach for upholding a myth of law as 'neutral'; which is to say distinct and separate from other disciplines such as politics, economics and sociology. By challenging this view, critical legal scholars have endeavoured to, 'draw attention to the way in which law's portrayal of people and organizations and the relationships between them helps to sustain the existing social order with all its inequalities and injustices' (King and Piper 1995: 63).

In the context of children this has served to challenge what is sometimes described as a 'progressive narrative'. According to this account, the recognition of children's individual personhood, upholding their interests and to a certain degree their 'rights', has increased slowly but steadily, albeit with clear room for improvement. The challenge to this narrative is made by revealing the values, beliefs and interests that inform legal decisions, but which are often silenced or obscured by the very fact that in western societies it is increasingly the 'neutral' best interests of children that are the formal focus of law. In other words, it enquires into what is done in the name of children. Underlying this critical approach is a recognition that when children are identified and referred to in law – for example, in court cases and in statutes, while the focus on the surface may appear to be 'real' embodied children it is more accurate to describe the representations of children as 'semantic artefacts' (King and Piper 1995: 63) or as 'contingent discursive constructs' (O'Donovan 1993: 90).

To demonstrate the implications and uses of this critical engagement with law this chapter, adopting a historical perspective, focuses on three issues: post-divorce family disputes; child sexuality; and youth justice. These three case studies do not, of course, provide a comprehensive coverage of child law.[1] However, they demonstrate that there is no uniform, coherent image of children in law but, rather, that law tells many different stories of childhood.

Post-divorce family disputes

'Child law', as a distinct legal category, is relatively new. It originated as a subcategory of family law, and the coupling of the 'child' with the 'family' continues to this day in student courses, academic journals and legal practice. This legal categorization is not incidental or a mere matter of convenience; rather it reflects and upholds the centrality of the institution of the family as the key determinant of children's identity, role and place within society.

In disputes arising on divorce or separation, the explicit function of law is to protect children, and courts do this by determining what is in children's 'best interests'. However, despite this 'child centred' focus the courts determine these interests in accordance with shifting conceptualizations of family life and gendered assumptions about the role of parents. In other words, judicial assumptions about child welfare are contingent upon construction(s) of the 'ideal' family. Neale and Smart (1999) identify three conceptualizations of the 'model' family underlying post-divorce disputes: marriage for life; lone/reconstituted family; and co-parenting/biological families, and they provide a helpful framework for tracing the shifting approach to child welfare. While each model constructs child welfare in distinct ways, what remains consistent is the construction of childhood in this context as one of passivity, without agency, a victim of parental failings.

'Marriage for life'

Prior to the Divorce Reform Act 1969, divorce was expensive, complex and rare. Legal practice in this way upheld the prevailing view, based on religious tenets, that marriage was, ideally, an institution entered into for life. Furthermore, in accordance with the dominant patriarchal view of society, the family was perceived in the eyes of the law not as a complex set of relationships between individual adults and children, but as a single unit, headed by the man, whom both women and children were expected to obey. Prior to the nineteenth century this was achieved by constructing children as the property of the father. However, the gradual recognition of the independent interests of children did not challenge father's rights, as the traditional role of the father was simply reinforced through a construction of child welfare based on the 'laws of nature'. For example, in a custody dispute in 1883 a judge held that 'it is for the *general interest of children*, and really for the interest of the particular infant, that the court should not except in very extreme cases, interfere with the discretion of the father but leave him to the responsibility of exercising that power *which nature has given him* by the birth of the child'.[2] In a similar way, it was arguments based on child welfare that were used to deny women who committed adultery, or left their husbands for whatever reason, any right to custody of their children, the assumption being that a 'bad wife' was, by definition, a 'bad mother'.[3]

In the latter part of the twentieth century the English courts developed a set of assumptions about children's 'best interests', a particularly crucial one being the 'tender years' or 'maternal preference' doctrine.[4] This resulted in most children remaining with their mothers post-divorce but was upheld by the courts on the basis of the laws of nature; as one judge commented in 1978, 'however good a man may be, he cannot perform the functions which a mother performs by nature'.[5] The recognition of the importance of the mother-child bond and the harmful consequences of separation reflected and legitimized the work of child psychologists Bowlby and Winnicott (Mitchell and Goody 1999); and their influence represents the increasing dominance of 'science' and the 'psy-discourses' in judicial constructions of child welfare. Subsequent critics, however, have highlighted how this approach to child welfare reinforced an essentialist construction of mothers and 'supported the intentions of the government of the day to reconstruct "the family" as the cornerstone of a stable and prosperous society' (Bainham *et al.* 1999: 4).

Lone/reconstituted family

The Divorce Act 1969 and procedural changes introduced in the 1970s made divorce considerably easier. As the divorce rate increased dramatically after 1969 it was argued by moral traditionalists that the law was condoning family breakdown and undermining the institution of marriage. However, the legal reforms were largely a pragmatic response to the fact that increasing numbers of people were separating and forming new relationships without getting divorced. Consequently, while the legal reforms did not save individual marriages, by making it easier for people to remarry, as opposed to 'living in sin', they reinstated and upheld marriage as the preferred institutional basis for family life, or, to put it another way, 'the unbreakable marriage was replaced with serial monogamy' (Neale and Smart 1999: 36).

In supporting the 'lone/reconstituted' model as the 'ideal' post-divorce family, the courts were again able to draw on new 'scientific' understandings of child welfare. These now emphasized the child's need for continuity of care, stability/one home and the avoidance of conflict.[6] Together with increasing use of 'clean break' financial settlements this new approach to child welfare cohered with legal support for the lone/reconstituted family by enabling parents to construct new relationships unencumbered by their previous marriage. In practice this cohered with the 'maternal preference' doctrine, as in most cases it was, and still is, the mother that is the primary carer. However, the shift was reflected in the language of the courts as explicitly gendered assumptions about the 'natural' role of the mothers were gradually replaced by gender-neutral references to the importance of the 'primary care giver'.

While the assumptions about 'maternal preference' and 'stability of care' frequently coincided, the potential for conflict was evident in custody cases relating to lesbian mothers. In these cases custody was often awarded to the father – especially where he had remarried and could offer a 'reconstructed' family that reflected the ideal norm (Reece 1996; Golombok 1999). These cases demonstrate the extent to which legal assumptions about child welfare reinforced traditional morality, while at the same time appearing to be 'child centred'. Moreover, they demonstrate the extent to which psychological or social parentage – an implicit factor in the embracement of the reconstituted family model – could often be privileged in legal discourse above biological or genetic parentage.[7]

Co-parenting/biological family

The Children Act 1989, hailed as a 'children's rights charter', made substantial changes to the legal conceptualization of the relationship between children and parents, and this was reflected in new terminology: 'custody' was replaced by 'residence' and 'access' by 'contact'. Moreover, it provided that married parents would both automatically have parental responsibility. In this way the law reflected the emerging claim that while marriage may be temporary, parenting is for life. The implicit message for families was that 'If they can't remain together under one roof (still of course the preferred option) then . . . it [the family] must reinvent itself as a bi-nuclear family' (Neale and Smart 1999: 37). The emphasis on biological parentage and co-parenting post-divorce represented a radical shift from the norm of parenting within the lone/ reconstituted family, and was reinforced, once again, by changing ideas of child welfare which *now* argued that children needed contact with both biological parents and in particular the 'absent father' (Wallerstein and Kelly 1980). This perspective on child welfare cohered with conservative 'moral panics' and neo-liberal economic concerns about single-parent families and the perceived negative consequences of children not having male role models (Abbott and Wallace 1992). In a more complex and less explicitly politicized manner it also cohered with increasing fears and uncertainties about developments in reproductive medicine (Sheldon 2001b).

The shift towards the co-parenting/biological model has had a significant impact on law, most notably the Child Support Act 1991 and the recent change in the law relating to the status of unmarried fathers (Sheldon 2001a). In the context of post-divorce disputes the impact is most clearly detected in the courts' approach to contact. It is important to note, however, that when parents separate or divorce, the issue of contact is adjudicated by the court only when the parents themselves cannot agree. Furthermore, it is assumed that it is in the child's best interest that parents should ideally make these agreements without recourse to the courts; legal conflict is perceived as harmful for children and this is one of the motivations behind the current emphasis on mediation (Piper 1996). However, court decisions have an indirect impact on 'agreements', through the intervention of mediators and especially solicitors; for in advising parents they reconstruct the problems of their clients within their own, sometimes simplified, understanding of law (Diduck 2000).

In determining disputes relating to contact the paramount principle for the courts is the welfare of the individual child (Children Act 1989, Section 1). Despite this flexibility and formal recognition of the uniqueness of each child, the courts have adopted an approach that makes a refusal to allow contact highly exceptional. This approach is based on an assumption that contact is 'a fundamental emotional need'.[8] As a result, contact has been held to be in the best interests of the child in the following circumstances: where the child has little previous contact with the parent;[9] where the children themselves expressly oppose contact;[10] where contact could be a cause of disruption to the child;[11] and where there is an acknowledged history of violence against the mother by the father[12] (Kaganas 1999). Mothers who have attempted to resist contact have been described by the courts as 'implacably hostile' and threatened with the removal of the child[13] and even imprisonment.[14] Underlying this approach is the normative ideal of co-parenting, as the mother who objects to contact is perceived as 'undermining the potential for the creation of a "good" post-divorce family both because she is fomenting conflict and because she is "robbing" her child of a relationship with the non-resident parent' (Kaganas 1999: 102). Within this legal discourse the child is constructed as a victim, whose 'right to contact' has been infringed by the resident parent. This demonstrates one of the dangers of the discourse of 'rights'. For the historical 'proprietary' and 'natural' rights of fathers, while seemingly distinct from the contemporary acknowledgement of a child's right to have contact with both parents, can in reality lead to similar outcomes – namely the exposure of children to the dangers of violent fathers.

In a recent judgement, the Court of Appeal held that contact with a violent parent was not in the child's best interest and that courts should examine more carefully the behaviour of the parent requesting contact, rather than simply focusing on the parent resisting contact.[15] This judgement represented an acknowledgement of extensive research which demonstrated that 'In practice children may be victims of contact rather than lack of contact' (Piper 1996: 371). Moreover, focusing on the *quality of parenting*, as opposed to awarding contact simply on the basis of *parental status*, to a certain extent represents an attempt to incorporate within law an understanding of family life as a site of negotiated practices and complex relationships (Neale and Smart: 1999). However, it is important not to overstate this new trend, for uncritical assumptions about the benefits of contact have been reinforced by a report of the Children Act Sub-Committee of the Lord Chancellor's Advisory Board on Family Law (Eekelaar 2002). Moreover, focusing on the quality of parenting, like 'child welfare', is open to conflicting interpretations. As a result, contact disputes are more likely to remain a site for upholding contingent and highly romanticized ideals of family life, rather than a space for listening and responding to the voices of real children.

Child sexuality

Sexuality, perhaps more than any other issue, helps define and uphold the fragile distinction between adulthood and childhood; it is an area where 'maturity' in a child is frequently perceived as a problem to be dealt with (or, as is often the case, ignored), rather than a normal part of development to be encouraged or praised. The current age at which children can, in law, consent to sexual relations is 16. The criminal law, in this way, imposes a symbolic threshold; below 16 children are constructed as essentially non-sexual or sexual innocents, while on reaching 16 they are constructed as autonomous sexual beings with a variety of sexual identities and complex subjectivities. There is a clear cultural and historical dimension to this age limit. In the nineteenth century, the age limit was 13 and even within western European countries today the age of consent varies from 13 to 18. However, legal prohibitions are a crude form of control and protection (as the high level of sexual activity among those under 16 attests) and children themselves within their own communities and peer groups have their own views on the role and value of the age of consent laws (Thomson 2000).

Consequently, there is a tension between denying child sexuality in order to uphold the deeply embedded myth of sexual innocence (Stainton Rogers and Stainton Rogers 1999; Piper 2000) and acknowledging its existence, in order to protect children from obvious dangers such as STDs and HIV/AIDS; from consequences of sexual activity such as teenage pregnancy; and from forms of sexual identity, such as homosexuality, that public policy and dominant morality has deemed to be not in children's 'best interests' (Monk 1998a, 1998b). Law plays an important role in resolving this tension by legitimizing conflicting constructions of the child within distinct locations. To demonstrate this, the issue of sex education and access to contraception in the contexts of education and health will be explored in more detail.

Education

The law relating to sex education is complex and has been amended and further amended on numerous occasions throughout the last 15 years against a background of highly politicized campaigns and debates between traditional moralists and children's rights advocates (Thomson 1994; Monk 2001). Underlying this conflict are two versions of protection, 'one of *sexual beings* from harm because of their immaturity and ignorance, the other of the *non-sexual* from the "perversity" of sexual indoctrination' (Evans 1993: 216). While in recent years there has been a marked shift towards the former form of protection, in the context of the school the construction of children as non-sexual prevails. This has been achieved in part by the statutory structure of the curriculum and by privileging the rights of parents.

Since the Education Reform Act 1988, sex education has been divided between biology lessons, within the centrally controlled National Curriculum for Science, and sex and relationship education (SRE), which is controlled by school governors accountable to parents. While the control of each aspect is clear from the legislation the distinction in terms of content is not. The contingent meaning of biology came to the fore in 1991, when the then Secretary of State attempted to include information about STDs and HIV/AIDS within the National Curriculum for Science. This was successfully opposed by traditional moralists on the basis that it would expose children to 'immoral' material and that by locating this subject matter within the National Curriculum parents would be denied any influence. Underlying this criticism was a clear distinction between biology and SRE – the former being constructed as universal and unproblematic 'truths' and the latter as controversial and cultural, and consequently contested, values. Knowledge that is defined as 'biology' is in this way privileged and serves to uphold and legitimize particular normative values under the 'neutral' label of science. In other words, the current position whereby biology is interpreted in such a way as to include fertility treatment but to exclude information about HIV and practical sexual advice has little to do with science but more to do with upholding traditional sexual ideals of monogamy and marriage and with denying the reality of child sexuality.

Within SRE practical information about contraception has been highly controversial. While government guidance, issued in 1994, advised that sex education in this context could make 'a substantial contribution' to attempts to reduce the rate of teenage pregnancies, it went on to state that it could do so by being taught 'within a clear framework of values and an awareness of the law on sexual behaviour' (DES 1994: para. 8). By referring to the criminal law, the guidance clearly favoured enforcing abstinence rather than providing practical information about contraception, and in doing so reinforced the construction of the child as ideally non-sexual. However, the guidance issued in 2000 states that SRE has an important role in providing 'knowledge of the different types of contraception, and of access to, and availability of contraception' (DFEE 2000: para. 2.10). While this represents a radical shift, the new guidance legitimizes this approach not by acknowledging children's right to information, or to autonomy in making sexual choices, but by emphasizing the physical and emotional benefits of *delaying* sexual activity and the negative consequences of sex, such as abuse, disease and unwanted pregnancy. By drawing on the discourse of protection – the traditional 'child saving' welfare approach – it reconciles providing practical advice with the image of the child as innocent and dependant. This approach is reinforced in the new guidance by the absence of any mention of sexual pleasure and by a repeated emphasis on the necessity of involving and consulting parents, as opposed to children, in the development of sex education policies generally. In doing so it represents a strategic challenge to the claim that sex education 'sexualizes' children and conflicts with parental rights (Monk 2001), while simultaneously legitimizing practical information.

The privileging of parental rights over those of children is most explicit in the context of confidentiality – as the guidance states that 'it is only in the most exceptional circumstances that schools should be in the position of having to handle information without parental knowledge' (DFEE 2000: para. 7.2). This restriction on the role of teachers was similarly stated in the previous guidance and was described by Bainham, a leading child lawyer, as 'a thinly veiled attempt to intimidate the teaching profession . . . that is without foundation in criminal and civil law' (1996: 38). Significantly, however, the guidance states that medical and health professionals can offer confidentiality. The legal distinction drawn here between the legitimate roles of the two professions is not highly questionable in law, as Bainham and others have suggested, but hints at a very different image of the child within the context of health.

Health

The legal regulation of the relationship between doctors and children (and their parents) has come under judicial scrutiny in a wide range of situations, from forced treatment for anorexia and blood transfusions contrary to religious convictions, to tattooing and body piercing (Bridgeman 2000). The most famous case is the 1986 House of Lords decision in *Gillick* v. *West Norfolk and Wisbech Area Health Authority* and it is particularly relevant in this context as it dealt with the issue of contraception.[16] Mrs Gillick challenged the lawfulness of guidance provided by her health authority that advised GPs that they could, in certain circumstances, provide contraception to girls under the age of 16 without informing the child's parents. The Court of Appeal held in favour of Mrs Gillick, arguing, not illogically, that to decide otherwise would be contrary to existing criminal and medical law, which provided that a child could not lawfully consent to sexual intercourse under the age of 16 and that parental consent was required for medical treatment for children under that age. In a groundbreaking decision, a majority of the House of Lords overturned the Court of Appeal. The judgement is lengthy and complex but three key points can be identified. First, that the law should attempt to reflect real life, in the words of Lord Scarman: 'If the law should impose upon the process of 'growing up' fixed limits where nature knows only a continuous process, the price would be artificiality and a lack of realism' (p. 855).

Second, that parental rights are not absolute, but, rather, legitimate only to the extent that they uphold and are exercised in accordance with the child's best interests (in other words that they are, in effect, 'responsibilities' rather than 'rights'). Third, linking the above, that in exercising parental rights, responsible parenting should take account of the child's development. Again in the words of Lord Scarman: 'the parental right yields to the child's right to make his own decisions when he reaches a sufficient understanding and intelligence to be capable of making up his own mind on the matter requiring decision' (p. 186).

The case was hailed as a breakthrough for the cause of children's rights. However it is important not to overstate such a claim for a number of reasons. While the court called for a flexible, less age-based approach, in doing so it upheld a *developmental* construction of childhood – within which childhood is a process, the purpose and end result of which is becoming an adult. This is problematic, for as Bridgeman argues, it results in real children being judged 'with reference to either (abiding by norms of) adulthood or conformity to expectations of childhood' (2000: 217). The implications of this are acute, for while Lord Scarman referred to the 'child's right', the House of Lords judgement in *Gillick* did not envisage or permit girls under the age of 16 to determine for themselves whether they were mature enough to consent to contraception, but, rather, left this decision firmly in the hands of the medical profession. In other words, while it acknowledged that children could, and should (sometimes) be treated in effect *like* adults, it did not treat them *as* autonomous adult subjects. Consequently, while it effectively *decriminalizes* sexually active under 16-year-olds, at the same time it *pathologizes* them, and they become judged and objectified not by the judiciary or by parents, but by the 'parallel judges' of the medical profession.

Despite this critical reading of *Gillick* there is a very real distinction between the construction of childhood in the contexts of education and health. In education the ideal normative view of childhood as non-sexual prevails. The school, like the family, can be understood in this way to represent a 'child-appropriate' space within which children are 'protected' from the adult world, but, consequently, required to behave as children. Moreover, while the new guidance encourages the provision of information about contraception, it does so in a way that does not challenge the ideal image of the non-sexual child, but, rather, is legitimized in such a way that it simply acknowledges, with explicit regret, that some children, for whatever reason, fail to live up to the ideal. In other words, while it acknowledges that children may be sexually active, the limits placed on the role of teachers ensures that these pupils are constructed as having 'health problems' as opposed to 'normal' educational or social needs that might be best addressed in the National Curriculum. By contrast, in the context of health, the possibility of child sexuality is explicitly recognized and while the *Gillick* judgement falls short of respecting their autonomy, it legitimizes a construction of the child as, potentially, sexually mature and capable of making adult-like decisions.

There is a clear conflict between the two images of the child in these locations. However, it is possible to view this conflict not as contradictory and illogical but, rather, as coherent to the extent that it enables the ideal of the non-sexual child to coexist with a pragmatic acknowledgement that it is simply a romantic and idealized norm. The conflicting approach serves to marginalize sexual children, but at the same time enables their needs to be addressed and the political aim of reducing teenage pregnancies to be met. In this way the legal boundary between health and education is not simply a matter of professional or geographical location but enables two conflicting images of children to coexist and legitimizes two distinct forms of control or 'governance'. This approach again requires a critical engagement with the discourse of rights, in particular it suggests that acknowledging children's rights is not always principled, which is to say that it is not simply a matter of acknowledging their individual subjectivities and personhood but, rather, pragmatic, which is to say that it is contingent on social and political calculations as to what is and is not appropriate child behaviour.

Children, youth justice and crime

Children pose numerous problems for the criminal justice system – whether they be the victim, a witness or the perpetrator of a crime. As victims, concerns focus on the harm caused by requiring a child to participate in the prosecution process, both at the investigation and trial stages. Such is the extent of these potential harms, or 'secondary abuse', that some children's rights commentators have seriously questioned whether child abuse should be criminalized at all (Wattam 1999). The child as a witness raises similar concerns (and, of course, the role of victim and witness can sometimes overlap). However, it also raises distinct questions regarding the validity of the evidence of a child and the weight to be accorded to it. This concern impacts on the child in the role of offender; for if children's understanding or capacity to give evidence is questionable, so too is their capacity to plead guilty or innocent. This raises the question as to whether or not a child can be considered to have actually committed an offence, as all criminal offences have both a physical element (the *actus reus* or 'guilty act') and a mental element (the *mens rea* or 'guilty mind'). Furthermore, where a child is convicted of an offence, questions arise as to the appropriate form of sentence.

Underlying all these problems and concerns is the construction within the criminal justice system of adults as rational, autonomous, morally-conscious beings who, consequently, can be called upon to provide reliable evidence and should be held responsible for their actions; and it is the extent to which children are considered unable to 'fit' into this role that requires and justifies a differentiated response. However, in resolving these problems the task of policy makers is not simply to establish the 'truth' about the capabilities of children or their 'lack' of adult qualities – even if such a task was possible. For it is first necessary to establish what is the function or purpose of the criminal justice system. This is a complex issue but debates are often constructed in terms of a tension between the conflicting discourses of 'justice' and 'welfare' (Muncie 1999).

The conflict is particularly acute in the context of youth justice as the emphasis within the justice discourse on retribution, punishment and deterrent is clearly dependent on the dominant construction of adulthood and it is the assumptions about the differences between adults and children that add legitimacy to the emphasis on welfare. For if young offenders are considered mentally 'incapable' of committing a crime, the case for welfare-based initiatives, which attempt to understand and address the reasons behind the criminal behaviour, are more likely to outweigh the demands of justice for adult-like punishment. Similarly, if child victims are considered less able than adults to withstand the rigours of a criminal investigation and trial, the case for welfare-based protective initiatives increases. In this way, assumptions about the capabilities and needs of children have a direct impact on law and policy. Portraying children as innately 'innocent', dependent and vulnerable legitimizes the demands for welfare, while portraying them as 'knowing', morally culpable and innately, or at least capable of, 'evil' legitimizes the demands for justice.

In recent years the emphasis on justice has come to dominate legal and policy responses to young offenders. While the rise and fall of the welfare discourse in this context is explored in more detail below, it is significant to note that in the context of children as victims and witnesses the welfare approach has generally been more entrenched, and children here are increasingly viewed as 'lacking in moral consciousness' (Fionda 2001; Levy 2001). The lack of coherence in law's image of the child is acute here and the dichotomous construction can coexist within a single piece of legislation (Fionda 2000). This highlights both the contingency of the legal construction of childhood and the extent to which it has little to do with real children.

Welfare/justice and youth crime

Prior to the mid-nineteenth century the criminal justice system treated children in the same way as adults. The modern youth justice system has its origins in the introduction of custodial institutions specifically for children. One of the first of these institutions was Pankhurst Prison, established in 1842, and Borstals for children between the ages of 16–20 were introduced by the Prevention of Crime Act 1907. These initiatives coincided with the enactment of legal restrictions on the employment of children in factories and the move towards compulsory education. Consequently the introduction of child-specific custodial institutions reflected a broader shift whereby childhood was increasingly being defined and demarcated by spatial boundaries (James *et al.* 1998: 37–58). Locating children in particular environments represented both a 'child-saving' welfare-based acknowledgement of the different needs of children, but also a more complex shift in understandings of the causes of crime. Moreover it enabled the state to intervene more directly in the governance of children.

This new approach was most clearly reflected in the Children Act 1908, as it addressed not simply the treatment of convicted young offenders, but established a separate juvenile court with specially trained magistrates and removed the death penalty for under 18-year-olds convicted of murder. The growing emphasis on welfare was further strengthened by the Children and Young Persons Act 1933, which provided that 'Every court in dealing with a child or young person who is brought before it, either as . . . an offender or otherwise, shall have regard to the welfare of the child or young person' (Section 44). By incorporating juvenile justice within a broader framework of child law the 1933 Act represented an explicit endorsement of a more child-centred approach as it required the courts to, in effect, treat child offenders as children first and offenders second.

The 1960s, culminating in the Children and Young Persons Act 1969, marked the 'heyday of welfarism' (Muncie 1997). However, this was followed by a return to a more punitive justice-based approach and the more radical aspects of the 1969 Act were never enacted. While the 1969 Act consequently had little practical impact, it offers important insights – for example, the stark contrast between the approach it legitimized and the current approach demonstrates the extent to which dominant constructions of childhood can shift dramatically within a relatively short space of time. The 1969 Act proposed a gradual replacement of criminal proceedings and custodial sentences with care proceedings and cautioning, with an emphasis on guidance, counselling and community-based initiatives, and would have resulted in decision making and control shifting from the police and magistrates to local authorities and social workers. It also proposed a rise in the age of criminal responsibility from 10 to 14. Underlying this radical embracement of a welfare-based approach, with its emphasis on protection, guidance and support as opposed to individual responsibility, guilt and punishment, was a 'developmental' conceptualization of youth crime as 'no more than a symptom of the rebellious adolescent phase of child development, which would with adequate guidance, naturally cease as the young person matured into adulthood' (Fionda 2001: 82). From this perspective, child offending, unless of a very serious form, was constructed not as an aberration but, rather, as a normal and temporary component of childhood. Significantly, this image of the child was again reinforced through spatial boundaries, as the welfare approach located the child within the wider community as opposed to a policy of incarceration. While the statutory enactment of this approach was short lived and the 1970s saw a return to a harsh punitive approach, with a subsequent dramatic increase in custodial sentences, the approach in the 1980s was more ambiguous. The Criminal Justice Act 1982, motivated by overcrowded prisons, imposed strict criteria for custodial sentences and this, together with the DHSS Intermediate Treatment Initiative and a shift in attitudes of probation workers and social workers resulted in a marked reduction in the use of custody (Freeman 1997; Muncie 1997; Fionda 2001).

The Criminal Justice Act 1991 has been described as 'the beginning of the end of a child specific youth justice system' (Fionda 2001: 82). By introducing a sentencing framework which required that the 'punishment fit the crime', it marginalized welfare concerns that implicitly focused on the criminal more than the crime. The return to an authoritarian justice approach was subsequently reinforced by the Criminal Justice and Public Order Act 1994, which introduced secure training orders that, in effect, enabled custodial sentences for children as young as 12, and the Crime and Disorder Act 1998, which abolished the *doli incapax* ('incapable of guilt') presumption for children between the age of 10 and 14. This presumption, which has its origins in the common law (judge-made law) and dated back to the fourteenth century, created a flexible middle ground between the age under which statute decreed that children could in no circumstances be held criminally responsible and the age where children are treated as adults. In this respect it was similar to the approach adopted in the *Gillick* case, to the extent that it explicitly recognized that children's understanding and maturity cannot be assessed by age alone. The abolition of *doli incapax*, which means that children over 10 can be held responsible for criminal acts without the prosecution being required to prove their capacity, has been severely criticized for conflicting with international legal norms (Fortin 1999) and for being out of step with almost every other European country which have a much higher age of responsibility.[17] Comparative perspectives are significant as they serve to remind us that the age limits are 'more about when we choose to punish children and only partly about their mental capacities' (Fionda 2001: 85), for it is obviously not the case that English children mature earlier or have a more developed sense of morality than, for example, German or Belgian children. Consequently, in attempting to explain the abolition of *doli incapax* and why from the early 1990s to the present time the justice approach has dominated youth justice policy it is necessary to look not at children but at the broader social and political environment. Numerous commentators have explained the shift as reflecting a 'moral panic' about 'persistent', 'hard core' offenders, and have highlighted the way in which inaccurate and exaggerated media-fuelled fears about young offenders, and 'youth' in general, provided politically convenient scapegoats (Freeman 1997; Muncie 1997). Similarly, others have suggested that in a time of change and lack of certainties young offenders represent a complex form of 'folk devil' that provides a 'reassuring' boundary between normality and abnormality, morality and immorality and 'us' and 'them' (Jenks 1996; Goldson 2001).

The Bulger trial

One of the key events during the 1990s that fed this climate of fear and helped legitimize subsequent legislation was the exceptionally brutal murder in 1993 of 2-year-old James Bulger by two 10-year-old boys. The treatment of the two boys, by both the media and politicians, has been compared to the 'kind of moral outrage reserved for the enemy in times of war' (King 1997: 115). Commenting on the demonization of the boys, Jenks argues that 'by refusing children who commit acts of violence acceptance within the category of child, the public was reaffirming to itself the essence of what children are' (1996: 129). Law was used to legitimize this construction in two distinct ways. First, the law required that children between the ages of 10 and 17 charged with murder be tried in the Crown Court as opposed to the Youth Court.[18] As a result the two boys were denied the status of 'child' but subjected to adult trial by judge and jury and no concessions were made for their age. In this way, the trial and legal procedures upheld the 'impossibility' and incompatibility of being simultaneously a 'child' *and* a 'murderer'. The second key application of law related to the issue of capacity. As the trial took place prior to the abolition of the presumption of *doli incapax*, it was necessary for the prosecution to rebut the presumption before the trial could take place. In determining this question, the law looked to psychiatry and the 'science' of child welfare. King has argued that the construction of the 'truth' about the two boys by psychiatry would inevitably challenge and conflict with that of morality; for, in what he acknowledges are crude terms, '"mad" usually excludes "bad", and "bad" usually excludes "mad"' (1997: 119). In this case, examining the psychological condition of the two boys would have revealed two exceptionally disturbed, neglected children from violent, disrupted homes and almost certainly evidence of sexual abuse (Freeman 1997). However, within the context of the law, the role of the psychiatrists was not to comment on the possible *causes* of the crime but, rather, simply to determine whether or not the boys had the necessary mental capacity to commit the offence. Using standard intelligence tests they found that they did and the presumption of *doli incapax* was consequently rebutted. The remit of the psychiatrists was further restricted by legal rules that deny therapeutic treatment prior to trial on the basis that such intervention might compromise the evidence. In this way 'science was "enslaved" by law', and acted as, 'a censor for scientific . . . amorality' (King 1997: 118, 123), and as a result the moral public demand for justice subjugated the private need for welfare. Moreover, the law ensured that the construction of the boys as 'mentally ill', 'sick' or 'victims of abuse' was denied public legitimacy and effectively 'postponed' until after the trial, at which point care and treatment was permitted.

In these ways the law had a significant impact in institutionalizing the moral outrage at the murder of James Bulger and in legitimizing the description of his death as 'murder' and the two boys as 'criminals'. However, it is important to remember that this was not inevitable and that the law could have had a radically different impact. The extent to which an alternative treatment of child killers is possible was demonstrated by the response in Norway to a similar event. In that case the children were never named and were placed in the care of psychologists and returned to school within a couple of weeks (Hattenstone 2000). While there are no doubt cultural and historical reasons for this stark contrast, had the 1969 Act been fully enacted and the age of responsibility consequently raised to 14, the Bulger trial would not have taken place.

Conclusion

The brief review of the law in these three distinct areas suggests a degree of caution in accepting the 'progressive' narrative, the notion that law has steadily become more responsive to the needs of children. In support of this optimistic claim, one could point to the fact that their interests are now 'paramount' in family dispute proceedings, that they are, in certain circumstances, entitled to contraceptive advice and that the creation of a distinct youth justice system protects many of them from the rigours of adult criminal justice. In these ways the law has, arguably, been an important tool in improving the lives of real children. However, in order to 'protect' children, the law does not simply impose rules but has to 'know' children; and exploring the ways in which knowledge of children has been constructed within legal discourse reveals more complex and ambivalent narratives. In post-divorce disputes the 'welfare of the child' has been constructed in such a way as to uphold shifting conceptualizations of the ideal family; in the context of sex education, 'protecting' children has translated into policies that deny or problematize child sexuality; while in the context of youth justice, acknowledging children's capacity has legitimized political and social demands for justice at the expense of focusing on the interests of child offenders. In this way, legal discourse upholds a variety of constructions of childhood – at times 'passive', 'innocent' and 'victim', while at other times 'knowing' and 'evil'. There is within law no coherent unified construction; rather, it represents a site of struggle between competing and often conflicting moral, 'scientific' and political discursive understandings of childhood. Legal practice is however, by necessity, a-historical – it focuses on the here and now and this fact combined with a traditional reading of law as a system of neutral rules obscures the productive role of law and upholds the myth of law as neutral. Consequently the legitimizing of a particular understanding of childhood within the law has a significant 'claim to truth'. Thinking critically about the law is not to suggest that it cannot improve the lives of real children, but when this is the formal justification for laws and legal decisions it behoves us to rigorously enquire: in whose best interests?

Notes

1   For an analysis of the relationship between childhood and some of the areas of law not addressed here see: Wakeley (2001) (social security), Cowan and Dearing, (2001) (housing), Masson and Winn Oakley (1999), Lindley *et al.* (2001) (care proceedings and child protection), Monk (2000) (school exclusions and special educational needs) and Buss 2000 (international law).
2   *Re Agar-Ellis, Agar-Ellis* v. *Lascelles* [1883] 24 Ch D 317, per Cotton LJ (emphasis added).
3   *Re L* [1962] 1 WLR at pp. 889–90.
4   See for example *Re B* [1962] 1 All ER 872; *Re S* [1958] 1 All ER 783.
5   *M* v. *M* [1978] 1 FLR 77.
6   A key text in this context here was Goldstein *et al.* (1979).
7   See Bainham (1999) for analysis of the distinctions between social, psychological, genetic and biological parentage.
8   *Re M (Contact: Welfare Test)* 1995 1 FLR 274, per Wilson J.
9   *Re F (Minors) (Contact: Mothers Anxiety)* [1993] 2 FLR 830; *Re D (Contact Reasons for Refusal)*.
10 *Re H (Minors) (Access)* [1992] 1 FLR 148.
11 *Re R (A Minor) (Contact)*[1993] 2 FLR 762.
12 *Re P (Contact: Supervision)* [1996] 2 FLR 314. See Barnett 2000.
13 *Re O (Contact: Supervision)* [1995] 2 FLR 124.
14 *Re A* v. *N (Committal: Refusal of Contact)* [1997] 1 FLR 533; *F* v. *F (Contact: Committal)* [1998] 2 LFR 237.
15 *Re L, V, M and H (Contact: Domestic Violence)* [2000] 2 FLR 334.

16 [1985] 3 WLR 830; [1986] AC 112, HL.
17 For example 13 in France, 14 in Germany, 15 in Sweden, 16 in Spain, 18 in Belgium.
18 Powers of the Criminal Courts (Sentencing) Act 2000 s. 91. (This provision was introduced, however, by the Children and Young Persons Act 1933.)

References

Abbott, P. and Wallace, C. (1992) *The Family and the New Right*. London: Pluto Press.

Alderson, P. (1993) *Children's Consent to Surgery* Buckingham: Open University Press.

Alderson, P. (2000) *Young Children's Rights: Exploring Beliefs, Principles and Practice*. London: Jessica Kingsley.

Alloway, N. and Gilbert, P. (1998) Video game culture: playing with masculinity, violence and pleasure, in S. Howard (ed.) *Wired Up: Young People and the Electronic Media*. London: UCL Press.

Alston, P. (1994) *The Best Interests of the Child: Reconciling Culture and Human Rights*. Oxford: Clarendon Press.

Archard, D. (1993) *Children: Rights and Childhood*. London: Routledge.

Ariès, P. ([1960] 1986) *Centuries of Childhood: A Social History of Family Life*, Harmondsworth: Penguin.

Arnold, G. (1980) *Held Fast For England: G.A. Henty, Imperialist Boys' Writer*. London: Hamish Hamilton.

Bainham, A. (1996) Sex education: a family lawyer's perspective, in N. Harris (ed.) *Children, Sex Education and the Law*. London: National Children's Bureau.

Bainham, A. (1999) Parentage, parenthood and parental responsibility: subtle, elusive yet important distinctions, in A. Bainham, S. Day Sclater and M. Richards (eds) *What is A Parent? A Socio-Legal Analysis*. Oxford: Hart.

Baldwin, A.L., Baldwin, C. and Cole, R.E. (1990) Street-resistant families and stress-resistant children, in J.E. Rolf, A.S. Masten, D. Cicchetti and S. Weintraub (eds) *Risk and Protective Factors in the Development of Psychopathology*, pp. 257–80. Cambridge: Cambridge University Press.

Barnett, A. (2000) Contact and domestic violence: the ideological divide, in J. Bridgeman and D. Monk (eds) *Feminist Perspectives on Child Law*. London: Cavendish.

Barthes, R. ([1972] 1987) *Mythologies*. London: Paladin.

Barton, A. (1988) *Vietnam and the Chinese Model*. USA: Woodside Press.

Beck, U.(1992) *Risk Society: Towards a New Modernity*. London: Sage.

Berger, P. and Luckmann, T. (1966) *The Social Construction of Reality*. Harmondsworth: Penguin.

Bond, T. (1996) *Street Children in Ho Chi Minh City*. Ho Chi Minh City, Vietnam: Report for Terres des Hommes.

Bowlby, J. (1969) *Attachment and Loss: Volume 1, Attachment*. London: Hogarth Press.

Bowlby, J. (1980) *Attachment and Loss. Volume 3, Loss*. London: Hogarth Press.

Boyden, J. (1990) Childhood and the policy makers: a comparative perspective on the globalisation of childhood, in A. James and A. Prout *Constructing and Reconstructing Childhood*. London: Falmer Press.

Bridge, S. (1999) Assisted reproduction and the legal definition of parentage, in A. Bainham, S. Day Sclater and M. Richards (eds) (1999) *What is A Parent? A Socio-Legal Analysis*. Oxford: Hart.

Barnardo's (1999) *Giving Children Back Their Future*. Ilford: Barnardo's.

Bridgeman, J. (2000) Embodying our hopes and fears? in J. Bridgeman and D. Monk (eds) *Feminist Perspectives on Child Law*. London: Cavendish Publishing.

Buckingham, D. (1993a) *Children Talking Television: The Making of Television Literacy*. London: Falmer.

Buckingham, D. (1993b) Just playing games, *English and Media Magazine*, 28: 21–5.

Buckingham, D. (1996) *Moving Images: Understanding Children's Emotional Responses to Television*. Manchester: Manchester University Press.

Buckingham, D. (2000) *After the Death of Childhood: Growing Up in the Age of Electronic Media*. Cambridge: Polity.

Buckingham, D. (2002a) The electronic generation? Children and new media in L. Lievrouw and S. Livingstone (eds) *Handbook of New Media*. London: Sage.

Buckingham, D. (ed.) (2002b) *Small Screens: Television for Children*. Leicester: Leicester University Press.

Buckingham, D. and Sefton-Green, J. (1997) From regulation to education, *English and Media Magazine*, 36: 28–32.

Buckingham, D. and Sefton-Green, J. (2002) Gotta catch 'em all: structure, agency and pedagogy in children's media culture, *Media, Culture and Society*, in press.

Buckingham, D., Davies, H., Jones, K. and Kelley, P. (1999) *Children's Television in Britain: History, Discourse and Policy*. London: British Film Institute.

Burr, R. and Montgomery, H.K. (2003) Children and rights, in M. Woodhead and H.K. Montgomery (eds) *Understanding Childhood: An Interdisciplinary Approach*. Chichester: Wiley/The Open University.

Buss, D. (2000) How the UN stole childhood: the Christian Right and the International Rights of the Child, in J. Bridgeman and D. Monk (eds) *Feminist Perspectives on Child Law*. London: Cavendish Publishing.

Butler, J. (1910) *Personal Reminiscences of a Great Crusade*. London: Horace Marshall.

Cadogan, M. and Craig, P. (1986) *You're A Brick, Angela! The Girls' Story 1839–1985*. London: Gollancz.

Cadogan, M. and Schutte, D. (1990) *The William Companion*. London: Macmillan.

Calvert, K. (1982) Children in American family portraiture 1670–1810, *William and Mary Quarterly*, special issue on the family in early America, 3rd series, xxxix (1): January.

Campbell, A., Converse, P.E. and Rodgers, W.L. (1976) *The Quality of American Life: Perceptions, Evaluations and Satisfactions*. New York: Russell Sage Foundation.

Carpenter, H. (1985) *Secret Gardens: the Golden Age of Children's Literature*. London: Allen & Unwin.

Casas, F. (1998) *Infancia: Perspectivas Psicosociales*. Barcelona: Paidós.

Casas, F. (2000) *Quality of Life and the Life Experience of Children*. Ghent: International Interdisciplinary Course on Children's Rights.

Castenada, C. (2002) *Figurations*. Durham, NC: Duke University Press.

Center for Media Education (1997) *Web of Deception: Threats to Children from Online Marketing*. Washington, DC: Center for Media Education.

Chaplin, E. (1994) *Sociology and Visual Representation*. London: Routledge.

Cicourel, A. (1964) *Method and Measurement in Sociology*. New York: Free Press.

Cole, M. and Scribner, S. (1990) *The Psychology of Literacy* MA: Harvard University Press.

Corsaro, W. (1985) *Friendship and Peer Culture in the Early Years*. Norwood, NJ: Ablex.

Cowan, D. and Dearing, N. (2001) The minor as (a) subject: the case of housing law, in J. Fionda (ed.) *Legal Concepts of Childhood*. Oxford: Hart.

Crocker, W. and Crocker, J. (1994) *The Canela: Bonding through Kinship, Ritual and Sex*. Fort Worth, Tx: Harcourt Brace College Publishers.

Cuban, L. (1986) *Teachers and Machines*. New York: Teachers College Press.

Cunningham, H. (1991) *Children of the Poor: Representations of Childhood since the Seventeenth Century*. Oxford: Blackwell.

Cupitt, M. and Stockbridge, S. (1996) *Families and Electronic Entertainment*. Sydney: Australian Broadcasting Corporation/Office of Film and Literature Classification.

Cutt, M.N. (1974) *Mrs. Sherwood and her Books for Children*. London: Oxford University Press.

Danziger, K. (ed.) (1971) *Readings in Child Socialization*, Oxford: Pergamon.

Darwin, C. (1887) A biographical sketch of an infant, *Mind, 7*.

Davis, H. and Bourhill, M. (1997) 'Crisis': the demonisation of children and young people, in P. Scraton (ed.) *'Childhood' in Crisis*. London: UCL Press.

Dawe, A. (1970) 'Two sociologies', *British Journal of Sociology*, de Mause, L. (1976) *The History of Childhood*. London: Souvenir Press.

Deleuze, G. and Guattari, F. (1988) *A Thousand Plateaus: Capitalism and Schizophrenia*. London: Athlone.

Demos, J. (1970) *A Little Commonwealth: Family Life in Plymouth Colony*. New York: OUP.

Denzin, N. (1977) *Childhood Socialization*. San Francisco: Jossey-Bass.

Denzin, N. (1982) The work of little children, in C. Jenks (ed.) *The Sociology of Childhood*. London: Batsford.

DES (Department for Education and Science) (1994) *Education Act 1993: Sex Education in Schools* (Circular 5/94). London: DES.

DfEE (Department for Education and Employment) (2000) *Sex and Relationship Education Guidance* (Circular 0116/2000). London: DfEE.

Diduck, A. (2000) Solicitors and legal subjects, in J. Bridgeman and D. Monk (eds) *Feminist Perspectives on Child Law*. London: Cavendish Publishing.

Durkheim, E. ([1938] 1982) *The Rules of the Sociological Method*, trans. W. Halls. London: Macmillan.

Dutton, M.R. (1992) *Policing and Punishment in China: From Partriarchy to the 'People'*. Cambridge: Cambridge University Press.

Eekelaar, J. (2002) 'Contact – over the limit', *Family Law*, 271.

Elkin, F. and Handel, G. (1972) *The Child and Society: The Process of Socialization*. New York: Random House.

Engelhardt, T. (1986) Children's television: the shortcake strategy, in T. Gitlin (ed.) *Watching Television*. New York: Pantheon.

Ennew, J. (1986) *The Sexual Exploitation of Children*. Cambridge: Polity.

Evans, D. (1993) *Sexual Citizenship: The Material Construction of Sexualities*. London: Routledge.

Facer, K., Furlong, J., Furlong, R. and Sutherland, R. (2001) Home is where the hardware is: young people, the domestic environment and 'access' to new technologies, in I. Hutchby and J. Moran-Ellis (eds) *Children, Technology and Culture*. London: RoutledgeFalmer.

Fine, A. (2000) Postscript, in H. Anderson and M. Styles (eds) *Teaching Through Texts: Promoting Literacy Through Popular and Literary Texts in the Primary Classroom*. London: Routledge.

Fionda, J. (2001) Youth and justice, in J. Fionda (ed.) *Legal Concepts of Childhood*. Oxford: Hart.

Fogelman, P. (2000) For Every Child. Geneva: UNICEF.

Fonagy, P., Steel, M., Steele, H., Higgit, A. and Target, M. (1994) The theory and practice of resilience, *Journal of Child Psychology and Psychiatry*, 33(2): 231–57.

Fortin, J. (1999) *Children's Rights and the Developing Law*. London: Butterworths.

Foucault, M. (1979) *Discipline and Punish*. Harmondsworth: Penguin.

Foucault, M. (1976) *The History of Sexuality: Volume 1*, trans. R. Hurley, Harmondsworth: Penguin.

Frank, G. (1971) *The Sociology of Development and the Undevelopment of Sociology*. London: Pluto Press.

Franklin, B. and Petley, J. (1996) Killing the age of innocence: newspaper reporting of the death of James Bulger, in J. Pilcher and S. Wagg (eds) *Thatcher's Children: Politics, Childhood and Society in the 1980s and 1990s*. London: Falmer Press.

Freeman, D. (1999) *The Fateful Hoaxing of Margaret Mead*. Co: Westview.

Freeman, M. (1997) The James Bulger tragedy: childish innocence and the construction of guilt, in A. McGillivray (ed.) *Governing Childhood*. Aldershot: Dartmouth.

Freud, S. ([1909] 1965) Infantile sexuality, in W. Kessen (ed.) *The Child*. New York: Wiley.

Frones, I. (1994) Dimensions of childhood, in J. Qvortrup, M. Bardy, G. Sgritta and H. Wintersberger (eds) *Childhood Matters: Social Theory, Practice and Politics*. Aldershot: Avebury.

Frosh, S., Phoenix, A. and Pattman, R. (2002) *Young Masculinities*. Basingstoke: Palgrave.

Garfinkel, H. (1967) *Studies in Ethnomethodology*. Englewood Cliffs, NJ: Prentice Hall.

Giddens, A. (1991) *Modernity and Self-Identity*. Cambridge: Polity.

Gillis, J. (1981) *Youth and History: Tradition and Change in European Age Relations, 1790–Present*. London: Academic Press.

Gittins, D. (1998) *The Child in Question*. Basingstoke: Macmillan.

Goldson, B. (2001) The demonization of children: from the symbolic to the institutional, in P. Foley, J. Roche and S. Tucker (eds) *Children in Society*. Basingstoke: Palgrave.

Goldstein, J., Freud, A. and Solnit, A. (1979) *Beyond the Best Interests of the Child*, 2nd edn. New York: Free Press.

Golombok, S. (1999) Lesbian mother families, in A. Bainham, S. Day Sclater and M. Richards (eds) *What is A Parent? A Socio-Legal Analysis*. Oxford: Hart.

Goodman, R. (2000) *Children of the Japanese State*. Oxford: Oxford University Press.

Gorman, D. (1978) The maiden tribute of modern babylon re-examined: child prostitution and the idea of childhood in late-Victorian England, *Victorian Studies*, 21: 353–79.

Goslin, D. (ed.) (1969) *Handbook of Socialization Theory and Research*. Chicago: Rand McNally.

Green, B. and Bigum, C. (1993) Aliens in the classroom, *Australian Journal of Education*, 37(2): 119–41.

Gregor, T. (1985) *Anxious Pleasures*. Chicago: Chicago University Press.

Greven, P. (1970) *The Protestant Temperament: Patterns of Child Rearing, Religious Experience and the Self in Early America*. New York: Alfred Knopf.

Griffin, C. (1993) *Representations of Youth: The Study of Youth and Adolescence in Britain and America*. Cambridge: Polity Press.

Griffiths, M. (1996) Computer game playing in children and adolescents: a review of the literature, in T. Gill (ed.) *Electronic Children: How Children are Responding to the Information Revolution*. London: National Children's Bureau.

Grotberg, E. (1995) *A Guide to Promoting Resilience in Children: Strengthening the Human Spirit*. The Hague: Bernard Van Leer Foundation.

Hamilton, D. (1981) *On Simultaneous Instruction and the Early Evolution of Class Teaching*. Glasgow: University of Glasgow.

Haraway, D. (1991) Situated knowledges: the science question in feminism and the privilege of partial perspective, in D. Haraway *Simians, Cyborgs and Women: The Reinvention of Nature*. New York: Routledge.

Hardman, C. (1973) Can there be an anthropology of children? *Journal of the Anthropological Society of Oxford*, 4(1): 85–99.

Hattenstone, S. (2000) They were punished enough by what they did, *Guardian*, 30 October.

Haviland, V. (ed.) (1980) *The Openhearted Audience*. Washington, DC: Library of Congress.

Hendrick, H. (1990) Constructions and reconstructions of British childhood: an interpretive survey 1800 to the present, in A. James and A. Prout (eds) *Constructing and Reconstructing Childhood: Contemporary Issues in the Sociological Study of Childhood*. London: Falmer Press.

Henriques J. *et al.* (1998) *Changing the Subject: Psychology, Social Regulation and Subjectivity*, 2nd edn. London: Routledge.

Herdt, G. (1993) *Semen Transactions in Sambia Culture: in Ritualized Homosexuality in Melanesia*. Berkeley, CA: University of California Press.

Hey, V. (1997) *The Company She Keeps: An Ethnography of Girls' Friendships*. Buckingham: Open University Press.

Hill, M. (1999) What's the problem? Who can help? The perspectives of children and young people on their well-being and on helping professionals, *Journal of Social Work Practice*, 13(2): 17–21.

Hirst, P. (1975) *Durkheim, Bernard and Epistemology*. London: Routledge & Kegan Paul.

Hodge, B. and Tripp, D. (1986) *Children and Television: A Semiotic Approach*. Cambridge: Polity.

Hofstede, G. (1980) *Culture's Consequences: International Differences in Work-related Values*. Beverly Hills, CA: Sage.

Holland, P. (1992) *What is a Child? Popular Images of Childhood*. London: Virago Press.

Holland, P. (1996) 'I've just seen a hole in the reality barrier!' Children, childishness and the media in the ruins of the twentieth century, in J. Pilcher and S. Wagg (eds) *Thatcher's Children: Politics, Childhood and Society in the 1980s and 1990s*. London: Falmer.

Hollis, M. (1977) *Models of Man*. Cambridge: Cambridge University Press.

Hunt, P. (2001) *Children's Literature: An Anthology, 1801–1902*. Oxford: Blackwell.

Jackson, S. (1982) *Childhood and Sexuality*. Oxford: Basil Blackwell.

James, A. and Prout, A. (ed.) (1990) *Constructing and Reconstructing Childhood*. Basingstoke: Falmer.

James, A. and Prout, A. (eds) (1997) *Constructing and Reconstructing Childhood: Contemporary Issues in the Sociological Study of Childhood*, 2nd edn. London: Falmer.

James, A., Jenks, C. and Prout, A. (1998) *Theorising Childhood*. Cambridge: Polity.

Jenkins, H. (1993) ' "x logic": repositioning Nintendo in children's lives', *Quarterly Review of Film and Video*, 14(4): 55–70.

Jenks, C. (1982 and 1992) *The Sociology of Childhood*. Aldershot: Batsford.

Jenks, C. (1996) *Childhood*. London: Routledge.

Jessen, C. (1999) *Children's Computer Culture: Three Essays on Children and Computers*. Odense, Denmark: Odense University.

Jones, D. and Watkins, A. (eds) (2000) *A Necessary Fantasy? The Heroic Figure in Children's Popular Culture*. New York: Garland.

Jones, K. and Williamson, J. (1979) The birth of the schoolroom, *Ideology and Consciousness*, 6: 59–110.

Jordanova, L. (1986) Naturalising the family: literature and the bio-medical sciences in the late eighteenth century, in L. Jordanova (ed.) *Languages of Nature: Critical Essays on Science and Literature*. London: Free Association Press.

Jordanova, L. (1989) Children in history: concepts of nature and society, in G. Scarre (ed.) *Children, Parents and Politics*. Cambridge: Cambridge University Press.

Jowett, G.S., Jarvie, I.C. and Fuller, K.H. (eds) (1996) *Children and the Movies: Media Influence and The Payne Fund Controversy*. Cambridge: Cambridge University Press.

Justice, J. (1986) *Policies, Plans and People: Culture and Health Development in Nepal*. Berkeley, CA: University of California Press.

Kaganas, F. (1999) Contact, conflict and risk, in S. Day Sclater and C. Piper (eds) *Undercurrents of Divorce*. Aldershot: Ashgate/Dartmouth.

Kappeler, S. (1986) *The Pornography of Representation*. Oxford: Polity.

Katz, J. (1997) *Virtuous Reality: How America Surrendered Discussion of Moral Values to Opportunists, Nitwits and Blockheads like William Bennett*. New York: Random House.

Kehily, M.J. and Swann, J. (eds) (2003) *Children's Cultural Worlds*. Chichester: Wiley/The Open University.

Kellmer Pringle, M.L. (1974) *The Needs of Children*. London: Hutchinson.

Khanh, D. (1996) Juvenile delinquency a growing menace, *The Vietnam News*: 4.

Kincaid, J.R. (1992) *Child-Loving. The Erotic Child and Victorian Culture*. New York: Routledge.

Kinder, M. (1991) *Playing with Power in Movies, Television and Video Games: From Muppet Babies to Teenage Mutant Ninja Turtles*. Berkeley, CA: University of California Press.

King, M. (1997) *A Better World for Children?* London: Routledge.

Kitzinger, C. (in press) Intersex and psychology of women, *The Psychologist*.

Kitzinger, J. (1990) Who are you kidding? Children, power and the struggle against sexual abuse, in A. James and A. Prout (eds) *Constructing and Reconstructing Childhood: Contemporary Issues in the Study of Childhood*. London: Falmer Press.

Kline, S. (1993) *Out of the Garden: Toys and Children's Culture in the Age of TV Marketing*. London: Verso.

Lalljee, M. (2000) The interpreting self: a social constructionist perspective, in R. Stevens (ed.) *Understanding the Self*, London: Sage.

Lanham, R. (1993) *The Electronic Word: Democracy, Technology and the Arts*. Chicago: University of Chicago Press.

Lansdown, G. (2001) Children's welfare and children's rights, in P. Foley, J. Roche and S. Tucker (eds) *Children in Society: Contemporary Theory, Policy and Practice.* Basingstoke: Palgrave/The Open University.

Lave, J. and Wenger, E. (1991) *Situated Learning: Legitimate Peripheral Participation.* Cambridge: Cambridge University Press.

Law, J. and Moser, I. (2002) *Managing Subjectivities and Desires.* Lancaster: Centre for Science Studies, University of Lancaster.

Lee, N. (2001) *Childhood and Society.* Buckingham: Open University Press.

Levy, A. (2001) Children in court, in J. Fionda (ed.) *Legal Concepts of Childhood.* Oxford: Hart.

Lindley, B., Herring, J. and Wyld, N. (2001) Public law children's cases: whose decision is it anyway? in J. Herring (ed.) *Family Law: Issues, Debates, Policy.* Devon: Willan.

Livingstone, S. (2002) *Young People and New Media.* London: Sage.

Locke, M. and Scheper-Hughes, N. (1997) The mindful body: prolegomenon to future work in medical anthropology, *Medical Anthropology Quarterly*, 1(1): 6–41.

Luke, C. (1989) *Pedagogy, Printing and Protestantism: The Discourse on Childhood.* Albany, NY: SUNY Press.

MacKay, R. (1973) Conceptions of children and models of socialization, in H.P. Dreitzel (ed.) *Recent Sociology No.5 – Childhood and Socialization.* New York: Macmillan.

Manville-Fenn, G. (1976) Henty and his books, in L. Salway (ed.) *A Peculiar Gift: Nineteenth Century.* London: Kestrel.

Martindale, A. (1994) The child in the picture: a medieval perspective, in D. Wood (ed.) *The Church and Childhood* (Vol. 31 of *Studies in Church History*). Oxford: Blackwell.

Masson, J. and Winn Oakley, M. (1999) *Out of Hearing: Representing Children in Care Proceedings.* London: Wiley.

Mayall, B. (ed.) (1994) *Childrens' Childhoods Observed and Experienced.* London: Falmer.

Mayall, B. (2002) *Towards a Sociology for Childhood: Thinking from Children's Lives.* Buckingham: Open University Press.

Mayhew, H. (1861) *London Labour and the London Poor.* London: Griffin, Bohn & Company.

Mead, M. ([1928] 1972) Coming of Age in Samoa. London: Penguin.

Mead, M. and Wolfenstein, M. (1954) *Childhood in Contemporary Cultures.* Chicago: Chicago University Press.

Melody, W. (1973) *Children's Television: The Economics of Exploitation.* New Haven, CT: Yale University Press.

Merleau-Ponty, M. (1967) *The Primacy of Perception.* Paris: Gallimard.

Mitchell, J. and Goody, J. (1999) Family or familiarity? in A. Bainham, S. Day Sclater and M. Richards (eds) *What is a Parent? A Socio-legal Analysis.* Oxford: Hart.

Monk, D. (1998a) Sex education and the problematisation of teenage pregnancy: a genealogy of law and governance, *Social and Legal Studies*, 7(2): 239–59.

Monk, D. (1998b) Beyond Section 28: law, governance and sex education, in L. Moran, D. Monk and S. Beresford (eds) *Legal Queeries: Lesbian, Gay and Transgender Legal Studies*. London: Cassell.

Monk, D. (2000) Theorizing education law and childhood, *British Journal of Sociology of Education*, 21(3): 355–70.

Monk, D. (2001) New guidance/old problems: recent developments in sex education, *Journal of Social Welfare and Family Law*, 23(3): 271–91.

Montgomery, H. (2001) *Modern Babylon? Prostituting children in Thailand*. Oxford: Berghahn.

Montgomery, H. (2003) Childhood in time and place, in M. Woodhead and H. Montgomery (eds) *Understanding Childhood, An Interdisciplinary Approach*. Chichester: Wiley/The Open University.

Moreno, A. (1998) Am I a man or a woman? *19 Magazine*, September: 16–18.

Morrison, A. and McIntyre, D. (1971) *Schools and Socialization*. Harmondsworth: Penguin.

Morrison, B. (1998) *As If*. London: Granta.

Muncie, J. (1997) Shifting sands: care, community and custody in youth justice discourse, in J. Roche and S. Tucker (eds) *Youth in Society*. London: Sage.

Muncie, J. (1999) *Youth and Crime: A Critical Introduction*. London: Sage.

Nabokov, V. (1955) *Lolita*. Harmondsworth: Penguin.

National Assembly of the Socialist Republic of Vietnam (1991) *National Law on Child Protection, Care and Education*. Hanoi: National Assembly.

Ncube, W. (1998) *Law, Culture, Tradition and Children's Rights in Eastern and Southern Africa*. Aldershot: Ashgate.

Neale, B. and Smart, C. (1999) In whose best interests? Theorising family life following parental separation or divorce, in S. Day Sclater and C. Piper (eds) *Undercurrents of Divorce*. Aldershot: Ashgate/Dartmouth.

Nelson, C. (1991) *Boys Will be Girls: The Feminine Ethic and British Children's Fiction, 1857–1917*. New Brunswick, NJ: Rutgers University Press.

Nelson, J. (1994) Parents, children and the church in earlier Middle Ages, in D. Wood (ed.) *The Church and Childhood* (Vol. 31 of *Studies in Church History*). Oxford: Blackwell.

Neuman, S. (1995) *Literacy in the Television Age: The Myth of the Television Effect*, 2nd edn. Norwood, NJ: Ablex.

Newburn, T. (1996) Back to the future? Youth crime, youth justice and the rediscovery of 'authoritarian populism', in J. Pilcher and S. Wagg (eds) *Thatcher's Children? Politics, Childhood and Society in the 1980s and 1990s*. London: Falmer.

Nixon, H. (1998) Fun and games are serious business, in J. Sefton-Green (ed.) *Digital Diversions: Youth Culture in the Age of Multimedia*. London: UCL Press.

O'Dell, L. (1998) Damaged goods and victims? Challenging the assumptions within academic research into the effects of child sexual abuse. Unpublished doctoral dissertation, The Open University.

O'Donovan, K. (1993) *Family Law Matters*. London: Pluto Press.

O'Neill, J. (1994) *The Missing Child in Liberal Theory*. Toronto: University of Toronto Press.

Oakley, A. (1994) Women and children first and last: parallels and differences between women's and children's studies, in B. Mayall (ed.) *Childrens' Childhoods*. London: Falmer.

Ong, W. (1982) *Orality and Literacy*. London: Methuen.

Opie, I. and Opie, P. (1959) *The Lore and Language of Schoolchildren*. Oxford: Oxford University Press.

Opie, P. and Opie, I. (1969) *Children's Games in Street and Playground*. Oxford: Oxford University Press.

Orme, N. (2001) *Medieval Children*. Princeton, NJ: Yale University Press.

Orr Vered, K. (1998) Blue group boys play *Incredible Machine*, girls play hopscotch: social discourse and gendered play at the computer, in J. Sefton-Green (ed.) *Digital Diversions: Youth Culture in the Age of Multimedia*. London: UCL Press.

Oswell, D. (2002) *Television, Childhood and the Home: A History of the Making of the Child Television Audience in Britain*. Oxford: Oxford University Press.

Papert, S. (1993) *The Children's Machine: Rethinking School in the Age of the Computer*. New York: Basic Books.

Parsons, T. (1964) *The Social System*. New York: Free Press.

Parsons, T. (1968) *The Structure of Social Action* (Vols 1 & 2). New York: Free Press.

Parton, N. (1991) *Governing the Family: Child Care, Child Protection and the State*. London: Macmillan.

Piachaud, D. and Sutherland, H. (2000) How effective is the British government's attempt to reduce child poverty? *Innocenti Working Papers 77* (Innocenti Research Centre/UNICEF).

Piaget, J. (1972) *Psychology and Epistemology*, trans. P. Wells. Harmondsworth: Penguin.

Piaget, J. (1977) *The Language and Thought of the Child*. London: Routledge & Kegan Paul.

Piper, C. (1996) Divorce reform and the image of the child, *Journal of Law and Society*, 23(3): 364–82.

Piper, C. (2000) Historical constructions of childhood innocence: removing sexuality, in E. Heinze (ed.) *Of Innocence and Autonomy: Children, Sex and Human Rights*. Aldershot: Ashgate/Dartmouth.

Podmore, B. (1996) The NAWE interview with Anne Fine: another little spanner? *Writing in Education*, 8 (Supplement): i–viii.

Pollock, L. (1983) *Forgotten Children: Parent-child Relations from 1500–1900*. Cambridge: Cambridge University Press.

Pollock, L. (1987) *A Lasting Relationship: Parents and Children over Three Centuries*. London: Fourth Estate.

Postman, N. (1983) *The Disappearance of Childhood*. London: W.H. Allen.

Postman, N. (1992) *Technopoly: The Surrender of Culture to Technology*. New York: Knopf.

Pratchett, T. (1993) *Only You Can Save Mankind*. London: Corgi.

Pratchett, T. (1996) *Hogfather*. London: Corgi.

Pringle, K. (1998) *Children and Social Welfare in Europe*. Buckingham: Open University Press.

Provenzo, E. (1991) *Video Kids: Making Sense of Nintendo*. Cambridge, MA: Harvard University Press.

Qvortrup, J. (ed.) (1993) *Childhood as a Social Phenomenon: Lessons from an International Project* (Eurosocial report 47). Vienna: European Centre.

Qvortrup, J. (1994) Childhood matters: an introduction, in J. Qvortrup, M. Bardy, G. Sgritta and H. Wintersberger (eds) *Childhood Matters: Social Theory, Practice and Politics*. Aldershot: Avebury.

Reece, H. (1996) The paramountcy principle – consensus or construct? *Current Legal Problems*, 49: 267.

Reynolds, K. and Yates, P. (1998) Too soon: representations of childhood death in literature for children, in K. Lesnik-Oberstein (ed.) *Children in Culture*. Houndmills: Macmillan.

Ritchie, O. and Kollar, M. (1964) *The Sociology of Childhood*. New York: Appleton Century Crofts.

Roche, J. (1992) Children's rights and the welfare of the child, in W. Stainton Rogers, D. Hevey, J. Roche and E. Ash (eds) *Child Abuse and Neglect: Facing the Challenge*. London: Batsford/The Open University.

Roche, J. (2001) Quality of Life for Children, in P. Foley, J. Roche and S. Tucker (eds) *Children in Society*. Basingstoke: Palgrave.

Rose, N. (1985) *The Psychological Complex*. London: Routledge.

Rose, N. (1990) *Governing the Soul*. London: Routledge.

Rotman, B. (1980) *Mathematics: An Essay in Semiotics*. Bristol: University of Bristol.

Rudd, D. (2000) *Enid Blyton and the Mystery of Children's Literature*. London: Macmillan.

Sanders, B. (1995) *A is for Ox: The Collapse of Literacy and the Rise of Violence in the Electronic Age*. New York: Vintage.

Schutz, A. (1964) *Collected Papers (Vol. 1)*. The Hague: Martinus Nijhoff.

Schwartz, S.H., Bardi, A. and Bianchi, G. (2000) Value adaptation to the imposition and collapse of communist regimes in East-Central Europe, in S.A. Renshon and D. Duckitt (eds) *Political Psychology: Cultural and Cross-cultural Foundations*. London: Macmillan.

Scraton, P. (ed.) (1997) *'Childhood' in Crisis*. London: UCL Press.

Sefton-Green, J. (ed.) (1998) *Digital Diversions: Youth Culture in the Age of Multimedia*. London: UCL Press.

Sefton-Green, J. and Buckingham, D. (1996) Digital visions: children's 'creative' uses of multimedia technologies, *Convergence* 2(2): 47–79.

Seiter, E. (1993) *Sold Separately: Parents and Children in Consumer Culture.* New Brunswick, NJ: Rutgers University Press.

Sheldon, S. (2001a) Unmarried fathers and parental responsibility: a case for reform? *Feminist Legal Studies*, 9(2): 93–118.

Sheldon, S. (2001b) 'Sperm bandits': birth control fraud and the battle of the sexes, *Legal Studies*, 21(3): 460–80.

Shorter, E. (1975) *The Making of the Modern Family.* London: Fontana/Collins.

Simmonds, M. (2003) Patients and parents in decision making and management, in A. Balen, S. Creighton, M. Davies, J. McDougall and R. Stanhope (eds) *Multi-disciplinary Approaches to Paediatric and Adolescent Gynaecology.* Cambridge: Cambridge University Press.

Smith, D.J. (1994) *The Sleep of Reason.* London: Random House.

Speier, M. (1970) The everyday world of the child, in J. Douglas (ed.) *Understanding Everyday Life.* London: Routledge & Kegan Paul.

Spigel, L. (1992) *Make Room for TV: Television and the Family Ideal in Postwar America.* Chicago: University of Chicago Press.

Spufford, F. (2002) *The Child that Books Built: A Memoir of Childhood and Reading.* London: Faber & Faber.

Stainton Rogers, R. and Stainton Rogers, W. (1992) *Stories of Childhood: Shifting Agendas of Child Concern.* Hemel Hempstead: Harvester Wheatsheaf.

Stainton Rogers, W. and Stainton Rogers, R. (1999) What is good and bad sex for children? in M. King (ed.) *Moral Agendas for Children's Welfare.* London: Routledge.

Stainton Rogers, W. and Stainton Rogers, R. (2001) *The Psychology of Gender and Sexuality.* Buckingham: Open University Press.

Stainton Rogers, W., Hevey, D., Roche, J. and Ash, E. (1991) *Child Abuse and Neglect: Facing the Challenge.* London: Batsford in association with The Open University.

Stead, W.T. (1885) *Maiden Tribute of Modern Babylon.* London: *Pall Mall Gazette*, Secret Commission.

Stearns, P. (1975) *European Society in Upheaval.* London: Macmillan.

Steedman, C. (1990) *Childhood, Culture and Class in Britain, Margaret McMillan 1860–1931.* London: Virago.

Steedman, C. (1995) *Strange Dislocations: Childhood and the Idea of Human Interiority 1780–1930.* London: Time Warner Books.

Stewart, W.A.C. (1972) *Progressives and Radicals in English Education 1750–1970.* London: Macmillan.

Stone, G. (1965) The play of little children, *Quest, 4.*

Stone, L. (1977) *The Family, Sex and Marriage in England 1500–1800.* London: Weidenfeld & Nicolson.

Tapscott, D. (1998) *Growing Up Digital: The Rise of the Net Generation.* New York: McGraw-Hill.

Temple Black, S. (1988) *Child Star, An Autobiography*. London: Headline Press. *The African Charter for Children* (1991).

Thomson, R. (1994) Prevention, promotion and adolescent sexuality: the politics of school sex education in England and Wales, *Sexual and Marital Therapy*, 9(2): 115–26.

Thomson, R. (2000) Legal, protected and timely: young people's perspectives on the heterosexual age of consent, in J. Bridgeman and D. Monk (eds) *Feminist Perspectives on Child Law*. London: Cavendish Publishing.

Thorne, B. (1993) *Gender Play: Girls and Boys at School*. New Brunswick, NJ: Rutgers University Press.

Thwaite, Ann (1990) *A.A. Milne: His Life*. London: Faber & Faber.

Tobin, J. (1998) An American *otaku* (or, a boy's virtual life on the net), in J. Sefton Green (ed.) *Digital Diversions: Youth Culture in the Age of Multimedia*. London: UCL Press.

Tobin, J. (2000) *'Good Guys Don't Wear Hats': Children's Talk About the Media*. New York: Teachers College Press.

Tucker, N. (1998) Madame Spitfire, *Independent Saturday Magazine*, 14 February.

Turkle, S. (1995) *Life on Screen: Identity in the Age of the Internet*. New York: Simon & Schuster.

Ungar, M. (2003) *Nurturing Hidden Resilience in Troubled Youth*. Toronto: University of Toronto Press.

United Nations (1959) *The United Nations Declaration on the Rights of the Child*. Geneva: United Nations.

Vance, C. (1991) Anthropology rediscovers sexuality: a theoretical comment, *Social Science and Medicine*, 33(8): 875–84.

Venn, C. (1984) The subject of psychology, in J. Henriques *et al. Changing the Subject: Psychology, Social Regulation and Subjectivity*, 2nd edn. London: Routledge.

Wagg, S. (1992) One I made earlier: media, popular culture and the politics of childhood in D. Strinati and S. Wagg (eds) *Come on Down? Popular Media Culture in Post-War Britain*. London: Routledge.

Walkerdine, V. (1984) Developmental psychology and the child-centred pedagogy: the insertion of Piaget into early education, in J. Henriques *et al. Changing the Subject: Psychology, Social Regulation and Subjectivity*, 2nd edn. London: Routledge.

Walkerdine, V. (1989) *Counting Girls Out*. London: Virago.

Walkerdine, V. (1997) *Daddy's Girl: Young Girls and Popular Culture*. Basingstoke: Macmillan.

Walkerdine, V. (1998) Popular culture and the eroticisation of girls, in H. Jenkins (ed.) *The Children's Culture Reader*. New York: New York University Press.

Wallace, J. and Mangan, M. (1996) *Sex, Laws and Cyberspace*. New York: Henry Holt.

Wallerstein, J. and Kelly, J. (1980) *Surviving the Breakup*. New York: Basic Books.

Waltermann, J. and Machill, M. (eds) (2000) *Protecting Our Children on the Internet.* Gutersloh, Germany: Bertelsmann Foundation.

Walther, L. (1979) The invention of childhood in Victorian autobiography, in G. Landon *Approaches to Victorian Autobiography.* Athens, OH: Ohio University Press.

Waltz, S. (2002) Reclaiming and rebuilding the history of the Universal Declaration of Human Rights, *Third World Quarterly*, 23(3): 437–48.

Warner, M. (1994) *Managing Monsters: The Reith lectures.* London: Vintage.

Wattam, C. (1999) Criminalisation of child harm and injury: in the interests of the child? *Children and Society*, 11: 97–107.

White, G. (1977) *Socialization.* London: Longman.

White, P. (ed.) (1986) *Memoirs of Many in One.* Harmondsworth: Penguin.

WHO (World Health Organization) (1993) (Quality of Life Group) *Measuring Quality of Life: The Development of the World Health Organization's Quality of Life Instrument.* Geneva: WHO.

Williams, R. (1961) *The Long Revolution.* London: Columbia University Press.

Williams, R. (1974) *Television, Technology and Cultural Form.* Glasgow: Fontana.

Williams, R. (1989) *Resources of Hope, Culture, Democracy, Socialism*, ed. R. Gale. London: Verso.

Woodhead, M. (1996) *In Search of the Rainbow: Pathways to Quality in Large-scale Programmes for Young Disadvantaged Children.* The Hague: Bernard Leer Foundation.

Woodhead, M. (1997) Psychology and the cultural construction of children's needs, in A. James and A. Prout (eds) *Constructing and Reconstructing Childhood: Contemporary Issues in the Sociological Study of Childhood.* London: Falmer.

Woodhead, M. (2003) Childhood studies: past, present and future. Paper presented at Open University conference, 'Childhood Reconsidered', 27 June.

Wrong, D. (1961) The oversocialised conception of man in modern sociology, *American Sociological Review*, XXV: 1 April.

Zelitzer, V. (1985) *Pricing the Priceless Child: The Changing Social Value of Children.* New York: Basic Books.

Zordano, J.L. (2001) *Inventing the Child: Culture, Ideology, and the Story of Childhood.* New York: Garland.

Index

Related books from Open University Press

Purchase from www.openup.co.uk or order through your local bookseller

---

TOWARDS A SOCIOLOGY OF CHILDHOOD
THINKING FROM CHILDREN'S LIVES

Berry Mayall

This important book moves the sociology of childhood forward. Berry Mayall argues, that, since childhood is a permanent component of society, in order to understand how society works, we must take account of children as well as adults, otherwise our explanation omits an important social group. Children's lives are shaped by policies and practices, but they are also agents, who make a life for themselves through their relationships with adults and other children. This book argues that feminist theory and practice is useful for understanding childhood; we should start from the children's own accounts to show how the organisation of social relations provides an explanation for their social position.

This is a political book: through analysis of children's own descriptions and evaluations of childhood, it argues for an improved social status of childhood, including respecting children's rights. The book also shows that in order to understand childhood we must take account of both child-adult relations (generational relations) and gender relations.

It is essential reading for childhood sociologists and feminists, and for all those seeking to raise the social status of childhood. It is highly recommended to students of childhood studies, at all levels.

Contents
Introduction – Studying childhood – Studying relational processes – Relations with parents – Childhood work – The moral status of childhood – Towards a child standpoint – Comparing childhoods – Generation and gender – Appendix – Bibliography – Index.

224pp   0 335 20842 8 (Paperback)

DOING EARLY CHILDHOOD RESEARCH
THEORY AND PRACTICE

Glenda MacNaughton, Sharne Rolfe and Iram Siraj-Blatchford (eds)

Research training is an important element in both undergraduate and postgraduate degrees in early childhood education and there is a genuine need for an accessible textbook that addresses the particular research issues which are a feature of this important field. *Doing Early Childhood Research* introduces the most common qualitative and quantitative methods in the early childhood context. The contributors cover a wide range of conventional and newer approaches including observation, surveys, action research, ethnography, policy analysis and poststructuralist approaches. The reader is shown step by step how to select a topic, review the literature, design their research project, analyse data and produce a report.

Throughout the emphasis is on practical application of the methods and the text is illustrated by a wide range of examples and case studies. Each chapter includes checklists, explanations of key concepts, annotated further reading and questions for reflection.

Written by leading international early childhood researchers, this book is a standard introduction to research in the early childhood field.

Contents
Introduction – Glossary – Part 1: The nature of research – Research as a tool – The research process – Research paradigms, perspectives and methods – Doing research for the first time – Ethics in early childhood research – Part 2: Analysis and design – Design issues – Quantitative designs and statistical analysis – Qualitative designs and analysis – Equity issues in research design – Part 3: The research process in action – Surveys and questionnaires – Interviewing children – Interviewing adults – An ethnographic approach to researching young children's learning – Action research – Direct observation – Policy research – Case study – Appendices – Index.

320pp   0 335 20902 5 (Paperback)

CHILDHOOD AND SOCIETY
GROWING UP IN THE AGE OF UNCERTAINTY
Nick Lee

- What happens to childhood when the nature of adulthood becomes uncertain?
- What impact is globalization having on adult-child relationships?
- How are we to study 'growing up' today?

Traditionally, children and adults have been treated as different kinds of person, with adults seen as complete, stable and self-controlling, and children seen as incomplete, changeable and in need of control. This ground-breaking book argues that in the early twenty-first century, 'growing up' can no longer be understood as a movement toward personal completion and stability. Careers, intimate relationships, even identities, are increasingly provisional, bringing into question the division between the mature and the immature and thereby differences between adults and children.

Childhood and Society charts the emergence of the conceptual and institutional divisions between adult 'human beings' and child 'human becomings' over the course of the modern era. It then examines the contemporary economic and ideological trends that are eroding the foundations of these divisions. The consequences of this age of uncertainty are examined through an assessment of sociological theories of childhood and through a survey of children's varied positions in a globalizing and highly mediated social world. In all, this accessible text provides a clear, up-to-date and original insight into the sociological study of childhood for undergraduates and researchers alike. It also develops a new set of conceptual tools for studying 'growing up'.

Contents
Introduction – Part one Human beings and human becomings – What do you want to be when you grow up? – Defining the dependent child? – Beings in their own right?: The recognition and misrecognition of children – Part two Ambiguities of childhood – Children out of place: ambiguity and social order – Children in their place: home, school and media – New places for children: voice, rights and decision making – Part three Human becomings and social research – Childhood and extension: the multiplication of becoming – Towards an immature sociology – Conclusion: growing up and slowing down – References – Index.

192pp   0 335 20608 5 (Paperback)   0 335 20609 3 (Hardback)